CLEP Courseware
U.S. History I:
Colonization to 1877

Published by: Perfect Score Software.

Email: info@perfectscoresoftware.com

ISBN 0-9798516-8-8 (Paperback)

Manufactured in the United States of America

10 9 8 7 6 5 4 3 2 1

CONTENTS

HISTORY OF THE UNITED STATES I - EARLY COLONIZATION TO 1877

DESCRIPTION OF THE EXAMINATION

The History of the United States I: Early Colonization to 1877 examination covers material that is usually taught in the first semester of a two-semester course in United States history. The examination covers the period of United States history from early European colonizations to the end of Reconstruction, with the majority of the questions on the period of 1790-1877. In the part covering the seventeenth and eighteenth centuries, emphasis is placed on the English colonies.

The examination contains 120 quuestions to be answered in 90 minutes. Some of these are pretest questions that will not be scored. Any time candidates spend on tutorials and providing personal information is in addition to the actual testing time.

KNOWLEDGE AND SKILLS REQUIRED

Questions on the History of the United States I examination require candidates to demonstrate one or more of the following abilities:

- Identification and description of historical phenomena
- Analysis and interpretation of historical phenomena
- Comparison and contrast of historical phenomena

The subject matter of the History of the United States I examination is drawn from the following topics. The percentages next to the main topics indicate the approximate percentages of exam questions on those topics.

Topical Specifications

> 35% Political institutions and behavior and public policy
> 25% Social developments
> 10% Economic developments
> 15% Cultural and intellectual developments
> 15% Diplomacy and international relations

Chronological Specifications

- 30% 1500–1789
- 70% 1790–1877

The following themes are reflected in a comprehensive introductory survey course:

- The nature of indigenous societies in North America
- The origins and nature of black slavery and resistance
- Immigration and the history of ethnic minorities
- Major movements and individual figures in the history of women and the family
- The development and character of colonial societies
- British relations with the Atlantic colonies of North America
- The changing role of religion in American society
- The content of the Constitution and its amendments, and their interpretation by the Supreme Court
- The development and expansion of participatory democracy
- The growth of and changes in political parties
- The changing role of government in American life
- The intellectual and political expressions of nationalism
- Major movements and individual figures in the history of American literature, art, and popular culture
- Abolitionism and reform movements
- Long-term democratic trends (immigration and internal migration)
- The motivations for and character of American expansionism
- The process of economic growth and development
- The causes and impacts of major wars in U.S. history

You are entitled to a free download version of an electronic simulated test bank that simulates the actual exam. This test bank contains over 350 questions and provides you will three full length computer based exams. To receive your electronic please send a copy of your receipt to sales@perfectscoresoftware.com.

CHAPTER 1 - THE FRENCH AND INDIAN WAR (1754-1763)

The French and Indian War, a colonial extension of the Seven Years War that ravaged Europe from 1756 to 1763, was the bloodiest American war in the 18th century. It took more lives than the American Revolution, involved people on three continents, including the Caribbean. The war was the product of an imperial struggle, a clash between the French and English over colonial territory and wealth. Within these global forces, the war can also be seen as a product of the localized rivalry between British and French colonists.

Tensions between the British and French in America had been rising for some time, as each side wanted to increase its land holdings. What is now considered the French and Indian War (though at the time the war was undeclared), began in November 1753, when the young Virginian major George Washington and a number of men headed out into the Ohio region with the mission to deliver a message to a French captain demanding that French troops withdraw from the territory. The demand was rejected. In 1754, Washington received authorization to build a fort near the present site of Pittsburgh. He was unsuccessful because of the strong French presence in the area. In May, Washington's troops clashed with local French forces, a skirmish that ultimately resulted in Washington having to surrender the meager fort he had managed to build just one month later. The incident set off a string of small battles. In 1755, The British sent General Edward Braddock to oversee the British Colonial forces, but on his way to oust the French from Fort Duquesne he was surprised by the French and badly routed, losing his life in the process.

After a year and a half of undeclared war, the French and the English formally declared war in May 1756. For the first three years of the war, the outnumbered French dominated the battlefield, soundly defeating the English in battles at Fort Oswego and Ticonderoga. Perhaps the most notorious battle of the war was the French victory at Fort William Henry, which ended in a massacre of British soldiers by Indians allied with the French. The battle and ensuing massacre was captured for history--though not accurately--by James Fenimore Cooper in his classic The Last of the Mohicans .

The tide turned for the British in 1758, as they began to make peace with important Indian allies and, under the direction of Lord William Pitt began adapting their war strategies to fit the territory and landscape of the American frontier. The British had a further stroke of good fortune when the French were abandoned by many of their Indian allies. Exhausted by years of battle, outnumbered and outgunned by the British, the French collapsed during the years 1758-59, climaxing with a massive defeat at Quebec in September 1759.

By September 1760, the British controlled all of the North American frontier; the war between the two countries was effectively over. The 1763 Treaty of Paris, which also ended the European Seven Years War, set the terms by which France would capitulate. Under the treaty, France was forced to surrender all of her American possessions to the British and the Spanish.

Although the war with the French ended in 1763, the British continued to fight with the Indians over the issue of land claims. "Pontiac's War" flared shortly after the Treaty of Paris was signed, and many of the battlefields--including Detroit, Fort Pitt, and Niagara--were the same. The Indians, however, already exhausted by many years of war, quickly capitulated under the ferocious British retaliation; still, the issue remained a problem for many years to come.

The results of the war effectively ended French political and cultural influence in North America. England gained massive amounts of land and vastly strengthened its hold on the continent. The war, however, also had subtler results. It badly eroded the relationship between England and Native Americans; and, though the war seemed to strengthen England's hold on the colonies, the effects of the French and Indian War played a major role in the worsening relationship between England and its colonies that eventually led into the Revolutionary War.

The French and Indian War, a colonial manifestation of the same forces and tensions that erupted in the European Seven Years' War, was, quite simply, a war about imperialism. The French and the English were competing for land and trading rights in North America; these strivings resulted in a great deal of disputed land, particularly that of the rich Ohio Valley. Each nation saw this territory as vital in its effort to increase its own power and wealth while simultaneously limiting the strength of its rival. Although the war itself therefore stemmed from a fairly simple motivation, its consequences were far-reaching. The English victory in the war decided the colonial fate of North America, and yet at the same time sowed the seeds of the eventual colonial revolution. After the war, the British ended their century-long policy of salutary neglect, attempting to keep the colonials under a more watchful eye. The British also raised taxes in an effort to pay for the war. Both of these postwar policies resulted in massive colonial discontent and added to the budding nationalism that eventually exploded in the Revolutionary War.

The French and Indian War also had lasting (and devastating) effects for the Native American tribes of North America. The British took retribution against Native American nations that fought on the side of the French by cutting off their supplies and then forcibly compelling the tribes to obey the rules of the new mother country. Native Americans that had fought on the side of the British with the understanding that their cooperation would lead to an end to European encroachment on their land were unpleasantly surprised when many new settlers began to move in. Furthermore, with the French presence gone, there was little to distract the British government from focusing its stifling attention on whatever Native American tribes lay within its grasp. All of these factors played into the multinational Indian uprising called "Pontiac's War" that erupted directly following the end of the French and Indian War.

Before the French and Indian War broke out, the main issue facing the two colonial powers was division of the continent. The English were settled along the eastern seaboard, in Georgia, the Carolinas, and what is now the Northeastern United States. The French controlled Louisiana in the South and, to the far North, Acadia (Nova Scotia) and Northeast Canada. The Cherokee, Catawabas, Creeks, Choctaws and Chickasaws inhabited the mountainous region in between the two powers and attempted to maintain their autonomy by trading with both nations. Based primarily on the travels of the explorer Rene-Robert Cavelier de Salle in 1682, France regarded itself as possessor of all disputed lands in the west, including the Ohio Valley. The English needless to say, disputed the French claim. Although the French lay claim to far more territory than the English did, the French territory was sparsely populated. Often French territory was not marked by the existence of outposts or towns but simple forts manned by only a few men. English territory, by contrast, was rapidly being populated. The pressures of a growing population, the desire for expansion, and impatience to gain access to the profitable fur trade of the Great Lakes region impelled an intense English desire to extend westward during the 18th century.

During the first half of the 18th century, the British slowly moved to expand their land base. In 1727, they constructed a trading fort, Oswego, on the banks of Lake Ontario. In 1749, the Ohio Company, a consortium of Virginian speculators, successfully petitioned the English crown for lands in the Ohio region with the purpose of building a permanent settlement. That same year the French began sending diplomats to the British, demanding that Fort Oswego be abandoned and that England recognize French land boundaries. The next year a conference was held in Paris in an attempt to sort out some of the conflicting claims. No progress was made. In 1752, the Marquis Duquesne assumed the office of governor of New France, with specific instructions to secure possession of the Ohio Valley. All of these small agitations set the stage for the French and Indian War to explode.

While the War has often been portrayed as merely a fight between England and France, the many Indian nations that lived in these regions played a pivotal role in both the instigation and the outcome of the conflict. The fight for control of the continent was a fight between three nations, and until the late 18th century it was not at all certain which one would win. The Indians, especially the Five nations of the Iroquois, were exceptionally good at playing the French and the English against each other in order to maximize their own benefits. The French and Indian War was a guerrilla war of small skirmishes and surprise attacks. The terrain was unfamiliar to both the French and the English; the involvement of the Indian nations as allies in battle made an enormous difference. In fact, some historians have hypothesized that the turning point in the war came when many of the Indian nations changed their war policies and turned their backs on the French. Faced with the greater resources of the British and lacking the advantage of their Indian allies, the French were left with little hope, and soon lost the continent.

IMPORTANT PEOPLE AND PLACES

British and colonials

- Earl of Loundoun - Appointed commander-in-chief of the British forces in 1756, Loundoun presided over, and caused, many devastating failures for the British.
- Major General Edward Braddock - The first general to arrive from Britain. He was killed in 1755 at the first battle for Fort Duquesne.
- Lieutenant Governor Robert Dinwiddie - The colonial leader of Virginia in 1754, Dinwiddie was concerned about French encroachment on the Virginia border. In late 1753, he sends a 21-year-old major in the Virginia military named George Washington to tell the French to back away from the border.
- William Johnson - Johnson began his career as the Indian agent for the colony of New York. During this period he was one of the most successful negotiators with many Indian nations, especially the Iroquois. During the war he became a war hero as well, leading the British to victory at the Battle of Lake George in 1755.
- Lieutenant Colonel George Munro - In history, Munro met defeat as the leader of Fort William Henry in 1757. In literary history, he is a central figure in James Fenimore Cooper's classic The Last of the Mohicans.
- William Pitt - Pitt assumed leadership of the British ministry in December 1756. His aggressive new policies for the war were a crucial part of turning the tide in Britain's favor in the latter half of the war.
- Captain Robert Rogers - Leader of the Rangers, a rough-and-tumble force of men from New Hampshire. Operated as spies and participated in guerrilla warfare against the French to great success throughout the war.

- George Washington - Washington began his career as a brash and careless diplomat and military leader. After being asked to resign after the Fort Necessity fiasco, he returns as a volunteer under British authority. The French and Indian War is where Washington learned how to be a leader.
- James Wolfe - Major British general who led the British to victory in the Battle of Quebec.

French and Colonials

- Louis-Joseph de Montcalm - Beginning in 1756, Montcalm took over as commander-in-chief of the French forces in North America. He was a much-feared and respected general.
- Marquis de Vaudreuil - In 1755, he became the governor of Canada, replacing the Marquis Duquesne.
- Forts and Places
- Fort George/Fort Duquesne/Fort Pitt - This centrally located fort in what is now Pittsburgh, PA changed hands many times during the war. It was the site of England's first disastrous battle, in which Braddock lost his life.
- Fort Necessity - This hastily constructed fort in Great Meadows, PA was the site of George Washington's first defeat in 1754. Later in American history, it oddly came to symbolize the rugged spirit of the colonials.
- Fort William Henry - Site of the most notorious massacre in colonial history, this fort located near the Hudson River fell to the French in 1757.
- Louisbourg - An important city on the east coast of Canada (in present-day Nova Scotia). It was a French stronghold of arms and supplies.
- Ticonderoga - A major French fort and city north of Albany. The British failed repeatedly to seize it; they finally succeeded in 1759.

TIMELINE

- March 15, 1744-October 18, 1748: King George's War The warm-up to the French and Indain War between France and England, also fought for domination over North America. Ends with the treaty of Aix-la-Chapelle and no clear victor.
- 1752-1753: Agitation grows Tension grows between France and England over competing land and trading claims. Minor skirmishes break out, particularly in rural areas.
- November-December 1753: The message George Washington carries Virginia's ultimatum over French encroachment to Captain Legardeur de Saint-Pierre at Riviere aux Boeufs. He rejects it.
- May 28, 1754: The first battle Washington defeats the French in a surprise attack. His troops retreat to Great Meadows and build Fort Necessity.
- July 3, 1754: The French take Fort Necessity
- July 17, 1754: Washington's resignation Blamed for Fort Necessity, Washington resigns. He will later return as a volunteer under British authority.
- June 17, 1755: The British seize Acadia (Nova Scotia)
- July 9, 1755: The Battle of the Wilderness British General Braddock's forces are defeated near Fort Duquesne in Pennsylvania, leaving the backwoods of British territory undefended.
- September 9, 1755: The Battle of Lake George British Colonel William Johnson's forces win, making Johnson the first British hero of the war.
- May 8-9, 1756: Declarations of War Great Britain declares war on France. France declares war on Great Britain.

- August 14, 1756: Fort Oswego The French capture this fort on the banks of the Great Lakes.
- August 8, 1757: Fort William Henry The commander-in-chief of the French forces, Louis-Joseph de Montcalm takes Fort William Henry. The infamous massacre occurs, later dramatized in James Fenimore Cooper's The Last of the Mohicans.
- July 8, 1758: The French take Fort Ticonderoga
- July 26, 1758: Louisbourg The British seize Louisbourg, opening the route to Canada.
- August 27, 1758: Fort Frontenac The French surrender this fort on Lake Ontario, effectively destroying their ability to communicate with their troops in the Ohio Valley.
- October 21, 1758: British/Indian Peace The British make peace with the Iroquois, Shawnee, and Delaware Indians.
- November 26, 1758: The British recapture Fort Duquesne It is renamed "Pittsburgh."
- May 1, 1759: The British capture the French island of Guadeloupe in the Caribbean
- June 26, 1759: The British take Fort Ticonderoga
- July 25, 1759: A Slow Route to Victory The British take Fort Niagara; the French abandon Crown Point. After these two victories, the British control the entire western frontier.
- September 13, 1759: Quebec The British win the decisive Battle of Quebec. Montcalm and Wolfe, the commanding generals of both armies, perish in battle.
- May 16, 1760: French Siege of Quebec fails
- September 8, 1760: Montreal Montreal falls to the British; letters are signed finishing the surrender of Canada.
- (circa) September 15, 1760: The functional end of the war The British flag is raised over Detroit, effectively ending the war.
- 1761: The British make peace with the Cherokee Indians
- September 18, 1762: French attempt to retake Newfoundland fails
- February 10, 1763: Treaty of Paris All French possessions east of the Mississippi, except New Orleans, are given to the British. All French possessions west of the Mississippi are given to the Spanish. France regains Martinique, Guadeloupe and St. Lucia.
- April 27, 1763: Indian Wars Pontiac, the Ottowa Chief, proposes a coalition of Ottowas, Potawatomies and Hurons for the purpose of attacking Detroit.
- May 9, 1763: Battle of Detroit Pontiac's forces lay siege to Detroit. That summer, his allies destroy forts at Venango, Le Boeuf and Presque Isle.
- July 1763: Smallpox Men of the garrison at Fort Pitt infect besieging chiefs with blankets from the smallpox hospital. Soon faced with an epidemic, the Indians retreat.
- October 31, 1763: Pontiac capitulates at Detroit Indian power in the Ohio Valley is broken.

EARLY BATTLES AND FORT NECESSITY

In 1753, French forces began to build a series of Forts along the Allegheny River in Ohio territory, impinging upon land claimed by Virginia in its charter of 1609. Robert Dinwiddie, the Virginia's Lieutenant Governor, sent George Washington, a 21-year-old major, to warn the French captain Legareur de Saint-Pierre of his troops' trespass. On his way to deliver Dinwiddie's message, Washington attempted to enlist the help of a large group of Ohio Indians, with no success. Once he did arrive, the message was ignored; the French refused to recognize the Virginia charter. Though he returned to Virginia with nothing to show for his trip, Washington was nonetheless promoted to Lieutenant Colonel and, in the spring of 1754, given the mission of removing the French from the Ohio region.

Because of the powerful presence of the French, who had completed their string of forts along the Allegheny, Washington was unsuccessful in is attempt to build a fort near Pittsburgh. Then, at dawn on May 28, 1754, a Mingo Indian named Tanaghrisson who had agreed to scout for Washington spotted a French patrol stalking Washington's men. Tanaghrisson showed Washington how to surprise the French; in the ensuing attack the French commander Jumonville was killed. That the French would retaliate was obvious, and Washington's men retreated to Great Meadows, PA, where, against the advice of their Indian guides, they hastily threw up a stockade, nicknamed Necessity. The Indians, disgusted, abandoned Washington and his small contingent of Virginia militiamen. Sure enough, the French outnumbered him and took the fort easily on July 4, 1754.

This battle proved a catalyst in the deteriorating relationship between the English and the French. In a famous affadivit, the French claimed that Jumonville had been "assassinated." The English insisted that this word be translated as Jumonville's "defeat." The battle thus precipitated a war of propaganda right along with the physical battles that were to follow.

Washington returned to Virginia on July 17 and gave an account of the battle at Great Meadows to the Virginia council. The council blamed him for most of the failure. Humiliated, Washington resigned his position, though he later returned to battle as a volunteer under General Edward Braddock.

In the years leading up to 1753, the English had far less territory than the French. English settlements clustered between the Appalachian Mountains and the Atlantic coast, though many colonies had charters granting them land west of the mountains. French settlements, though more sparsely populated covered far more land, originating out of fur-trading outposts, extended through the interior of the continent, as far north as Quebec, as far south as New Orleans, and all the way to St. Louis in the west. The French hoped to keep the British pinned between the mountains and the ocean. The British, alternatively, desperately wanted to expand westward, as a speculative outlet for their growing population and because they wanted further access to the profitable fur trade. Competing land claims and disputes over encroachment had been going on between the French and the English for almost a hundred years and through three minor wars, by the early 1750s, tensions had begun to swell once more.

Virginia was a particularly crowded territory and could not expand, since it was hemmed in on all three sides by French territory and natural obstacles. Robert Dinwiddie had no illusions about the circumstances his colony faced: he expected his message to the French to meet with the failure that it did. He did not, however, anticipate Washington's tremendous miscalculation the following spring.

Though George Washington later gained fame as a war hero, he cut his teeth during the French and Indian War-- and, like most newcomers, he failed miserably. It was his difficult experience during the French and Indian, some argue, that helped to make him the general he eventually became. Interestingly enough, though, even Washington's early failures have come to take on a heroic cast in American history. After Washington's great success in the Revolutionary War, Fort Necessity came to stand as a metaphor for the rugged colonial spirit. That metaphor persists even today, although historians have proven that the fort was little more than a few logs lashed together to surround Washington's hapless army.

THE FAILURE OF GENERAL BRADDOCK

Soon after the capitulation of Fort Necessity, the British crown and Parliament learned that 78 French troops had been deployed to attack the British fort Oswego in Canada. Parliament responded by allocating more money to the colonies for the purpose of funding an expanded militia. They also sent British regiments to the colonies. In February 1755, the first British general to ever set foot in the colonies, Edward Braddock, arrived in Virginia.

Braddock was a general in the tradition of British generals, well versed in European warfare and completely ignorant of the possibilities and necessities of New World warfare. Soon after reaching shore, Braddock crafted a three-pronged strategy for defeating the French. The Massachusetts regiments were sent to reinforce the defenses at Oswego, with the expectation that they would then go on to capture Fort Niagara on the south shore of Lake Erie. Colonel William Johnson was assigned to capture Fort Frederick at Crown Point, on the banks of Lake Champlain. Braddock himself was to take Fort Duquesne in Pennsylvania.

The first battle after arrival of Braddock actually had nothing to do with Braddock's plan. In May and June of 1755, about 2,000 militiamen moved into French controlled Acadia (now Nova Scotia), and quite easily brought about the fall of the region in May and June of 1755. Many of the battles were small and almost uncontested, as the region was sparsely occupied. Some of the forts were won after a few days of musket fire, without any direct conflict between the troops. The governor of Nova Scotia, Charles Lawrence, sent about 6,000 Acadians, some half of those living in the region, to the colonies after the battle. Quite a few of these Acadians settled in New Orleans, where they became known as "Cajuns" and created an earthy, rich culture of their own in the United States. For the French, the loss of Acadia certainly stung, but it was no great tragedy; Acadia had little strategic value.

The first significant battle of 1755 was Braddock's battle for Fort Duquesne. Despite the fact that the British outnumbered the French by two to one, 2,200 men to 1,000 men, the French won in a colossal rout. In approaching the fort, Braddock arranged his men to cross the Monongahela River in columns, thereby allowing the French to easily ambush the British forces while using the surrounding trees as cover. In all, the British lost 977 men to the French's 9. Braddock was also killed. The British disaster would have been even worse had the French, shocked by their easy victory, decided to pursue the retreating army.

When news of Braddock's defeat reached the regiments approaching Fort Oswego, morale sank and there were many desertions. The attack on Fort Niagara was deferred until the next year, and the troops reinforcing Oswego were left with the prospect of facing an invigorated and more-experienced French army. The loss at Fort Duquesne sent the British forces into a tailspin from which they did not quickly recover; a three-year period the British termed "the years of losing."

The story of General Edward Braddock's defeat can be interpreted as a lack of cultural knowledge. Braddock's fighting style was suited to the plains of England and Europe, where columns of men in red jackets marching in an intimidating line towards the enemy was designed to create the image of an impenetrable force. In Europe, this strategy worked. However, the regions in which the French and Indian War took place were not plains; the battles of the war took place in mountains, forests, and fierce wildernesses. Trees, rivers, waterfalls, mountains, and hills twisted the landscape, making straight-on combat virtually impossible and highly unlikely. The type of battle most suited to this natural landscape was not Braddock's style, but rather sniping gunfire from the cover of trees, ambushes, surprise attacks, and guerrilla warfare. One of the primary reasons the French were able to hold an advantage in the war for four years despite being outnumbered and underfunded, was their tactical understanding of the landscape, and their ability and willingness to act on that tactical understanding. The French owed a great deal of their understanding to their Indian allies, who taught them invaluable things about fighting in the American landscape.

The example of Braddock demonstrates how far the British were in the early stages of the war from comprehending the realities of warfare in the colonies. It was only after Lord Pitt took charge of the army and reorganized it according to the necessities of the colonies that the British began to turn the tide of the war.

UNDECLARED WAR

Despite General Edward Braddock's massive failure and the unrest of the regiments at Fort Oswego, there was good news for the British in 1755. William Johnson's troops had a surprising victory at Crown Point on Lake Champlain, taking Fort Frederick's. Johnson, an Irish immigrant, emerged as the first hero of the war and set himself on a quick rise to fame and historical importance.

One of the reasons for Johnson's success was due to his renowned ability to negotiate with the Indians. While George Washington had failed abysmally in his attempt to procure the help of tribes near Fort Necessity, Johnson recruited allies from the Mohawk and Iroquois to accompany his colonial troops. Included in his forces was Captain Robert Rogers, a 23-year-old recruit from New Hampshire who went on to lead the Rangers. Johnson's forces approached Crown Point in early September. On September 8, the English forces surrounded the French and attacked from behind a breastwork of trees and overturned wagons. As the French advanced, the British climbed over the breastwork for hand-to-hand combat; the French fled in disarray. Johnson, who was wounded in the battle, performed a feat that was not to be repeated until 1758--defeating a French army with a colonial army unfortified by British professionals. Johnson received a baronetcy for his troubles.

All during the year of 1755 the British colonial forces suffered a lack of support (and, perhaps more importantly, funding) from both the colonies and the crown. The colonies were reluctant to provide funding for a war that they felt, perhaps rightly, was not their own. After all, it was Britain who had bullied the French for more territory. The British crown, meanwhile, was reluctant to send money to the colonies for war when catastrophes like Braddock's continued to take place. A similar scenario took place on the French side, though with perhaps even more neglect. The French crown had less money to send their colonies, and France's attention was in Europe, where Prussia was becoming increasingly antagonistic and was on the verge of invading Saxony in 1756, setting off the Seven Year's War.

William Johnson's role as an Indian leader made a crucial difference in both his ability to recruit allies and his ability to lead a successful battle against the French. Without a doubt, Britain had a more difficult time crafting successful Indian policy and getting the Indians to cooperate as allies in war than did the French. This can be attributed, in large part, to a difference in colonial policy on behalf of the French and the English. In general, the British policy towards the Indians was to make them into Englishmen, to "reduce them to civility." The British thought the Indians were hopelessly arrogant, savage, and pagan. These beliefs led to a general feeling of cultural superiority that affected all of their relations with the Indians. They were eager to convert the Indians to Protestant

Christianity, change their customs, and induct them into the British way of life. Often they were so adamant about the superiority of the British way of life that they did not listen to the Indians on practical matters, like fighting the French in the American wilderness.

Though the French were no more humane towards the Indians, they were traditionally much less interested in altering the history and cultures of the peoples they encountered. (This can also be seen in comparisons of French and British colonial history around the world.) They certainly believed in the superiority of the French way of life, and they did all they could to convert the Indians to Catholicism, but in their relations with the Indians they left room for a sort of cultural blending to take place. For example, if the Indians were more likely to believe in Catholicism when they could also worship their own idols as "saints," the French were happy to encourage them. As such, the French were usually more successful at making Indian allies and negotiating with the Indians. This lent them a crucial advantage in war.

DECLARED WAR AND FRENCH DOMINANCE

The years 1756 and 1757 brought three things: the arrival of Louis-Joseph de Montcalm, newly appointed commander-in-chief of the French forces in North America, declarations of war by the two mother countries, and a string of French victories in forts along the Northeast frontier.

While General Edward Braddock's defeat at Fort Duquesne was offset by William Johnson's victory at Crown Point, 1756 and 1757 brought nothing but bad news for the English. With the arrival of Montcalm in March 1756, an exceptionally talented strategist and warrior, the French forces gained a new level of professionalism, savvy, and strength. The British, meanwhile, were disorganized and fighting among themselves. Conflicts between British officers and colonial militiamen were common, culminating in the summer of 1756, when the regiments headed to Crown Point were upset by a small "mutiny."

After almost two years of battles, England and France finally declared war on each other in May 1756. The declaration brought an influx of funding colonies and the arrival of even more British troops. The Earl of Loundoun was appointed commander-in-chief of the British troops in America, but he shortly proved himself as inept as Braddock in the all-important areas of Indian policy and frontier battle strategy. It was under Loundoun's command that the "mutiny" of colonial militiamen exploded, and it was under his command that the British suffered some of the worst defeats of the war.

One of most devastating of these defeats was the fall of Fort Oswego on August 14, 1756. The loss of the fort shocked the British, though in hindsight it's fall seems unsurprising. The fort was devastated by long periods of neglect. The surrounding tribes were already hostile to the British, and Montcalm swayed them further to the French side by spreading a rumor of plunder as a reward for all Indians who came to fight. The fort offered little resistance, and it fell to the French easily. This was an important strategic gain for the French, as it offered them control of Lake Ontario and access to all of the provisions and equipment that had been painfully transported to the fort.

The "mutiny" at Crown Point was another example of British failure to think clearly regarding colonial policy. Loundoun humiliated colonial officers by placing ceilings upon their rank, announcing that a regular British captain would outrank even the highest-ranking colonial. Loundoun caused further consternation by ordering that the troops be incorporated into a single body. His intention was clearly to fortify the colonial troops with British men; the colonial men did not take kindly to the implicit assumption of their inferiority. When Loundoun's orders met with resistance, he denounced the colonials as mutinous and sent many of them home.

Both England and France resisted declaring war on each other for as long as possible. To the mother countries, war meant expense, and colonies were meant to be pure profit--a declaration of war would cut into their budgets and make the colonies less profitable, possibly for years to come. The French and English were willing to wage an undeclared and even partially neglected war in North America. However, when Prussia invaded Saxony in 1756, triggering a European war, called the Seven Year's War in which France, Sweden, Russia, and Austria-Hungary sided against the Prussians and English, the pressure became too great: France and England declared war on each other. The Seven Year's War has been called the first modern world war: it encompassed several continents and three separate names. There were campaigns not just in North America (The French and Indian War), but Europe (Seven Year's War), India (Third Carnatic War), Africa, and the Caribbean. Other European countries, including Austria, Russia, Prussia, and Spain were also drawn into the conflict.

Montcalm and Loundoun had incredibly different approaches to war, and this explains the general pattern of French success and English failure over the first two years of declared conflict. Montcalm was flexible enough to adapt his own strategies to the North American continent, wise enough to sway Indian nations over to the French cause, and brutal enough to use campaigns of terror and massacre on both civilians and militias. Loundoun, on the other hand, was loutish and unwilling to budge on important issues like Indian policy and battle strategy. His openly condescending behavior toward the colonial troops shows how far out of touch most of the British were with life in the colonies, and underlines conflicts to come between the mother country and its American colonies.

THE MASSACRE AT FORT WILLIAM HENRY

The fall of Fort William Henry and the ensuing "massacre" of the surrendered English on August 8, 1757 is one of the most famous incidents in American history. As dramatized by James Fenimore Cooper in The Last of the Mohicans , the fall of the fort was an incredible tragedy of epic proportions, an illustration of the nobility of the British and the savagery of both the French and the Indians, and an example of brutal primal rage. The real picture is more complicated.

On August 2, 1757 Major General Daniel Webb learned of a concentration of French forces preparing to attack Fort William Henry, which was on the southern end of Lake George along the route to Montreal. With the poor foresight typical among the British officers up to that point in the war, Webb decided to retreat, leaving Lieutenant Colonel George Munro in charge. When Munro, who was left to defend the fort with 2,300 men (only 1,600 of whom were fit for battle) learned that Louis-Joseph de Montcalm was preparing to attack the fort with over 7,000 men, he appealed to Webb for reinforcements. Though Webb had a good number of ready and able reinforcements at his side, he refused Munro's request, and sent back a letter advising Munro to settle on the best possible terms. Amazingly, Munro held out against the French for four days. But the odds were virtually impossible, and he finally capitulated on August 9.

The British troops were disarmed as a condition of surrender, and made to march from the fort. As the inhabitants of the fort streamed out, the Ottawa, Abenaki, and Potawatomi Indians who fought with the French fell upon the British. The massacre began with the helpless-- the wounded and sick men that had been in the fort's hospital and were carried out last. Women and children, most likely families of the soldiers, were also murdered. Other victims included black and mulatto servants, Indian allies of the British, and retreating soldiers who were in sight when order broke down.

While the Indians attacked, the French did nothing to stop the massacre or go to the assistance of those who were being slaughtered. Montcalm excused his behavior with the following words: "I have been obliged here to gratify the Indian nations, who will not leave without me, and am obliged to pass my time with them in ceremonies as tiresome as they are necessary." Montcalm did attempt to restore hostages that the Indians carried off, and he was successful at rescuing many of them.

The number of casualties of the massacre continues to be disputed. It is certain that the French underestimated the death toll, and the English wildly overestimated it, both for propaganda purposes. Contemporary historians normally place the number at over 200, with over 300 captives taken.

The massacre at Fort William Henry became a vital part of American history, though Hawthorne's version often took precedence over the real facts. The massacre also became a cornerstone of colonial propaganda against the Indians, much the way the Battle of the Alamo was used to justify the Mexican War in 1846. While the massacre at Fort William Henry is less problematic than the Alamo, the "villains" of Fort William Henry had clear reasons for their behavior.

When the French recruited the Ottowas, Potowatomis and Abenakis to fight in the battle for the fort, they promised them the opportunity to plunder the fort after the battle was won. This clause was crucial to the Indians because a number of devastating forces?-including smallpox and starvation brought on by the disruptions of European settlers and the war--made every opportunity to get food, supplies, and money crucial for their survival. Indians were not usually paid by either the British or the French, except in gifts of rum, blankets, clothing, and trade goods. Depending on the Indian nation, "plunder" might be interpreted as including the opportunity to gather scalps from the enemy. As they had at Oswego, the French usually turned their backs while the Indians engaged in their scalping.

But at Fort William Henry, the French made other plans. In their negotiations with the British as to rights of surrender, they allowed the British to remove most of their personal belongings and goods from the fort. No Indians were present at these negotiations. As the troops filed out of the fort with all of their supplies, the Indians grew infuriated. The British were leaving with their only spoils of war, and it appeared as though the French had deceived them. The Indians reacted violently, by attacking the helpless sick and wounded at the end of the train, and chaos quickly broke out.

The Indians who seized scalps from the sick at the back of the train were indeed punished brutally for their actions--the scalps were infected with smallpox, which was transferred to the Indians and their communities, further weakening the Indians. But both the British and colonials used the massacre for years after the war as an example of the "savagery" of the Indians and a justification for seizing their lands. The truth, unfortunately, isn't quite so simple.

British Ascension (1758)

In December 1756, William Pitt became the leader of the British ministry. He adopted aggressive new policies that had a crucial effect on the latter half of the war. One of those policies was, in October 1757, to recall the Earl of Loundoun as commander-in-chief of British forces in North America.

The first battle of 1758 was, nonetheless, a failure for the British. They failed to take the Fort at Ticonderoga, despite having a force of 16,000 men to the French's 3,500 troops. The battle was a disaster, due mostly to a lack of British leadership. The only British allies to emerge from the battle with any credibility at all were Robert Rogers' Rangers, who were rapidly gaining fame and success for their skill at scouting, spying, and employing guerrilla tactics against the French.

Pitt's new tactics soon began to take hold, however, and, after Ticonderoga, things quickly began to change for the British. On July 26, 1758, the British finally captured Louisbourg after many attempts. This victory opened the route to Canada. Just a month later the British achieved another victory by taking Fort Frontenac on the shores of Lake Ontario, and thereby cutting off the ability of the French to communicate with their troops in the Ohio Valley. In November, the British captured Fort Duquesne, the site of Braddock's disaster and death. Duquesne was renamed Fort Pitt, after the new English leader, and eventually became known as Pittsburgh, PA.

With Pitt at the helm, England finally began to take advantage of its huge advantage in supplies and manpower, and the tide of the war quickly turned. In May 1759, the British captured the French island of Guadeloupe in the Caribbean. Guadeloupe was a wealthy, sugar-producing island and the French would certainly want it back in any peace negotiation--a chip the British planned to use for their advantage. They followed this victory with the seizure of Ticonderoga in June and Fort Niagara in July. The French abandoned their post at Crown Point shortly after, leaving the whole of the western frontier to the British.

Unlike previous British generals and rulers, William Pitt did not attempt to force the colonies to comply with British policy by waving the rights of the mother country in their faces. Instead, he asked for their cooperation, and he got it. He also made it clear in court that the way to win the war was not merely by defending the British's existing territory, but by striking at the heart of the French empire and attacking the possessions the French held most dear.

Pitt's policies were aided by a change of heart among a number of the Indian nations. Many abandoned their alliances with the French; some of them going so far as to fight against the French. In October 1758, the British made peace with the Shawnees, the Delaware, and the enormous Iroquois nation. Both the British and the French had for years coveted making an alliance with these three powerful Indian nations. Although all three refused to take an integral role in the fighting, their favor surely boosted the profile of the English with other Indian nations.

Battle of Quebec

After the French abandoned Crown Point, the British controlled the western frontier. However, the French strongholds were further north, in Quebec and Montreal. These were also the French cities and forts that were most heavily supplied, funded, and protected.

William Pitt emphasized the importance of gaining Quebec in assuring outright British victory; he gave the assignment of conquering the city to famed general James Wolfe. Wolfe and Vice-admiral Charles Saunders organized a team of ships and infantry to besiege the city. The battle began in June 1759 and lasted for three months. The ships ascended the St. Lawrence flawlessly and held out against massive French assaults of fire and cannon.

Despite the romantic glaze that hangs over the Quebec campaign, it was a desperate struggle that frequently became brutal. Wolfe, like Montcalm, was not immune to terrorizing the civilian population, and one of his first orders to scouting parties was to "burn and lay waste the country." Louis-Joseph de Montcalm responded with equal brutality, threatening the frightened civilians with "the savages" when they meekly appealed to him for surrender.

Because Quebec was so mighty and heavily fortified, Wolfe was forced to starve the French out for two and a half months. The British forces were not large enough to completely surround the city and cut off its supplies; though French food and materiel were rapidly dwindling they were still enough to keep the soldiers alive.

Finally, on September 13, Wolfe landed a small host of soldiers in the middle of the night at l'Anse au Foulon, upstream of the city. Sheer luck played as much a role as skill in this success--Wolfe was able to fool a sentry and a general by speaking French and gathered the rest of his troops for the invasion. Montcalm was so disoriented by this bizarre turn of events that he made many mistakes in defending the city. First, he gathered his troops at the wrong place - downstream of the city, in a place called Beaumont. When they finally caught up to the British, Montcalm ordered them to charge instead of waiting for reinforcements. The battle lasted only fifteen minutes and both Wolfe and Montcalm were killed.

After the capture of Quebec, the rest of Canada quickly fell. The French attempted a brief counter-siege from May 11-16, 1760, but quickly gave up. Montreal capitulated in September 1760, and the British General Amherst and the French Marquise de Vaudreuil signed letters of capitulation that finished the surrender of Canada. On or around September 15, the British flag was hoisted over the city of Detroit, effectively ending the war.

The victory at Quebec can be attributed to many factors. Although Quebec was heavily defended, the overall position of the French was extremely weak. They had lost many of their Indian allies. The army was strained to the limit after years of fighting against the greater resources of the British. British victories at Fort Duquesne and Niagara cut off French communication with the west, leaving the forces at Quebec without reinforcements of either men or supplies. All of this combined with James Wolfe's tactics of terror made the siege brutally effective.

It helped that Quebec's landscape was not twisted and wild like America's. The British soldiers could exercise their disciplined techniques of columns and volley fire without the threat of sniping and ambush that had worked so well for the French in the American colonies. Wolfe was also fortunate to be aided by several unflappable and highly skilled officers, including Saunders, who held up the pillars of the final battle.

After the fall of Quebec, the rest of the war was almost an afterthought. The French forces had been completely demoralized by a string of defeats, and the British were in position to dominate both the West and Canada. After a feeble attempt to win back Quebec, and a brave attempt to hold out against the British at Montreal, the French capitulated and turned their attention to gaining the best treaty possible.

A Tenuous Peace (1760-63)

After the surrender of Canada in 1760, the war was effectively over in North America. Nonetheless, fighting continued in other parts of the world for the next two years and small skirmishes--especially Indian raids--occasionally broke out in the colonies and along the Canadian border.

Despite this, the French and Indian War ended French political influence on the North American continent, a fact underscored by the Treaty of Paris, signed at the end of the Seven Year's War, in February 1763. As part of the negotiations for this treaty, France regained its wealthy sugar-producing islands in the Caribbean that had been lost to the British during the fighting--Martinique, Guadeloupe, and St. Lucia. With the exception of New Orleans, France surrendered all of its North American possessions east of the Mississippi to the British. All possessions west of the Mississippi were given to the Spanish.

Although the British won the war with the French, the British still faced pressing colonial problems that the Treaty of Paris only aggravated. The Indians in particular were angered by the provisions of peace that left little room for their concerns. One of the reasons they agreed to fight--on either side of the war--was to ensure that they would retain the sole rights to their land. Instead, the exhausted Indians were faced with the immediate encroachment of British speculators, traders, and settlers.

Disaffected and impoverished, a host of Indian nations organized in April 1763 under the leadership of an Ottawa chief named Pontiac. The forces included Ottawas, Chippewas, Potawatomis, Hurons, Shawnees, and Delawares. On May 9, 1763, the allies laid siege to Fort Detroit. That summer, they proceeded to destroy forts at Venango, LeBoeuf, and Presque Isle. They also attacked forts at Niagara and Pittsburgh.

The British reacted immediately and brutally. Their tactics included both ruthless bloodshed (Commander-in-chief of the British forces, Jeffrey Amherst, encouraged soldiers to "Put to death all that fall into your hands") and deception (the soldiers at Fort Pitt spread smallpox among the Delawares by presenting them with a "gift"--infected blankets from the hospital nearby). Their tactics weakened the Indians and forced Pontiac to capitulate Fort Detroit on October 31, 1763.

With the end of Pontiac's war, the fight for control over the North American empire east of the Mississippi was officially over, though small battles with the Indians continued for years. Their fear of "foreigners", both French and Indian, subsided, the British turned their attention to the colonies. Having spent so much time, money, men to keep the colonies, England was now determined to keep the colonies in line and make them as profitable as possible. To ensure that they attained these goals, the British gave up their longstanding policy of salutary neglect, and instituted harsh policies and high taxes for the colonials. England's harsh treatment of the colony's after 1763 had precisely the opposite of its desired result: instead of making the colony's profitable, it made them increasingly angry, and eventually led to another uprising--the Revolutionary War, which exploded just thirteen years later.

What really won the French and Indian War? On the surface, it seems that the British won out bulk rather than skill. It is certainly true that the French were more clever strategists and better at recruiting the Indians to their cause. But the British outnumbered them, and the British had greater material resources to devote to the war. In the end, what won the war was not the guerrilla warfare that dominated as the chief strategy of battle. It was the large battles--Louisbourg, Fort Duquesne, Quebec--that made all the difference. Even when the British lost major battles to the French, as they did at Ticonderoga and the first battle at Fort Duquesne, they killed French soldiers that were not easy to replace. By overwhelming the French with sheer numbers, the British weakened their overall fitness for war and managed to eventually exhaust French resources.

The Treaty of Paris ended the French and Indian War but not the issues that caused it: specifically, land encroachment. The only difference was the enemy that remained after the war ended. After the French had been removed from the North American continent, the British turned their attention to fighting the Indians for their lands. Like the French, the Indians fought back, but faced almost certain defeat because of their limited supplies, manpower, and the general lack of cohesion between Indian tribes.

The French and Indian War failed to solve another important problem: the growing estrangement between England and its colonies on the Atlantic. It was the hope of many that fighting a common enemy would pull England and its colonies together. But it did just the opposite. Living in close quarters with the British, subjected to constant humiliation and orders from British authorities, the colonials became even more aggravated at British arrogance and flagrant greed. After the war, the heavy taxes Britain levied on the colonies to pay for the war only made the colonials angrier.

And so the French and Indian War led to more wars, one with the Indians and one with the colonials. But it brought an imperialist conflict between France and Britain to an end and decided which country would have control over the North American continent, both in history and in cultural impact.

CHAPTER 2 - PRE-REVOLUTIONARY AMERICA (1763-1776)

The French and Indian War changed the balance of power in North America in favor of the British. The French were driven out by a coalition of Britons, colonists, and Indians. However, once peace returned, these groups began to quarrel, and the situation in North America became more fragile every day. The colonists and the British held deep resentment toward each other following the war, stemming most particularly from the poor relations between British and colonial troops. Indian tribes feared that the British would allow the colonists to invade their tribal lands, and thus conducted attacks against the British in North America in attempt to stave off western settlement. Eventually, the British passed the Proclamation of 1763, limiting colonial expansion to appease the tribes, but this angered the colonists, who thought that Britain should stay out of North American affairs all together.

The next ten years consisted of a string of British impositions on the colonies, as if to test the limits of Parliament's power in North America. The first of these impositions was the use of writs of assistance, which allowed customs agents to search any building or ship without a specific warrant. The colonists saw this as a great infringement upon their natural rights. The effect of the writs was compounded by the advent of the Sugar Act, which put tight regulations on American trade, and provided for jury-less trials for accused smugglers. The colonists were greatly inconvenienced by this act, but full- fledged opposition to the British was hesitant in coming.

Parliament passed the Stamp Act in March 1765, requiring all colonists to buy specific watermarked paper for all newspapers and legal documents. Due to the Stamp Act's wide effect throughout the colonies, and the fact that it placed an internal tax on the colonies, it roused significant opposition. As violence broke out all over the colonies, the groups such as the Loyal Nine and the Sons of Liberty took control of the resistance and mobilized the citizenry in efforts to pressure Parliament to repeal the act. The culmination of the Stamp Act crisis was the strategy of non-importation undertaken by colonial businessmen, severely damaging the British economy and forcing repeal.

However, it was not long before the British again offended the colonists. Tension rose up around the Quartering Act in New York in 1766, and Parliament threatened to remove the colony's power of self-government if it did not comply with British orders. In 1767, Parliament passed the Townshend duties, a series of taxes on certain imported goods clearly designed to raise revenue for the British treasury and undertaken by Parliament in the hope of establishing a fund with which to pay the salaries of colonial governors.

The corruption with which the Townshend duties were enforced caused the tide of colonial opposition to rise to new heights. After the Boston Massacre the colonists became convinced that the British government planned to suppress them by force and deny them the right to self-government. Organized political resistance arose in the form of the Committees of correspondence, which linked the colonies in a network of political thought and action. The committees of correspondence would help lead the colonists into the Revolutionary War.

Throughout most of the history of the American colonies up until the mid- eighteenth century, the colonists had been allowed to live in relative isolation under a policy called salutary neglect. Britain's hand was only felt lightly in the government of the individual colonies, each of which had a legislature that passed laws and taxed the colonial citizens as it saw fit. Despite this political isolation, the overwhelming majority of colonists remained loyal to the king, and recognized British Parliament as the ultimate source of governmental authority. Relations with Britain were amiable, and the colonies relied on British trade for economic success and on British protection from other nations with interests in North America.

In 1756, the French and Indian War broke out between the two dominant powers in North America: Britain and France. Basically an imperial struggle for land, by the end of the war in 1760 the British had effectively driven the French out of America, gaining control of the territory from the east coast to the Mississippi River. The 1763 Treaty of Paris ceded all French lands to Britain, and decided the colonial fate of the continent. Shortly after the end of the war, the British government dropped its policy of salutary neglect and attempted to gain tighter control over its holdings in North America.

Further, the British wished to force the colonies to share in the responsibility for the monumental debt built up during the French and Indian War.

Heightened interaction between the colonies and mother country led to a steady decline in the relationship between the two parties. During the period from 1763 to 1773, Parliament and the colonies grew increasingly antagonistic. The issues that would continue at the fore throughout the revolution were first brought to light during this period, and the lines of political battle were drawn. The ideology of revolution was built upon the principles that inspired the colonists to act during the decade leading up to the revolution. Most notable was the cry of "no taxation without representation," and later "no legislation without representation," which, raised by the colonists, defined their primary quarrel with the British government.

Also during this period of antagonism, opposition to parliamentary meddling in colonial affairs developed into organized political action. The colonies, which up until now had lived not only in isolation from Britain, but also in isolation from each other, began to communicate and unify. Groups such as the Sons of Liberty, who coordinated massive demonstrations throughout the colonies, transformed the initial anti-parliament opposition from disorganized rabble into well-directed, militaristic forces. The committees of correspondence kept the colonies informed and coordinated a united front of political action. The 1773 Stamp Act Congress was the first pan-colonial meeting of political leaders. All of these organizations were key in the development of the political unity and efficient communication among colonies that was necessary for the undertaking and winning of the Revolutionary War.

The period from 1763 to 1773 mobilized political actors in the colonies and gave them the issues on which to base a rebellion. This period set the stage for the rapid descent into the revolution that ended with the colonies breaking free from the grasp of the British king and parliament. Once the war was finished the newly formed United States undertook a long period of state building, during which the offenses of the British government in the period leading up to the revolution were very much on the minds of political leaders. 1763 to 1773 was both prelude and forge to the birth of a nation.

IMPORTANT TERMS, PEOPLE, AND EVENTS

Terms

- Committees of Correspondence - Committees of Correspondence were organized by New England patriot leader Samuel Adams and made up a system of communication between patriot leaders in the towns of New England and eventually throughout the colonies. Committees of Correspondence provided the political organization necessary to unite the colonies in opposition to Parliament.

- Declaratory Act - The Declaratory Act stated that Parliament could legislate for the colonies in all cases. Passed just after the repeal of the Stamp Act, most colonists interpreted the act as a face-saving mechanism and nothing more. However, Parliament continually interpreted the act to its broadest extent and continued to try to legislate in the colonies.

- Letters From a Pennsylvania Farmer - This series of twelve letters published by John Dickinson denounced the Townshend duties, demonstrating that many of the arguments employed against the Stamp Act were valid in regard to the Townshend duties as well. The letters inspired anti-parliament sentiment throughout the colonies.

- Loyal Nine - The Loyal Nine was a group of Boston merchants and artisans that formed during the Stamp Act crisis to lead the public in attempts to drive the stamp distributors from the city. This was one of the first steps toward political organization in the colonies.

- Quartering Act - The Quartering Act was enacted in 1765, requiring colonial assemblies to pay for certain supplies for troops stationed within their respective colonies. In 1767, New York, the colony in which the greatest number of troops were stationed, refused to comply with the law, provoking parliament to threaten the nullification of all laws passed by the New York colonial legislature.

- Salutary Neglect - Salutary neglect refers to the state of Anglo-American relations before the end of the French and Indian War. British Parliament did not interfere in the government of the colonies, and America existed in relative political isolation.

- Sons of Liberty - The Sons of Liberty were the successors of the Loyal Nine as the leaders of the opposition to the Stamp Act. They brought a new level of sophistication to the mass demonstrations, prohibiting their followers to carry weapons and using strict discipline and military formations to direct the protestors.

- Stamp Act - The Stamp Act required Americans to buy special watermarked paper for newspapers and all legal documents. Violators faced juryless trials in vice-admiralty courts, just as under the Sugar Act. The Stamp Act provoked the first truly organized response to British impositions.

- Sugar Act - The Sugar Act lowered the duty on foreign-produced molasses from six pence per gallon to 3 pence per gallon, in attempts to discourage smuggling. The act further stipulated that Americans could export many commodities, including lumber, iron, skins, and whalebone, to foreign countries, only if they passed through British ports first. The act also placed a heavy tax on formerly duty- free Madeira wine from Portugal. The terms of the act and its methods of enforcement outraged many colonists.

- Townshend Duties - Parliament passed the Revenue Act of 1767 on July 2, 1767. Popularly referred to as the Townshend duties, the Revenue Act taxed glass, lead, paint, paper, and tea entering the colonies. The colonists objected to the fact that it was clearly designed more to raise revenue than to regulate trade in a manner favorable to the British Empire.

- Virginia Resolves - In response to the Stamp Act, Patrick Henry persuaded the Virginia House of Burgesses to adopt several strongly worded resolutions that denied Parliament's right to tax the colonies.

These resolutions were known as the Virginia Resolves, and persuaded many other colonial legislatures to adopt similar positions.

- Virtual Representation - The concept of virtual representation was employed by Prime Minister George Grenville to explain why Parliament could legally tax the colonists even though the colonists could not elect any members of Parliament. The theory of virtual representation held that the members of Parliament did not only represent their specific geographical constituencies, but rather that they took into consideration the well being of all British subjects when deliberating on legislation.

- Writs of Assistance - Writs of assistance were general search warrants, which allowed customs officers to search any building or ship they thought might contain smuggled goods, even without probable cause for suspicion. The colonists considered the writs to be a grave infringement upon personal liberties.

People

- Samuel Adams - Samuel Adams played a key role in the defense of Colonial rights. He had been a leader of the Sons of Liberty, and suggested the formation of the committees of correspondence. Adams played a crucial role in spreading the principle of colonial rights throughout New England.

- John Dickinson - An influential political leader from Pennsylvania, Dickinson published Letters From a Pennsylvania Farmer in response to the Townshend duties, and provoked much colonial response thereby.

- Thomas Hutchinson - Hutchinson was a British official who played many roles in the years leading up to the American Revolution. He served as chief justice of the Massachusetts supreme court that heard James Otis' case against the writs of assistance; as lieutenant governor of Massachusetts during the Stamp Act crisis; and finally, as the royal governor. In 1773, Samuel Adams published a number of Hutchinson's letters, in which Hutchinson advocated "an abridgement of what are called British liberties," and "a great restraint of natural liberty" in the colonies.

- King George III - The king of England during this period, King George III exercised a greater hand in the government of the nation than many of his predecessors had. Colonists were torn between loyalty to the king and resistance to acts carried out in his name.

- Ebeneezer MacIntosh - MacIntosh, a shoemaker from the South End of Boston, was chosen by the Loyal Nine to lead the coalition of the North End and South End factions in Boston against the stamp distributor, Andrew Oliver. He oversaw the mob that drove Oliver out of town before he could collect stamp taxes.

- James Otis - James Otis was an influential Bostonian heavily involved in the fight for colonial rights. Most notably, he argued the case against the writs of assistance in front of the Massachusetts supreme court. Though unsuccessful in his case, Otis succeeded in illuminating the core of the colonists' opposition to Parliamentary actions in the colonies.

- Pontiac - Pontiac was an Ottawa Indian leader, who led a series of attacks against the British forts near the Great Lakes, eight of which he successfully sacked. He was a great proponent of driving the British out of Indian territory, fearing the British presence there would encourage the colonists to move west and overrun the tribal lands.

- Charles Townshend - Townshend was the chancellor of the exchequer under Prime Minister William Pitt. However, when Pitt fell ill, Townshend took effective control of the government. His most notable action was the passage of the Revenue Act of 1767, popularly called the Townshend duties. The act enraged the colonists and provoked widespread resistance.

- John Wilkes - Wilkes was a political dissident who had fled Britain to evade arrest. During the outcry against the Townshend duties, he returned to London to run for Parliament in 1768. He was elected, but denied his seat and jailed. A mass movement grew up in Britain and the colonies in support of Wilkes, and when he was finally released in 1770, he was hailed by one Boston celebration as "the illustrious martyr of liberty."

Events

- Boston Massacre - On March 5, 1770, a crowd led by sailor Crispus Attucks formed to demonstrate against the customs agents. When a British officer tried to disperse the crowd, he and his men were bombarded with rocks and dared to shoot by the unruly mob. After being knocked to the ground, one soldier finally did shoot, and others followed. Five people were killed, including Attucks, who is often considered the first casualty of the Revolutionary War.

- Massacre of St. George's Fields - After John Wilkes was denied his seat in Parliament, some 30,000 of his followers, known as Wilkesites, gathered on St. George's Fields, outside the prison where he was being held, to protest his arrest. When the protestors began throwing objects, soldiers fired into the crowd, killing eleven. The so- called Massacre of St. George's Fields emphasized the disagreement in Britain over colonial rights and spurred the movement that grew up in support of Wilkes' cause.

- Stamp Act Congress - In response to the Stamp Act, and representing a new level of pan-colonial political organization, on October 7, 1765, representatives of nine colonial assemblies met in New York City at the Stamp Act Congress. The colonies agreed widely on the principles that Parliament could not tax anyone outside of Great Britain, and could not deny anyone a fair trial, both of which had been done in the American colonies.

TIMELINE

- February 10, 1763: Treaty of Paris The Treaty of Paris ended the French and Indian War in North America, granting the Britain control of all land to the east of the Mississippi River.

- Spring - Summer 1763: Pontiac's War Begins An Indian leader, Pontiac, led Ottawa Indians in attacks against British forts near the Great Lakes, eight of which they sacked successfully. However, the British ultimately prevailed, and the Indians were forced to make peace.

- October 7, 1763: King George III signs the Proclamation of 1763 The Proclamation of 1763 declared that all land transactions made to the west of the Appalachian crest would be governed by the British government rather than by the colonies.

- April 5, 1764: The Sugar Act is Passed The Sugar Act lowered the import tax on foreign molasses in an attempt to deter smuggling, and placed a heavy tax on Madeira wine, which had traditionally been duty-free. The act mandated that many commodities shipped from the colonies had to pass through Britain before going to other European countries.

- March 1765: The Stamp Act is Passed To be enacted on November 1, 1765, the Stamp Act required all colonists to purchase watermarked, taxed paper for use in newspapers and legal documents. The Stamp Act was the first internal tax ever imposed on the colonies by Parliament and aroused great opposition.

- March 24, 1765: The Quartering Act Takes Effect The Quartering Act required colonial legislatures to pay for certain supplies for British troops stationed in each colony. The Quartering Act became controversial during 1766, when New York refuses to comply with it.

- May 30, 1765: The Virginia House of Burgesses passes the Virginia Resolves The Virginia Resolves denied Parliament's right to tax the colonies under the Stamp Act, igniting opposition to the act in other colonial assemblies.

- October 7, 1765: The Stamp Act Congress Meets in New York City The colonial legislatures sent representatives to New York, where they agreed broadly that Parliament had no right to tax the colonies or to deny colonists a fair trial.

- March 4, 1766: The Stamp Act is Repealed In response to colonial resistance, Parliament repealed the Stamp Act, and passed the Declaratory Act on March 18, which states that Parliament may legislate for the colonies in all cases.

- July 2, 1767: The Townshend duties are Enacted The Townshend duties was the popular name for the collected import taxes imposed by the Revenue Act of 1767. The Revenue Act taxed glass, lead, paint, paper, and tea entering the colonies. The duties were clearly passed in an effort to raise revenue for the British treasury rather than to regulate trade.

- December 1767 John Dickinson Publishes Letters From a Pennsylvania Farmer Dickinson's series of twelve letters are published in almost every colonial newspaper. The letters exhorted Americans to resist the Townshend duties, enumerating the political arguments against the constitutionality of the Revenue Act.

- February 11, 1768: Circular Letter Adopted by the Massachusetts House of Representatives The circular letter, drafted by Samuel Adams and sent to all of the other colonial legislatures, condemned taxation without representation and decried British efforts to make royal governors financially independent of the elected legislatures as a further deprivation of representative government. It spurred some other legislatures to draft similar letters, but most remain apathetic.

- October 1, 1768: Troops Begin to Land in Boston In response to growing political unrest in Massachusetts, Britain sent troops to occupy the city in the final months of 1768. Tensions mounted between the troops and the civilians.

- March 4, 1770: The Boston Massacre Troops in Boston squared off with a crowd of sailors led by Crispus Attucks. When the crowd knocked one soldier to the ground, the soldiers fired and killed 5 men.

- April 12, 1770: The Townshend Duties are Repealed Under financial pressure from the colonists' non-importation policy, Parliament repealed all of the Townshend duties except for the tax on tea.

- June 9, 1772: The Burning of the Gaspee In an act of open defiance against British rule, more than one hundred Rhode Island colonists burn the corrupt customs ship Gaspee to the waterline after it runs aground near Providence.

- July 1773: Samuel Adams Publishes the Letters of Thomas Hutchinson Through the Committees of Correspondence Massachusetts' royal governor, Hutchinson, in his letters, advocates "an abridgement of what are called British liberties," and "a great restraint of natural liberty" in the colonies. The publication of these letters convinces Americans of a British plot to destroy their political freedom.

THE COLONIES AND MOTHER COUNTRY AT THE CLOSE OF THE FRENCH AND INDIAN WAR

When the French and Indian War, and its European counterpart, the Seven Years War, officially came to a close with the Treaty of Paris in 1763, North America was divided territorially between the British and Spanish. Britain had driven the French from the continent, and extended its land claims west to the Mississippi River. It seemed that British holdings in North America and all over the world were more secure than ever, but there were signs of trouble brewing in the American colonies. The French had been driven from the continent by a coalition of Britons, colonists, and Native Americans. However, once peace was restored, this three-pronged alliance showed signs of crumbling.

One source of conflict arose between the colonial and British soldiers. In Britain, it was widely assumed that the professional troops sent to the colonies deserved full credit for British victory in the war. In reality, about 40 percent of the regular soldiers who served in the war enlisted in America. American soldiers complained constantly during and after the war that British public opinion drastically underestimated America's part.

British soldiers, for their part, bemoaned the ineptitude of the colonial troops. They claimed the colonials were useless in battle and had no real sense of duty, tending to return home, even in the midst of a campaign, when their terms were up or they were not paid on time. Colonial troops denied these charges, and complained of British arrogance and contemptuousness in dealings with the colonials.

British troops also quarreled with colonial civilians, who were often reluctant to provide food and shelter to the British, and consistently complained of the troops' poor behavior. Pennsylvania Quakers, as pacifists, voted against appropriating funds for the war effort, and Massachusetts and New York also took a stand against the quartering of British troops in their colonies. British Parliament, and King George III, viewed these actions as antagonistic to the British effort to defend imperial territories.

Another major area of contention was taxation. The colonies had profited greatly form the war. Military contracts and expenditures by British troops had meant a large inflow of British currency. Trade flourished, and many American's traded with the French West Indies. This trade was illegal in peace time, and seen as morally reprehensible during a war against the French, but it proved very profitable. Meanwhile, the British national debt had climbed from 72 million pounds before the war to 132 million at its end. To pay down this debt, Britain instituted a land tax at home, and imposed excise tax on many commonly traded goods.

However, the colonists felt burdened as well. During the war, prosperous colonists had developed a taste for imported goods. In fact, the annual value of British imports to the colonies had doubled. Once the wartime economic boom ended, many Americans went into debt trying to maintain their middle-class lifestyle. Colonial debts to Britain grew rapidly, and many began to suspect that the British were intentionally plotting to enslave the colonists economically.

The conflict between British and colonial soldiers was indicative of the evolving attitudes of the two regions toward one another. The colonies began to associate all things British with arrogance and condescension, and the British viewed Americans as inept, irresponsible, and primitive. The colonial units in the war were involved primarily in support roles, providing reserve forces in battles and holding British forts. This way, the more highly trained British professionals could lead the offensive against the French. Despite their separation of duties, the troops interacted often enough to decide that they disliked each other, and each side registered frequent complaints about the other.

The conflict of soldiers and civilians highlighted a major complaint of the colonists throughout the period of time leading up to the revolution. The colonists were perpetually wary of British meddling in colonial affairs, and saw the military as the primary on-site actors in this effort. Fearing the installation of standing armies, the colonies, throughout their histories, had been reluctant to supply and house British troops. During the French and Indian

War this reluctance caused King George and the Parliament to question the loyalty of some colonies and led the British government to commit even more strongly to keeping a strong British hand in colonial business.

The issue of taxation was one that would drive a wedge between the colonies and their mother country from this time until the end of the revolution. In Britain, citizens were forced to pay exorbitant taxes on land and traded goods in order to support Britain's skyrocketing debt. These citizens looked across the ocean to see the colonists not pulling anywhere close to equal weight, even though the colonists had been the primary beneficiaries of the war. Colonists continued to assert their freedom from taxation and reminded British rulers that they had not called for the war. Still, even though many Americans went through hard times because of the collapse of the wartime boom, the colonists could not deny the facts. The colonial debt totaled 2 million pounds to Britain's 132 million. In fact, just the interest charges on Britain's debt cost the empire 4 million pounds per year. Still, the colonists railed against taxation.

Emerging after the war was a new dynamic in Anglo-American relations. The British sought to control their colonial possessions more tightly, and sent greater numbers of officials to America, imposed regulations on trade, and restricted territorial expansion to this effect. The colonies, on the other hand, wished to be free to govern themselves, to trade as they desired, and to expand into the West. The French and Indian war was hailed as a victory for Britain in its attempt to control its colonies, but the conditions immediately after the war's close set the stage for a widening rift rather than the maintenance of affable relations.

THE BRITISH ON THE FRONTIER

Britain's need for revenue continued even after France was ejected from North America, primarily because of continuing struggles with the Native Americans. The conflict between the French and British had kept each side trying to gain the Indians' loyalty through gifts and concessions. However, once France left North America the British stopped giving these gifts to the tribes, and squatters from the colonies began to settle on Indian lands. The Native Americans, in turn, feared the British would support these movements. Tensions rose and both sides prepared for a long battle.

An Indian prophet from the Delaware tribe, named Neolin, attracted a large following among the natives, calling for a complete rejection of all things European, including culture and alliances. Pontiac, an Ottawa Indian, was another proponent of anti-British action. During the summer of 1763, he led the Ottawas in attacks against British forts around the great lakes, eight of which they successfully sacked. His efforts continued, but over the coming years conditions declined. The Ottawas experienced shortages of food and ammunition, and a smallpox epidemic broke out after the British deliberately distributed infected blankets as a peace offering. Finally, the hobbled Indians made peace with the British in 1766.

In efforts to conciliate the Indians, the British government issued the Proclamation of 1763 on October 7, 1763. The proclamation declared that all land transactions made to the west of the Appalachian crest would be governed by the British government rather than by the colonies. The British vowed to respect Native American land rights and stringently control colonial expansion.

As a result of the increased tension in North America, especially between the Native Americans and the British, the British government decided that rather than recall its entire army, 10,000 troops would remain behind to protect the empire's interests in the newly acquired territory. The British troops intimidated Indians, the remaining French, and the Spanish, all of which challenged Britain in certain areas of the continent. As it turned out, the troops also intimidated the colonists, some of whom reacted negatively to the decision to leave troops in North America. The expense for maintaining North American operations, including payment and supplies for troops, and the establishment of civil governments in Canada and Florida, totaled about six percent of Britain's peacetime budget. The British thought it was reasonable for the colonists to share in this expense, and began to deliberate on how best to tax the colonies. Most colonists, on the other hand, considered the payment of soldiers in North America and the establishment of colonial governments to be none of their responsibility.

The history of the colonization of North America is also the history of forced western migration for the continent's Native Americans. Constantly at odds with the settlers on the continent, the tribes had relied on their ability to play the major powers of France and Britain against each other to maintain their land claims west of the Appalachians. However, once France no longer occupied a large geographical area, this option disappeared. They feared that with all land east of the Mississippi in British hands, the British colonists along the east coast would rapidly move westward, and drive them further from their land. When colonial squatters did start to move into the western lands, the Indians saw no option but to react strongly. However, the lack of communication between tribes and the resulting lack in coordinated action made them easy prey for the British soldiers.

The Proclamation of 1763 was an attempt by the British government to restore order to colonial expansion, which until then had been left to the colonies themselves to regulate. The Proclamation was intended to assuage the fears of the Indian tribes by recognizing all existing Indian land titles everywhere west of the "proclamation line" until tribal governments agreed to cede the lands through treaties. The wording of the proclamation made it clear that the British expected the tribes to cede their lands at some point in the future, and that the British government intended to regulate, not stop, westward expansion. Though the proclamation calmed the Indians' fears to an extent, the colonists saw it as an unjust invasion of their rights, and decried its slowing effect on expansion. After the British became the controlling power in North America, many colonists had grown excited about the prospects of settling in the west, and expansion was universally considered to be the path to prosperity. The Proclamation of

1763 was added to the growing litany of British impositions, which the colonists complained restricted their freedoms.

Another British imposition on the colonies was the maintenance of British armed forces in North America after the close of the war. These troops appeared to many colonists as evidence of a British desire to install a standing army in the American colonies for the purpose of controlling the traditionally somewhat independent Americans. The troops seemed the manifestation of a British desire to have a stronger hand in the affairs of the colonies, especially in their role as enforcers of the Proclamation of 1763, which they undertook with vigor.

THE WRITS OF ASSISTANCE

Even before the French and Indian War ended, the British decided to heighten their level of control over trade in the colonies. Colonial assemblies had proven unable to stem trade with the French West Indies, and certain ports, such as Boston and Newport, Rhode Island, engaged heavily in trade with the enemy in the West Indies. Colonial smugglers that traded with the West Indies, not only sustained the enemy, but avoided duties imposed by the Molasses Act of 1733. The Molasses Act charged a duty of six pence a gallon on molasses, nine pence on a gallon of rum, and five shillings per 100 pounds of sugar on goods imported from non-British territories. Smuggling thus not only aided Britain's wartime enemy, but also deprived the British treasury of much needed revenue during the war.

In response, the British officials in the colonies called for a crackdown on smuggling. In 1760, governor Bernard of Massachusetts authorized the use by revenue officers of writs of assistance. Writs of assistance were documents which served as a general search warrant, allowing customs officials to enter any ship or building that they suspected for any reason might hold smuggled goods.

Writs of assistance proved an immediately useful tool in the fight against smuggling, and many buildings and ships were ransacked and seized. Shortly after their implementation, Boston merchants, the group primarily responsible for smuggling in the colonies, hired lawyer James Otis to challenge the constitutionality of the writs before the Massachusetts supreme court, which he did in 1761, in what is known as the Petition of Lechmere. A fiery orator, Otis argued that the writs were "against the fundamental principles of law," and claimed that even an act of Parliament "against the Constitution is void." It took two and a half years before the ruling in the case was delivered. After consulting extensively with authorities in Britain, and noting the use of similar writs in England, the court, heavily influenced by the opinions of Chief Justice Thomas Hutchinson, ruled against the Boston merchants and kept the writs in place.

The writs of assistance and Otis' arguments at trial convinced many that Britain had overstepped its bounds, and objections to their use was commonly heard at town meetings and in assemblies throughout the colonies. However, political opposition to the writs ended with the Boston merchants' loss in the Petition of Lechmere. It would take further impositions by the British government before the colonists would begin to truly question parliamentary authority.

Smuggling was a major problem in the American colonies during and after the war. It is clear that if there had been no smuggling the British government would have taken in more revenue from customs duties. Additionally, later evidence has shown that the influx of goods to the French West Indies provided by American smugglers was a primary reason the French were able to sustain their war effort in North America for as long as they did. During the war it was well known that smuggling accounted for a significant part of American income, but in the midst of the fighting the British found it nearly impossible to regulate trade effectively. Thus, partially because they had few other options and partially out of frustration and anger, the writs of assistance were granted and used.

Despite the assertion by the Massachusetts supreme court that the writs of assistance were within legal limits, most English authorities agreed that the writs violated the Constitution. Colonists and Many British observers were outraged at the blatant neglect of what had been traditionally considered British liberties. Most notably, the writs allowed officials to enter and ransack private homes without proving probable cause for suspicion, a traditional prerequisite to a search.

Although he lost the case against the writs of assistance, James Otis hit upon precisely the ideological cornerstone that would lead the colonies up to and into revolution. The British Constitution was not a written document; it was an unwritten collection of customs and traditions guaranteeing certain rights, and therefore an abstract and fungible thing. Most British subjects assumed that all laws made by Parliament were incorporated into the Constitution, and thus that Parliament could alter the Constitution as it wished, without question. The government was the sole judge of the constitutionality of its actions. However, Otis' primary argument in front of the supreme court centered on the growing sentiment in the colonies that even Parliament could not infringe on certain basic rights that stood at the core of the Constitution, often termed 'the rights of Englishmen.' Otis contended that in the principles of government, there existed certain limits, "beyond which if Parliaments go, their Acts bind not." This claim echoed the growing conception of the great majority of colonists as to the proper role of Parliament under the British Constitution. In the years to come, the colonists continued to complain that the British government had infringed upon this set of "inalienable" rights. This infringement was commonly claimed as the motive for revolution.

THE SUGAR ACT

In 1764 Parliament passed the Sugar Act, with the goal of raising 100,000 pounds, an amount equal to one-fifth of the military expenses in North America. The Sugar Act signaled the end of colonial exemption from revenue-raising taxation. Previous acts, such as the long-standing Navigation Acts, had been passed as protectionist measures, regulating trade to boost the economy of the British Empire as a whole. Under the Navigation Acts, taxes were paid by British importers alone, rather than the colonists, and brought in just 1,800 pounds in 1763, compared with a cost of 8,000 pounds just to enforce the acts.

The Sugar Act lowered the duty on foreign-produced molasses from six pence per gallon to 3 pence per gallon, in attempts to discourage smuggling. The act further stipulated that Americans could export many commodities, including lumber, iron, skins, and whalebone, to foreign countries, only if they passed through British ports first. The act also placed a heavy tax on formerly duty- free Madeira wine from Portugal.

The Sugar Act complicated trade for American shippers by requiring them to fill out a number of confusing forms in order to legalize their shipments. If even the smallest technicality was not attended to, ships' captains could have their entire cargo seized. Further, the act could be employed in some cases regarding local trade along the east coast, and in many cases put unrealistic restrictions on this trade.

In addition to a restriction of trade, many colonists felt the Sugar Act constituted a restriction of justice. The act allowed customs officials to transfer smuggling cases from colonial courts with juries to juryless vice- admiralty courts in Halifax, Nova Scotia. Until 1768, vice-admiralty judges were awarded five percent of all confiscated cargo and ships, a clear incentive to come to a guilty verdict. The vice-admiralty courts also reversed traditional judicial ideology, by burdening the defendant with the task of disproving the charge of smuggling rather than assuming innocence until guilt was proven.

British Prime Minister George Grenville ordered the navy to enforce the Sugar Act, and it did so vigorously. Still colonists continued to smuggle molasses until 1766, when the duty on foreign molasses was lowered to one penny.

The Sugar Act provided the British treasury with about 30,000 pounds per year between 1766 and 1775, a substantial source of income.

Nine provincial legislatures in America protested the passage of the Sugar Act, but seven of these objected on narrow grounds. Though many colonists objected to the act's revenue-raising taxation and regulation, opposition was minor, due to a lack of organization and the hesitancy of the legislatures to take a stand against Parliament.

The Sugar Act was one of the first tangible signs of Britain's intent to gain tighter control over colonial trade. Parliament predicted that if shippers had to stop at British ports en route to other destinations they would be more likely to purchase imperial goods to bring back with them to the colonies, and thus boost Britain's flailing economy. Parliament imagined it could further collect a great amount in revenue and discourage smuggling by lowering the duties. Parliamentary leaders reasoned that with the duty set at three pence, colonists would be less likely to smuggle than they had been when the duty was six pence, and thus more likely to pay, leading to a higher income for the British treasury. However, American smugglers had grown accustomed to paying one and a half pence per gallon of molasses to customs agents to look the other way, and continued this practice until 1776, when the duty was lowered to a penny, less than the amount smugglers had been paying in bribes. Meanwhile, the high tax on imported Madeira wine from the Azores and other Portuguese territories created a smuggling operation where none had existed before. Importing duty-free Portuguese wine had been a lucrative business for importers up until the passing of the Sugar Act, and they would not let it go easily.

The Sugar Act was another step in the direction of a strong British hand in colonial life. To the colonists, greater regulation of trade was not simply an economically restricting measure, but one which expanded the sphere of British involvement in the everyday activities of the colonists. The Sugar Act provided additional instances in which the writs of assistance might be employed. Further, the clause requiring shipping of many commodities through Britain struck many colonists as a symbol of Parliament's desire to strengthen both economic and governmental ties with the colonies while they strove to be free from British involvement.

Moreover, the Sugar Act seemed to many, in its methods of enforcement and adjudication, another defiance of the rights of Englishmen, namely, the right to a fair trial in front of a jury of one's peers. Not only did the Sugar Act provide for the relocation of trials from the colonies to Halifax, Nova Scotia, far from the setting in which infractions had taken place, it also allowed trials without a jury, in which the judge had a clear incentive to convict and the defendant was assumed to be guilty. This outraged many colonial leaders. However, most colonists were hesitant to claim that the Sugar Act was unconstitutional, because it seemed to be merely an amendment of the Molasses Act of 1733. Additionally, the tax burden fell most heavily upon Massachusetts New York, and Pennsylvania. While other colonies agreed that the Sugar Act was undesirable, they had less of an incentive to take a strong stand against Parliament, and organized opposition was never mounted.

THE STAMP ACT

Despite the revenue raised by the Sugar Act, Britain's financial situation continued to spiral out of control. In 1765, the average taxpayer in England paid 26 shillings per year in taxes, while the average colonist paid only one-half to one and a half shillings. Prime Minister Grenville thought that the American colonists should bear a heavier tax load. To this end, Parliament passed the Stamp Act in March 1765. The act required Americans to buy special watermarked paper for newspapers and all legal documents. Violators faced juryless trials in vice-admiralty courts, just as under the Sugar Act. Grenville optimistically predicted revenues of between 60,000 and 100,000 pounds.

William Pitt was the colonies' greatest defender in England. He argued that the colonies could not be taxed without representation in Parliament. Grenville and his followers claimed that they agreed with Pitt, and that the colonies were represented in Parliament, even though they did not elect any of the members. The Prime Minister claimed that Americans shared the same status as many British males, who did not have enough property to be granted the vote, or who lived in certain large cities that had no seats in Parliament. He claimed that all of these people were "virtually represented" in Parliament. The theory of virtual representation held that the members of Parliament did not only represent their specific geographical constituencies, but rather that they took into consideration the well-being of all British subjects when deliberating on legislation. Grenville further argued that Americans were not exempt from taxation, as many claimed, simply because they elected their own assemblies which legislated for and taxed the colonies. He compared colonial assemblies to Scottish town councils, claiming that they only exercised as much power as was granted to them by Parliament.

This position clashed directly with the contention of many colonists that their assemblies exercised legislative powers equal to those of the House of Commons in Britain. To many colonists, the Stamp Act seemed to represent all of the problems of Anglo-American relations. Moreover, it affected every one of the thirteen colonies equally, and every rank in society, since all colonists would at some time find reason to draw up a legal document such as a will, or to buy a newspaper. Throughout the colonies, town meetings and colonial assemblies heard violent demonstrations against the Stamp Act. Colonial agents in London and petitions from colonial legislatures warned against passage, but Parliament dismissed the petitions without even granting them a hearing.

In late May 1765, Patrick Henry persuaded the Virginia House of Burgesses to adopt several strongly worded resolutions. The Virginia Resolves, as they were known, were passed on May 30, 1765, and denied Parliament's right to tax the colonies under the Stamp Act. Word of Henry's resolutions spread throughout the colonies, taking on certain dramatic embellishments in many cases, and by the end of the year, eight other colonial legislatures had adopted similar positions.

Unlike the Sugar Act, which was an external tax (i.e. it taxed only goods imported into the colonies), the Stamp Act was an internal tax, levied directly upon the property and goods of the colonists. Internal taxes had far wider effects. While external taxes were paid primarily by merchants and ship captains, internal taxes, especially the Stamp Act, were not so discriminatory. Anyone who made a will or bought a newspaper would pay the tax on paper. The colonies had never been taxed internally by Britain before, and had traditionally taxed themselves through their colonial assemblies. Taxation was a primary function of the self-government to which the colonists so passionately clung. The Stamp Act refuted the claim to a measure of self-government, painting the colonies not as an entity in a loosely bound federation centered in London, but rather as an extension of the British nation, subject to Parliamentary legislation and taxation.

The Stamp Act forced colonists to consider the issue of Parliamentary taxation without representation. Few colonists agreed with Grenville that they were virtually represented. Though most admired and respected Parliament, few imagined it represented their needs. They claimed that the theory that members of Parliament concerned themselves with the needs of all British subjects was not valid. In the common colonial view, unless a legislator shared, to some extent, the interests of his constituents, he could not be expected to consider their welfare. Since the needs of the American colonists differed substantially from the needs of inhabitants of England, they feared that were Parliament permitted to legislate for the colonies its members would be easily persuaded to vote against the Americans' best interest, especially if England stood to gain. It seemed to many that this was precisely what had happened in the case of the Stamp Act.

Colonists conceded that as they were British subjects, Parliament did reserve limited powers of legislation over them. They believed that Parliament could standardize legal protocol throughout the Empire in the interest of granting all subjects access to royal justice. The colonists also accepted the role that in the interest of broad economic goals Parliament had to play in the regulation of trade throughout the Empire, and even accepted that this regulation might at some times prove disadvantageous to the colonies. Further, they acknowledged the need for loyalty to the crown and considered their responsibility to defend the Empire in time of war undeniable. However, they insisted that in all other ways they should be self-governed--that colonial assemblies alone could tax the colonists, and that in return they would not interfere with laws that regulated the empire's trade. James Otis expressed the core of the American argument at a Boston town meeting in the spring of 1765. He said "by [the

British] Constitution, every man in the dominion is a free man: that no parts of His Majesty's dominions can be taxed without consent: that every part has a right to be represented in the supreme or some subordinate legislature."

COLONIAL OPPOSITION TO THE STAMP ACT

In late summer 1765, a group of Boston artisans, shopkeepers, and businessmen formed a group known as the Loyal Nine to oppose the Stamp Act. The Loyal Nine planned to lead the public in forcing stamp distributors, who alone could collect money for stamped paper, to resign before taxes were due on November 1, 1765.

Bostonians were in the habit of congregating in large groups to express themselves politically. On certain festival days it was not uncommon for large crowds from the North End and South End of the city to converge upon each other, throwing stones and whatever else they could find, and engaging in rowdy fistfights. The Loyal Nine, in an effort to harness the power of both groups, oversaw a truce between the two groups, which were united under the leadership of a South End shoemaker, Ebeneezer MacIntosh.

On the morning of August 14, 1765, Bostonians awoke to find an effigy of stamp collector Andrew Oliver hanged from a tree. Oliver did not take the hint to resign immediately, so at dusk, MacIntosh led several hundred men in destroying a new building that Oliver owned. At this point the Loyal Nine disappeared, and the mob moved on without their controlling influence. They demonstrated outside Oliver's house, "stamping" his effigy to pieces. They then ransacked his house, destroying it. Lieutenant Governor Thomas Hutchinson arrived with the sheriff driving off the mob with a barrage of stones. Oliver resigned.

Violence was contagious in the colonies. Twelve days later, Hutchinson's home was destroyed as well. Violence next struck in Newport, Rhode Island, where a crowd organized by local merchants grew beyond control. The crowd burned effigies and destroyed the homes of three stamp distributors, and then turned against the merchants. A sailor named John Webber assumed control, and threatened to destroy the merchants' homes and warehouses if they did not pay an enormous sum. He was caught and jailed before any destruction took place.

Political dissent became organized quickly. Groups calling themselves the Sons of Liberty formed throughout the colonies to control the widespread violence. They directed violent demonstrations against property rather than individuals, and ensured that no one was killed. They forbade their followers to carry weapons, and used military formations to maneuver large crowds. On October 7, 1765, representatives of nine colonial assemblies met in New York City, at the Stamp Act Congress. The colonies agreed widely on the principles that Parliament could not tax anyone outside of Great Britain, and could not deny anyone a fair trial, both of which had been done in the American colonies.

By late 1765, most stamp distributors had resigned, and legal and business proceedings only continued because the colonial legislatures threatened to withhold the salaries of those in a position to halt them. By the end of 1765, almost every colony was functional, without stamped paper.

By this point, social and political elites had assumed leadership of the colonial opposition to the Stamp Act. On October 31, 1765, New York's merchants decided to boycott British goods, and they were soon joined by other cities. This move put the British economy, which exported about 40 percent of its manufactures to America, in considerable danger. Soon Britain's businessmen were clamoring for the repeal of the Stamp Act.

In mid 1765, the Marquis of Rockingham had succeeded Prime Minister Grenville. He hesitated to advocate repeal and offend the House of Commons, which was outraged and resentful of colonial resistance. However, led by William Pitt, support for repeal grew. In March 1766 Parliament finally repealed the Stamp Act, and passed the Declaratory Act, which stated that Parliament had the authority to legislate for the colonies in all cases.

It was not surprising that Boston emerged as the center of resistance to the Stamp Act. In 1765, Bostonians were not living particularly well. The port city, which relied on trade, had been substantially hurt by British restrictions--more so than other cities in the colonies. Moreover, in 1760 the city suffered a great fire that burned nearly 200 warehouses down and left ten percent of the city's population homeless. By 1765, the city had still not completely recovered. The majority of the population blamed British policy for the continued hard times that followed the French and Indian War. Additionally, the Boston town meeting was known for its somewhat radical views on self-government. Many of the most vociferous critics of Parliament, including James Otis and Samuel Adams, lived in Boston.

It is therefore understandable that the first demonstrations against the British took place in Boston. It is also understandable that the primary feature of the so-called Stamp Act crisis, organized political action, would have risen up in Boston. The formation of the Loyal Nine was the first step on a road to what would eventually become unified thinking and action spanning the colonies. Without organization, violence would have been without direction, as it was in the incident in Rhode Island. The Loyal Nine took the first step in channeling the power of the people, uniting two groups that would otherwise have been antagonistic toward each other, and directing that energy against a common foe. This sort of coalition building would prove crucial in the years to come as political leaders went about uniting the thirteen distinctive colonies in resistance.

From its beginnings in the Loyal Nine, grass-roots political organization took on even more sophistication with the leadership of the Sons of Liberty. Now, instead of simply pointing the masses in the right direction, the movement had goals, and the Sons of Liberty took distinct and successful measures to achieve those goals. Also, they exhibited a firm control over their followers that demonstrated an acute knowledge of social and political realities. For instance, they did not want to alienate elites with overly violent and disorganized mob tactics. Therefore they used the utmost discipline and did not permit their followers to carry guns. Knowing the value of martyrs, they decided early on that the only lives lost during the resistance would be American.

Without the organization of the Sons of liberty, elites would never have bought into the resistance. However, seeing that the masses were capable of controlled political expression, politicians and businessmen alike decided that they should join the opposition and lead it to an even more sophisticated, more publicly visible plane. These elites reigned in the scattered demonstrations of the masses, fearing that passion and turmoil would lead the opposition to an early death. It was the actions of the elites, most notably the boycott of British goods, which in the end led Parliament to repeal the Stamp Act.

Because the Declaratory Act's wording was vague, colonists chose to interpret it to their advantage. They saw it as a way for Parliament to save face after the Stamp Act had failed, and did not consider it to be a threat. However, Parliament chose to interpret the act broadly, to mean that the colonies could not claim exemption from any Parliamentary measure, including taxation. This fundamental disagreement would be the source of much future disagreement.

Despite the difficulties of 1765, most colonists soon put the year's strife behind them, and thanked king and Parliament for repealing the Stamp Act. The vast majority of the colonists still felt a deep emotional loyalty to Britain, but after 1765, they viewed the government in London with a higher level of scrutiny.

FURTHER IMPOSITIONS: THE QUARTERING ACT AND THE TOWNSHEND DUTIES

In August 1766, months after the repeal of the Stamp Act, King George III dismissed the Rockingham government and chose William Pitt as the new prime minister. Pitt opposed taxing the colonies, and the colonists widely supported this move. However, Pitt became seriously ill shortly after assuming office, and effective control of the government, and colonial policy, passed to Charles Townshend, the chancellor of the exchequer (treasurer).

During this transition of power, tensions arose in New York in regard to the 1765 Quartering Act. The Quartering Act required colonial legislatures to pay for certain goods for soldiers stationed within their borders. The goods were generally inexpensive, and the law only applied to soldiers in settled areas, not on the frontier. Most colonies were not dramatically affected by the payments, but New York, which had more soldiers stationed within its boundaries than any other colony, was more greatly burdened by the Quartering Act, and refused to comply with the law.

Townshend responded to this display of opposition by drafting the New York Suspension Act, which would have nullified any laws passed by New York's colonial legislature after October 1, 1767 unless the assembly voted to pay for the troops' supplies. Aiming to head off future trouble, the assembly caved.

Meanwhile, in Britain, elites were continuously outraged over the high taxes they paid in order to support British debt. In 1767, the elite landowners used their influence in the House of Commons to cut their taxes by one-fourth, leaving the British treasury short 500,000 pounds compared to the previous year. Townshend proposed laws to tax imports into the American colonies to make up for this lost revenue. Parliament passed the Revenue Act of 1767 on July 2, 1767. Popularly referred to as the Townshend duties, the Revenue Act taxed glass, lead, paint, paper, and tea entering the colonies.

The Revenue Act never yielded as much income as Townshend anticipated. Tea was the only major source of revenue, bringing in 20,000 pounds yearly, out of the total of 37,000 pounds the Revenue Act brought in. This high revenue was only possible because the British had lowered the price of British tea so that Americans would purchase it over less expensive smuggled tea. To accomplish this, Parliament had eliminated 60,000 pounds of import fees paid on British East Indian tea coming through Britain before being shipped out to the colonies. Thus the net product of the Townshend duties was a 23,000 pound loss for the British territory. Though ineffective in raising revenue, the Townshend duties proved remarkably effective in stirring up political dissent that had lain dormant since the repeal of the Stamp Act.

The colonists hailed the ascension of William Pitt as the best thing that could have happened to British government, since Pitt was the most respected English politician in America. Pitt, a friend of the colonies, had the potential to steer Anglo-American relations off of the disastrous course they had taken over the past several years. No one knows what might have happened had he not fallen ill so soon. Townshend, in contrast to Pitt, was no friend of the colonies and counted himself among those who were concerned that the colonists were not pulling their weight as British subjects. Townshend's colonial policy convinced the colonists that the Stamp Act had not been an isolated mistake, but rather a small piece in a larger antagonistic plan to undermine colonial efforts at self-government.

Before New York revived the tension between the colonies and the British government, the conflict had cooled dramatically. However, New York's defiance of what its legislature saw as an indirect tax reignited the cooling fires of anger and bitterness toward the American colonies in the House of Commons. The drafting of the New York Suspension Act demonstrated that British officials would not hesitate to defend parliamentary power by usurping a colony's self- governance, a sobering thought for colonists, which led them to begin to question the justice of British rule.

The Townshend duties called the justice of British rule into even further question. During the Stamp Act crisis, the colonists had made it clear that they objected to internal taxation, but had said very little about taxing imports. Townshend interpreted this to mean that the colonists would not object to any measure of external taxation. A now wiser former Prime Minister George Grenville warned, "they will laugh at you for your distinctions about regulations of trade," but Townshend did not heed this warning, and proceeded with the Revenue Act.

In the past, the colonists had submitted to external taxation as a legitimate regulatory measure. Even the Sugar Act had received only limited opposition due to its tax measures, compared to more serious complaints about impractical restrictions and the denial of a fair trial for offenders. However, the Townshend duties differed from past legitimate taxation in that past duties had been clearly protectionist in nature, excluding foreign goods from the colonial market by raising their cost to consumers. However, the Townshend duties set moderate duties that did not exclude foreign goods, but simply raised their prices within the range of the colonial market. The colonists deduced that the British government wanted the colonists to continue purchasing these goods, thus raising revenue for the British treasury at colonial expense. In this way, the Townshend duties could be construed as taxes similar to those under the Stamp Act.

Townshend claimed that the Revenue Act was intended to help solve the government's budgetary problems, but there were additional ulterior motives for his support of the act. Townshend planned to establish a fund through which to pay the salaries of the colonial royal governors. Traditionally, royal governors had been paid by the colonial assemblies, which thus exerted some measure of control over the actions of the governor. By taking away this power, Townshend hoped to give the royal governors the power to dominate colonial governments, yet another affront to colonial self-government.

REACTION TO THE TOWNSHEND DUTIES

At first, colonists were uncertain as to what the appropriate response to the Townshend duties would be. They could not use the same strong-arm tactics they had used against the stamp distributors against the British naval officers who collected the duties offshore. So resistance remained weak and unarticulated until December 1767, when John Dickinson published Letters From a Pennsylvania Farmer. Dickinson was actually a wealthy lawyer, but the title was used to appeal to the majority of colonists, who lived in rural areas. The 12 letters making up the work were published in nearly every colonial newspaper. Dickinson set forth the argument that although the Parliament could pass regulatory economic measures that provided incidental revenue, it had no right to tax the colonists specifically for the purpose of revenue.

Dickinson's writings were widely read and admired in the colonies, and political resistance to the Townshend duties sprung forth. In early 1768, the Massachusetts colonial assembly asked Samuel Adams to draft a circular letter to be sent to all other colonial legislatures regarding the Revenue Act. The circular letter, adopted by the Massachusetts colonial assembly on February 11, 1768, condemned taxation without representation and decried British efforts to make royal governors financially independent of the elected legislatures as a further deprivation of representative government. However, the letter did not challenge Parliament's position as the highest authority or advocate rebellion in any sense. Virginia's assembly approved the Massachusetts circular letter, and sent out its own statement on the subject, urging all colonies to actively oppose British policies that would "have an immediate tendency to enslave them."

Parliament saw in the circular letters the seeds of rebellion and reacted strongly. Lord Hillsborough, secretary of state for the colonies, ordered the Massachusetts assembly to recall its letter and forbade all overseas assemblies to endorse it. He commanded the royal governors to dissolve all colonial legislatures that violated these orders. The Massachusetts legislature voted 92 - 17 in defiance of Hillsborough's order, choosing not to recall Adams' letter. Other assemblies followed suit, endorsing the letter despite Hillsborough's threats. These assemblies were promptly dismissed by their respective royal governors, and the colonies reacted with anger.

In August 1768, Boston's merchants adopted an informal non-importation agreement, under which they refused to purchase British goods. Many other cities soon followed. However, some communities, such as Philadelphia and Baltimore, refused to cease importation of British goods, and the non- importation initiative probably kept no more than 40 percent of British imports out of the colonies.

The non-importation policies had a great effect on many British merchants and artisans, who clamored for a change in policy. Their desires were embodied by the political dissident John Wilkes, who had been forced to flee to Paris years earlier. Wilkes returned to London in 1768 despite a warrant for his arrest and ran for Parliament. He was elected, and promptly arrested and jailed. The next day, some 30,000 of his followers, known as Wilkesites, gathered on St. George's Fields, outside the prison, to protest his arrest. When the protestors began throwing objects, soldiers fired into the crowd, killing eleven. After the so-called Massacre of St. George's Fields a movement rapidly grew up around Wilkes' cause. He was elected to Parliament twice more and denied his seat. While in prison, he was in constant communication with many colonial political leaders, who considered him a hero. Upon his release from prison in April 1770 a Boston celebration hailed him as "the illustrious martyr of liberty."

The publication of John Dickinson's Letters From a Pennsylvania Farmer was certainly the first step in rousing opposition to the Townshend duties, but not because they proposed any new angle of criticism of parliamentary actions. All of Dickinson's arguments had been developed and employed earlier, during the Stamp Act crisis. His contribution to resistance lay in the fact that he convinced many Americans who were hesitant to object to the duties that many of the complaints that had informed opposition to the Stamp Act were equally applicable to the Townshend duties. In doing so, he recalled the fury of the Stamp Act crisis, and incited the colonists to oppose the Revenue Act.

The request that Samuel Adams draft a circular letter, which actually originated at a Boston town meeting chaired by James Otis, showed that the colonies' past run-ins with Parliament had shown them that it was best to present a united front consisting of all of the colonies. Massachusetts did not wish to sail into a struggle with Parliament alone. Instead, the colony sent out its circular letter to the other legislatures to explain its position, try to gain allies, and gauge the spirit of opposition throughout the colonies as a whole. As it turned out, the spirit of the other colonies varied considerably, from exuberant cooperation from Virginia to relative apathy from many other colonies. In fact, evidence suggests that resistance to the Townshend duties may well have faded away if Britain had not responded so quickly and strongly to the circular letters.

King George III later commented that he had "never met a man of less judgment than Lord Hillsborough." Hillsborough was in a delicate position in regard to the Townshend duties opposition. Had he read the situation better he might have acted more appropriately. He could have chosen a course that would have divided the colonists by appealing to a sense of loyalty to the crown, which many colonists continued to feel very strongly. Instead, he overreacted, and threatened to dismantle the symbol of self-government in the colonies, the assemblies. This move played right into the hands of political leaders Samuel Adams, James Otis, and John Dickinson, who were able to begin organizing mass political opposition to the British. Thanks to the earlier efforts of the Sons of Liberty and other leaders during the Stamp Act crisis, the American colonists were well versed in the art of political resistance and knew well the principles of their complaints. The patterns of oppositional action were easily duplicated in the form of mass demonstrations and an alliance by economic elites to prevent importation of British goods.

The events surrounding John Wilkes in London only magnified the drawing of political lines both in the colonies and in Britain. The outpouring of support for Wilkes demonstrated the displeasure many British citizens felt toward recent colonial policy, and lent further criticism to the theory of virtual representation, which was increasingly considered a sham within Britain itself.

CUSTOMS RACKETEERING AND THE REPEAL OF THE TOWNSHEND DUTIES

As corollary to the Townshend duties, the British tightened their supervision of colonial trade. The American Board of Customs Commissioners was created in 1767, raising the number of customs officials, constructing a colonial coast guard, and providing money to pay informers. However, the new board drew criticism due to its methods of enforcement. Like cases adjudicated under the Sugar Act, defendants were assumed guilty until they could prove otherwise. Informers were awarded one-third of all goods and ships confiscated from smugglers, an incentive to falsify charges and report shippers who committed even the slightest of offenses. Once the cases were transferred to vice-admiralty courts, they had a very high rate of conviction.

Customs officers enforced the duties vigorously and in underhanded manner, often relaxing certain technical restrictions for a time period and then suddenly clamping down. Customs officers would often claim that small items stored in a sailor's chest were undeclared cargo, and seize entire ships on that charge. The behavior of customs agents, often known as "customs racketeering," amounted to little more than legalized piracy. The activities of agents, and especially of informers, provoked considerable opposition from the colonists. Almost all cases of tarring and feathering during the years of the Townshend duties were instances of personal vengeance against informers. After 1767, riots led by sailors were increasingly common. Still, agents enforced the law strictly and tensions mounted.

In June 1768, John Hancock, the wealthiest of all Boston merchants, had a sloop, the Liberty, seized by customs agents on a perjured charge. A crowd of angry Bostonians formed, and tried to prevent the towing of the ship. Unsuccessful, they assaulted the customs agents in charge. The growing mob drove all of the revenue inspectors from the city.

By 1770, the British government began to reform the corrupt customs service. Charges against Hancock were dropped in fears that he would appeal to England, where honest officials would recognize the customs officers' deceit. In January 1770, Lord North became prime minister. He favored eliminating most of the Townshend duties to prevent a further split between the colonies and mother country. On April 12, 1770, Parliament did just this. However, Lord North insisted on maintaining the profitable tax on tea.

In response, Americans ended the policy of general non-importation, but maintained voluntary agreements not to consume British tea. Non-consumption kept the tea tax revenues far too low to pay the royal governors. The Townshend duties were effectively dead.

The behavior of the customs officials sent to enforce the Townshend duties convinced the colonists more than ever that their relationship with the British authorities had become one of enmity. The activities of informers and agents seemed to consist of petty needling at the colonists simply for the sake of antagonism, and as before, the colonists were outraged at the British concept of justice that accompanied the duties in the form of vice-admiralty courts.

Boston was an obvious target for unscrupulous customs agents, as the colonies' largest port and largest center of smuggling. John Hancock was also a major target, as a wealthy merchant and an influential advocate for colonial rights. Customs agents claimed falsely that the Liberty had avoided paying 700 pounds on Madeira wine worth 3,000 pounds and demanded triple payment on the wine, 9,000 pounds, about thirteen times the amount of the alleged tax evasion. Hancock refused to pay and the agents towed the Liberty. For many Americans, this was the last straw, proving that British authorities were out to cause suffering in the colonies and nothing more.

During the enforcement of the Townshend duties, many colonists began to question Parliament's ability to legislate for them, to an even greater extent than before. Previously, they had almost unanimously accepted the principle that Parliament could pass some laws pertaining to the colonies, but the infringement on liberty that accompanied the enforcement of the Townshend duties had convinced many, by 1770, that Parliament should not be permitted to legislate for the colonies in any case. The cry of "no taxation without representation" was gradually being expanded to "no legislation without representation." Though the reforms instituted by the British government largely ended the abuses of the customs agents, the enmities created could not be so easily bridged; the Townshend duties were a major step in the progressive alienation of the colonies from Britain.

The Repeal of the Townshend duties presented a dilemma for colonial leaders, who had to decide whether to continue all non-importation policies in protest of the continued tax on tea, the most profitable item, or to selectively boycott tea. Eventually, they decided on informal non-consumption agreements, which proved fairly effective. However, the tax on tea remained a visible reminder of Parliament's insistence on the broadest possible interpretation of the Declaratory Act. Tea would prove a divisive issue in the coming years as the colonies neared rebellion.

THE BOSTON MASSACRE AND THE COMMITTEES OF CORRESPONDENCE

As a consequence of continued violence in Massachusetts, 1700 British troops landed in Boston during the six weeks following October 1, 1768. Relations between the soldiers and civilians were not friendly, but 1769 passed without excessive conflict. However, passions were stirred when on February 22, 1770 a customs informer fired birdshot at a group of children pelting his house with stones, killing an eleven year-old German boy. Although the troops were not involved in the death, they were the natural target for aggression directed toward British authority, and were increasingly harassed.

One week after the German boy's funeral, on March 5, 1770, violence erupted outside the Boston customs office. A crowd led by sailor Crispus Attucks formed to demonstrate against the customs agents, and when a British officer tried to disperse the crowd, his men were bombarded with rocks and dared to shoot by the unruly mob. After being knocked to the ground one soldier finally did shoot, and others followed. In the end, five colonists died, including Attucks, who is often considered the first casualty of the Revolutionary War. The event quickly came to be known as the Boston Massacre, and marked the peak of colonial opposition to the Townshend duties, which were soon repealed. In trial, John Adams, a colonial leader and defender of colonial self-government, volunteered to defend the soldiers, and all but two of them were acquitted. Those convicted merely received brandings on their thumbs.

From 1770 to 1772, the British basically ignored the colonies, choosing to pursue less controversial policy initiatives in other areas. Tensions, which had reached a peak after the Boston Massacre, had cooled. However, the hiatus ended on June 9, 1772 when the customs schooner Gaspee ran aground near Providence, Rhode Island. The Gaspee was known to have been very much involved in customs racketeering, and the crew was known for its thievery and condescension toward the colonists. That night, helpless in the mud, the Gaspee was burnt to the water line by a crowd of over a hundred disguised men. This signaled the reopening of conflict between the colonists and British government.

In the fall of 1772, Lord North was preparing to begin paying royal governors out of customs revenue. In response to this threat, Samuel Adams convinced Boston's town meeting to request that every Massachusetts community appoint a group of individuals responsible for coordinating colony-wide measures to protect colonial rights. Within the year, Massachusetts had approximately 250 of these committees of correspondence, and the idea spread throughout New England.

In July 1773, Adams published letters of Massachusetts governor Thomas Hutchinson that had been obtained by Benjamin Franklin. In these letters, Hutchinson advocated "an abridgement of what are called British liberties," and "a great restraint of natural liberty" in the colonies. The publication of these letters convinced Americans of a British plot to destroy their political freedom. Meanwhile, in March 1773, Patrick Henry, Thomas Jefferson, and Richard Henry Lee had proposed that Virginia establish a committee of correspondence for the entire colony. By late 1773, nearly every colony had followed suit, and the political leaders of every colony were linked in resistance to the British. It was this situation that allowed the colonies to mobilize fully for rebellion over the coming years.

Bostonians regarded the troops stationed there as a standing army, and a clear violation of their rights as British subjects. Their presence was further resented by Bostonians because many of the soldiers were Irish Catholics, and a number were black. Most of the enlisted men were free to seek employment during the day after their duties were performed in the morning muster. They often agreed to work for much less than local laborers, and in so doing provoked outrage in a city with consistently high unemployment. As anti-British sentiment grew, the troops, as the physical manifestation of British authority, became more than ever a symbol of oppression. When the Boston Massacre occurred, many Bostonians, and other colonists, took it as proof that the troops had been sent to the colonies to suppress political opposition by force.

John Adams' defense of the seven soldiers tried for the Boston Massacre is a well-known story of the pre-Revolutionary period. Adams was an opponent of crowd actions, preferring instead non-violent protest by elite businessmen and political bodies. His intent in defending the soldiers was to demonstrate the colonists' commitment to impartial justice and to "lay before [the people of Boston] the Law as it stood, that they might be apprized of the Dangers ... which must arise from intemperate heats and irregular commotions." In effect, he was appealing to the masses to await a higher level of political organization.

The committees of correspondence provided this organization. The first large- scale attempt at close and continuous pan-colonial political cooperation over a large area, the committees linked all of the colonies as one political force. In Massachusetts the committees worked especially well. Linked to all of the interior communities, Samuel Adams was able to spread his message of political education, advancing the principles of colonial rights. The committees convinced local citizens that their rights were in danger and encouraged voting. The colony-wide committees provided a method through which colonial leaders could communicate, and established the framework of the colonies' early attempts at independent government.

The reaction to the Townshend duties spawned a gradual, drawn-out worsening of Anglo-American relations. Colonial allegiance was broken down substantially between 1767 and 1773, and the colonists grew increasingly defensive against the impositions of the mother country, eventually forming the committees of correspondence to coordinate a pan-colonial defense mechanism. With the colonies on guard and fed up with British meddling, the stage was set for the descent into rebellion, if the British did not back down. In late 1773, that descent began, and the American Revolution began.

CHAPTER 3 - THE AMERICAN REVOLUTION (1754–1781)

Before and during the French and Indian War, from about 1650 to 1763, Britain essentially left its American colonies to run themselves in an age of salutary neglect. Given relative freedom to do as they pleased, the North American settlers turned to unique forms of government to match their developing new identity as Americans. They established representative legislatures and democratic town meetings. They also enjoyed such rights as local judiciaries and trials by jury in which defendants were assumed innocent until proven guilty. American shipping, although theoretically regulated by the Navigation Act, functioned apart from the mighty British fleet for more than a hundred years. Finally, the promise of an expansive, untamed continent gave all settlers a sense of freedom and the ability to start fresh in the New World.

After the French and Indian War, the age of salutary neglect was finished. Britain, wanting to replenish its drained treasury, placed a larger tax burden on America and tightened regulations in the colonies. Over the years, Americans were forbidden to circulate local printed currencies, ordered to house British troops, made to comply with restrictive shipping policies, and forced to pay unpopular taxes. Furthermore, many of those failing to comply with the new rules found themselves facing a British judge without jury. Americans were shocked and offended by what they regarded as violations of their liberties. Over time, this shock turned to indignation, which ultimately grew into desire for rebellion. In a mere twelve years—between the end of the French and Indian War in 1763 and the outbreak of the Revolutionary War in 1775—the colonists moved from offering nightly toasts to King George III's health to demonstrations of outright hostility toward the British Crown.

The American Revolution had profound consequences, not only for the American colonists but for the rest of the world as well. Never before had a body of colonists so boldly declared their monarch and government incapable of governing a free people. The Thomas Jefferson–penned Declaration of Independence was as unique as it was reasonable, presenting a strong, concise case for American rebellion against a tyrannical government. Since then, his declaration has been a model for many groups and peoples fighting their own uphill battles.

The French and Indian War - The North American theater of the primarily European Seven Years' War was known as the French and Indian War. It was fought between Britain and France from 1754 to 1763 for colonial dominance in North America. British officials tried to rally public opinion for the war at the Albany Congress in 1754 but mustered only halfhearted support throughout the colonies. Nevertheless, American colonists dutifully fought alongside British soldiers, while the French allied themselves with several Native American tribes (hence the name "French and Indian War"). This war ended after the British captured most of France's major cities and forts in Canada and the Ohio Valley.

Pontiac's Rebellion - The powerful Ottawa chief Pontiac, who had no intention of allowing land-hungry whites to steal more tribal lands, united many of the tribes in the volatile Ohio Valley and led a series of raids on British forts and American settlements. British forces eventually squashed Pontiac's Rebellion. As a conciliatory gesture toward the Native Americans, Parliament issued the Proclamation of 1763, forbidding American colonists to settle on Native American territory unless native rights to the land had first been obtained by purchase or treaty.

The End of Salutary Neglect - The French and Indian War also motivated Parliament to end the age of salutary neglect. Prime Minister George Grenville began enforcing the ancient Navigation Acts in 1764, passed the Sugar Act to tax sugar, and passed the Currency Act to remove paper currencies (many from the French and Indian War period) from circulation. A year later, he passed the Stamp Act, which placed a tax on printed materials, and the Quartering Act, which required Americans to house and feed British troops.

Taxation Without Representation - The Sugar Act was the first fully enforced tax levied in America solely for the purpose of raising revenue. Americans throughout the thirteen colonies cried out against "taxation without representation" and made informal nonimportation agreements of certain British goods in protest. Several colonial leaders convened the Stamp Act Congress in New York to petition Parliament and King George III to repeal the tax. In 1766, Parliament bowed to public pressure and repealed the Stamp Act. But it also quietly passed the Declaratory Act, which stipulated that Parliament reserved the right to tax the colonies anytime it chose.

The Townshend Acts and Boston Massacre - In 1767, Parliament passed the Townshend Acts, which levied another series of taxes on lead, paints, and tea known as the Townshend Duties. In the same series of acts, Britain passed the Suspension Act, which suspended the New York assembly for not enforcing the Quartering Act. To prevent violent protests, Massachusetts Governor Thomas Hutchinson requested assistance from the British army, and in 1768, four thousand redcoats landed in the city to help maintain order. Nevertheless, on March 5, 1770, an angry mob clashed with several British troops. Five colonists died, and news of the Boston Massacre quickly spread throughout the colonies.

The Boston Tea Party - In 1773, Parliament passed the Tea Act, granting the financially troubled British East India Company a trade monopoly on the tea exported to the American colonies. In many American cities, tea agents resigned or canceled orders, and merchants refused consignments in response to the unpopular act. Governor Hutchinson of Massachusetts, determined to uphold the law, ordered that three ships arriving in Boston harbor should be allowed to deposit their cargoes and that appropriate payments should be made for the goods. On the night of December 16, 1773, while the ships lingered in the harbor, sixty men boarded the ships, disguised as Native Americans, and dumped the entire shipment of tea into the harbor. That event is now famously known as the Boston Tea Party.

The Intolerable and Quebec Acts - In January 1774, Parliament passed the Coercive Acts, also known as the Intolerable Acts, which shut down Boston Harbor until the British East India Company had been fully reimbursed for the tea destroyed in the Boston Tea Party. Americans throughout the colonies sent food and supplies to Boston via land to prevent death from hunger and cold in the bitter New England winter. Parliament also passed the Quebec Act at the same time, which granted more rights to French Canadian Catholics and extended French Canadian territory south to the western borders of New York and Pennsylvania.

The First Continental Congress and Boycott - To protest the Intolerable Acts, prominent colonials gathered in Philadelphia at the First Continental Congress in autumn of 1774. They once again petitioned Parliament, King George III, and the British people to repeal the acts and restore friendly relations. For additional motivation, they also decided to institute a boycott, or ban, of all British goods in the colonies.

Lexington, Concord, and the Second Continental Congress - On April 19, 1775, part of the British occupation force in Boston marched to the nearby town of Concord, Massachusetts, to seize a colonial militia arsenal. Militiamen of Lexington and Concord intercepted them and attacked. The first shot—the so-called "shot heard round the world" made famous by poet Ralph Waldo Emerson—was one of many that hounded the British and forced them to retreat to Boston. Thousands of militiamen from nearby colonies flocked to Boston to assist. In the meantime, leaders convened the Second Continental Congress to discuss options. In one final attempt for peaceful reconciliation, the Olive Branch Petition, they professed their love and loyalty to King George III and begged him to address their grievances. The king rejected the petition and formally declared that the colonies were in a state of rebellion.

The Declaration of Independence - The Second Continental Congress chose George Washington, a southerner, to command the militiamen besieging Boston in the north. They also appropriated money for a small navy and for transforming the undisciplined militias into the professional Continental Army. Encouraged by a strong colonial campaign in which the British scored only narrow victories (such as at Bunker Hill), many colonists began to advocate total independence as opposed to having full rights within the British Empire. The next year, the congressmen voted on July 2, 1776, to declare their independence. Thomas Jefferson, a young lawyer from Virginia, drafted the Declaration of Independence. The United States was born.

KEY PEOPLE & TERMS

People

- **John Adams** - A prominent Boston lawyer who first became famous for defending the British soldiers accused of murdering five civilians in the Boston Massacre. Adams was a delegate from Massachusetts in the Continental Congresses, where he rejected proposals for reconciliation with Britain. He served as vice president to George Washington and was president of the United States from 1797 to 1801.

- **Samuel Adams** - Second cousin to John Adams and a political activist. Adams was a failed Bostonian businessman who became an activist in the years leading up to the Revolutionary War. He organized the first Committee of Correspondence of Boston, which communicated with other similar organizations across the colonies, and was a delegate to both Continental Congresses in 1774 and 1775.

- **Joseph Brant** - A Mohawk chief and influential leader of the Iroquois tribes. Brant was one of the many Native American leaders who advocated an alliance with Britain against the Americans in the Revolutionary War. He and other tribal leaders hoped an alliance with the British might provide protection from land-hungry American settlers.

- **Benjamin Franklin** - A Philadelphia printer, inventor, and patriot. Franklin drew the famous "Join or Die" political cartoon for the Albany Congress. He was also a delegate for the Second Continental Congress and a member of the committee responsible for helping to draft the Declaration of Independence in 1776.

- **King George III** - King of Great Britain during the American Revolution. George III inherited the throne at the age of twelve. He ruled Britain throughout the Seven Years' War, the French and Indian War, the American Revolution, the Napoleonic Wars, and the War of 1812. After the conclusion of the French and Indian War, his popularity declined in the American colonies. In the Declaration of Independence, Thomas Jefferson vilifies George III and argues that his neglect and misuse of the American colonies justified their revolution.

- **George Grenville** - Prime minister of Parliament at the close of the French and Indian War. Grenville was responsible for enforcing the Navigation Act and for passing the Sugar Act, Stamp Act, Currency Act, and Quartering Act in the mid-1760s. He assumed, incorrectly, that colonists would be willing to bear a greater tax burden after Britain had invested so much in protecting them from the French and Native Americans.

- **Patrick Henry** - A radical colonist famous for his "Give me liberty or give me death" speech. Henry openly advocated rebellion against the Crown in the years prior to the Revolutionary War.

- **Thomas Hutchinson** - Royal official and governor of Massachusetts during the turbulent years of the 1760s and early 1770s. Hutchinson forbade the British East India Company's tea ships from leaving Boston Harbor until they had unloaded their cargo, prompting disguised colonists to destroy the tea in the Boston Tea Party.

- **Thomas Jefferson** - Virginian planter and lawyer who eventually became president of the United States. Jefferson was invaluable to the revolutionary cause. In 1776, he drafted the Declaration of Independence, which justified American independence from Britain. Later, he served as the first secretary of state under President George Washington and as vice president to John Adams. Jefferson then was elected president himself in 1800 and 1804.

- **Thomas Paine** - A radical philosopher who strongly supported republicanism and civic virtue. Paine's 1776 pamphlet Common Sense was a bestselling phenomenon in the American colonies and convinced thousands to rebel against the "royal brute," King George III. When subsequent radical writings of

Paine's, which supported republicanism and condemned monarchy, were published in Britain, Paine was tried in absentia, found guilty of seditious libel, and declared an outlaw in England.

- William Pitt, the Elder - British statesman who provided crucial leadership during the latter half of the French and Indian War. Pitt focused British war efforts so that Britain could defeat the French in Canada. Many have argued that without his leadership, Britain would have lost the war to the French and their allies.

- Pontiac - A prominent Ottawa chief. Pontiac, disillusioned by the French defeat in the French and Indian War, briefly united various tribes in the Ohio and Mississippi Valleys to raid colonists on the western frontiers of British North America between 1763 and 1766. He eventually was killed by another Native American after the British crushed his uprising. Hoping to forestall any future tribal insurrections, Parliament issued the Proclamation of 1763 as a conciliatory gesture toward Native Americans and as an attempt to check the encroachment of white settlers onto native lands.

- George Washington - A Virginia planter and militia officer who eventually became the first president of the United States. Washington participated in the first engagement of the French and Indian War in 1754 and later became commander in chief of the American forces during the Revolutionary War. In 1789, he became president of the United States. Although Washington actually lost most of the military battles he fought, his leadership skills were unparalleled and were integral to the creation of the United States.

Terms

- Albany Congress - A congress convened by British officials in 1754 promoting a unification of British colonies in North America for security and defense against the French. Although the Albany Congress failed to foster any solid colonial unity, it did bring together many colonial leaders who would later play key roles in the years before the Revolutionary War. To support the congress, Benjamin Franklin drew his famous political cartoon of a fragmented snake labeled "Join or Die."

- Battle of Lexington and Concord - Two battles, fought on April 19, 1775, that opened the Revolutionary War. When British troops engaged a small group of colonial militiamen in the small towns of Lexington and Concord, Massachusetts, the militiamen fought back and eventually forced the British to retreat, harrying the redcoats on the route back to Boston using guerrilla tactics. The battle sent shockwaves throughout the colonies and the world, as it was astonishing that farmers were able to beat the British forces. This battle marked a significant turning point because open military conflict made reconciliation between Britain and the colonies all the more unlikely.

- Battle of Saratoga - A 1777 British defeat that was a major turning point in the Revolutionary War. The defeat convinced the French to ally themselves with the United States and enter the war against Britain. Most historians agree that without help from France, the United States could not have won the war.

- Boston Massacre - An incident that occurred on March 5, 1770, when a mob of angry Bostonians began throwing rocks and sticks at the British troops who were occupying the city. The troops shot several members of the crowd, killing five. Patriots throughout the colonies dubbed the incident a "massacre" and used it to fuel anti-British sentiment.

- Boston Tea Party - An incident that took place on December 16, 1773, when a band of Bostonians led by the Sons of Liberty disguised themselves as Native Americans and destroyed chests of tea aboard ships in the harbor. The Tea Party prompted the passage of the Intolerable Acts to punish Bostonians and make them pay for the destroyed tea.

- First Continental Congress - A meeting convened in late 1774 that brought together delegates from twelve of the thirteen colonies (Georgia abstained) in order to protest the Intolerable Acts. Colonial leaders stood united against these and other British acts and implored Parliament and King George III to repeal them. The Congress also created an association to organize and supervise a boycott on all British goods. Although the delegates did not request home rule or desire independence, they believed that the colonies should be given more power to legislate themselves.

- French and Indian War - A war—part of the Seven Years' War fought in the mid-1700s among the major European powers—waged in North America from 1754 to 1763. The British and American colonists fought in the war against the French and their Native American allies, hence the American name for the war. After the war, the British emerged as the dominant European power on the eastern half of the continent.

- Loyalists - Those who chose to support Britain during the Revolutionary War. Loyalists were particularly numerous in the lower southern states, but they also had support from Anglican clergymen, wealthy citizens, and colonial officials. Thousands served in Loyalist militias or in the British army, while others fled to Canada, the West Indies, or England. A large majority of black slaves also chose to support Britain because they believed an American victory would only keep them enslaved. Native Americans sided with the British, too, fearing that American settlers would consume their lands if the United States won.

- Mercantilism - An economic theory predominant in the 1700s that stipulated that nations should amass wealth in order to increase their power. Under mercantilism, the European powers sought new colonies in the Americas, Africa, and Asia because they wanted sources of cheap natural resources such as gold, cotton, timber, tobacco, sugarcane, and furs. They shipped these materials back to Europe and converted them into manufactured goods, which they resold to the colonists at high prices.

- Patriots - Those who supported the war against Britain. In January 1776, the English émigré philosopher and radical Thomas Paine published the pamphlet Common Sense, which beseeched Americans to rebel against the "royal brute," King George III, declare independence, and establish a new republican government. The pamphlet sold an estimated 100,000 copies in just a few months and convinced many Americans that the time had come to be free of Britain forever.

- Pontiac's Rebellion - An uprising led by the Ottawa chief Pontiac against British settlers after the end of the French and Indian War. Pontiac united several Native American tribes in the Ohio Valley and attacked British and colonial settlements in the region. The forces under Pontiac laid siege to Detroit and succeeded in taking all but four of the fortified posts they attacked. Although the British army defeated Pontiac's warriors and squelched the rebellion, Parliament issued the Proclamation of 1763 as a conciliatory gesture to the Native Americans, recognizing their right to their territories.

- Second Continental Congress - A meeting convened in 1775 by colonial leaders to discuss how to proceed after the recent Battle of Lexington and Concord. The Congress decided to try one last time to restore peaceful relations with Britain by signing the Olive Branch Petition. In the meantime, they prepared for national defense by creating a navy and the Continental Army and installing George Washington in command of the latter. At this point, many believed that war was inevitable.

- Stamp Act Congress - A meeting convened in 1765 in New York to protest the Stamp Act. Delegates from nine colonies attended and signed petitions asking Parliament and King George III to repeal the tax. It was the first time colonial leaders united to protest an action by Parliament.

THE FRENCH AND INDIAN WAR: 1754–1763

- 1754 - George Washington's forces initiate French and Indian War Albany Congress convenes

- 1755 - Braddock defeated

- 1758 - British take Louisbourg

- 1759 - British take Quebec

- 1760 - British take Montreal

- 1763 - Treaty of Paris ends French and Indian War Pontiac attacks Detroit British issue Proclamation of 1763

- George Washington - American general whose forces helped start the French and Indian War in western Pennsylvania in 1754

- General Edward "Bulldog" Braddock - British general who proved ineffective in fighting Native American forces during the French and Indian War

- William Pitt - Major British statesman during second half of the French and Indian War; successfully focused war efforts on defeating French forces in Canada

- Pontiac - Ottawa chief disillusioned by the French defeat in the war; organized unsuccessful uprising against settlers after the war's end

THE BEGINNING OF THE WAR

Unlike the previous wars between European powers in the 1700s, the French and Indian War was begun in North America—in the heartland of the Ohio Valley, where both France and Britain held claims to land and trading rights. Westward-moving British colonists were particularly aggressive in their desire for new tracts of wilderness. The French, in order to prevent further British encroachment on what they believed to be French lands, began to construct a series of forts along the Ohio River. Eventually, the two sides came into conflict when a young lieutenant colonel from Virginia named George Washington attacked French troops with his small militia force and established Fort Necessity. Washington eventually surrendered after the French returned in greater numbers.

AMERICANS FIGHTING FOR THE BRITISH

The opportunity to serve side by side with British regulars during the war gave many Americans a sense of pride and confidence. It is estimated that some 20,000 Americans fought with the British against the French and Native American opposition. Washington, though he was defeated more than once during the war, was one of many colonists who gained valuable military and leadership skills that later proved useful during the Revolutionary War.

At the same time, though military service gave colonists a sense of pride, it also made many realize how different they were from the British regulars with whom they fought. Many British regulars disliked the colonists they were fighting to protect, and many British commanders refused to acknowledge the authority of high-ranking colonial militia officers.

COLONIAL DISUNITY

Furthermore, the British never managed to gain colonial support for the conflict. Many colonists, especially those living on the eastern seaboard far from the conflict, didn't particularly feel like fighting Britain's wars. Many colonial legislatures refused to support the war wholeheartedly until leading British statesman William Pitt offered to pay them for their expenses. Some colonial shippers were so disinterested in British policy that they actually shipped food to the French and its European allies during the conflict. In short, there was little colonial support for the war, but much colonial unity that was subversive to British war aims.

THE ALBANY CONGRESS

To bolster more colonial support for the French and Indian War, Britain called for an intercolonial congress to meet in Albany, New York, in 1754. To promote the Albany Congress, Philadelphia printer Benjamin Franklin created his now-famous political cartoon of a snake with the caption "Join or Die." Despite Franklin's efforts, delegates from only seven of the thirteen colonies chose to attend. The delegates at the Albany conference agreed to support the war and also reaffirmed their military alliance with the Iroquois against the French and their Native American allies. But somewhat surprisingly, the delegates at Albany also sent Parliament recommendations for increased colonial unity and a degree of home rule. British ministers in London—as well as the delegates' own colonial legislatures—balked at the idea.

WAR SPREADS TO EUROPE

American colonists and the French waged undeclared warfare for two years until 1756, when London formally declared war against France. The conflict quickly spread to Europe and soon engulfed the Old World powers in another continental war (in Europe, the war was referred to as the Seven Years' War).

For Britain and France, this expansion of the war shifted the war's center from the Americas to Europe and thus transformed the struggle entirely. The fighting in North America became secondary, and both powers focused their attention and resources in Europe. However, despite the diversion of resources and manpower to Europe, many key battles in the war continued to be fought in the New World.

FRANCE'S STRONG START

During the initial years of the war, the French maintained the upper hand, as they repeatedly dominated British forces. The most notorious British defeat in North America came in 1755, when British General Edward "Bulldog" Braddock and his aide George Washington chose to attack the French Fort Duquesne in the Ohio Valley. After hacking through endless wilderness, their forces were slaughtered by the French and their Native American allies. This seemingly easy victory encouraged Native American tribes throughout the frontier to attack the British settlers encroaching on their lands.

BRITAIN'S RESURGENCE

After Britain officially declared war on France in 1756, British troops—many of whom were American colonists—invaded French Canada and also assaulted French posts in the West Indies. Not until the "Great Commoner" statesman William Pitt took charge of operations in London did Britain begin to turn the tide against France. Pitt focused the war effort on achieving three goals: the capture of the French Canadian cities Louisbourg, Quebec, and Montreal. He succeeded: Louisbourg fell in 1758, Quebec in 1759, and Montreal in 1760, giving the British a victory.

The Treaty of Paris - The war ended formally with the Treaty of Paris, signed in 1763. Under the terms of the agreement, France was effectively driven out of Canada, leaving Britain the dominant North American power.

PONTIAC AND THE PROCLAMATION OF 1763

Despite the signing of the peace treaty, unofficial fighting between white settlers and Native Americans in the West continued for another three years. In one incident, a group of Native Americans, under the leadership of Ottawa chief Pontiac and supported by bitter French traders, killed roughly 2,000 British settlers, lay seige to Detroit, and captured most of the British forts on the western frontier. Though the British army quickly squelched Pontiac's Rebellion, Parliament, in order to appease Native Americans and to prevent further clashes, issued the Proclamation of 1763, which forbade British colonists from settling on Native American territory. The Proclamation of 1763 angered Americans intensely: during the French and Indian War, they had believed they were fighting, at least in part, for their right to expand and settle west of the Appalachians. Many firmly believed that this land was theirs for the taking. The proclamation thus came as a shock. Many colonists chose to ignore the proclamation and move westward anyway. This issue was the first of many that would ultimately split America from Britain.

THE SUGAR AND STAMP ACTS: 1763–1766

- 1764 - Britain begins to enforce the Navigation Act Parliament passes the Sugar and Currency Acts

- 1765 - Parliament passes the Stamp and Quartering Acts Stamp Act Congress convenes in New York

- 1766 - Parliament repeals the Stamp Act, passes the Declaratory Act

- George III - King of Great Britain throughout much of the colonial period; saw marked decline in popularity in the colonies after the French and Indian War

- George Grenville - Prime minister of Parliament; enforced the Navigation Act and passed the Sugar, Stamp, Currency, and Quartering Acts

- Sons of Liberty - Secretive groups of prominent citizens who led protests against British taxes and regulations; influence grew in 1765 after passage of the Stamp Act

GROWING DISCONTENTMENT WITH BRITAIN

During the period from 1763 to 1775, in the twelve years after the French and Indian War and before the outbreak of the Revolutionary War, colonial distrust of Britain grew markedly, and the emerging united national identity in America became more prominent. In just over a decade, proud British subjects in the American colonies became ardent anti-British patriots struggling for independence.

SALUTARY NEGLECT

Likewise, London's view of the colonies changed radically after the French and Indian War. Prior to the war, Parliament barely acknowledged the American colonists, treating them with a policy of salutary neglect. As long as the colonies exported cheap raw materials to Britain and imported finished goods from Britain (see Mercantilism, below), Britain was quite happy to leave them alone. After the war, though, the situation was radically different. By the end of the Seven Years' War, the British national debt had climbed over 100 million pounds, hundreds of thousands of which had been used to protect the British colonies in America.

MERCANTILISM

Britain's economy during the 1700s was based on mercantilist theories that taught that money was power: the more money a nation had in its reserves, the more powerful it was. Britain and other European powers, including France and Spain, actively sought new colonies in the Americas, Africa, and Asia to stimulate their economies and increase their wealth. Colonies provided cheap natural resources such as gold, cotton, timber, tobacco, sugarcane, and furs. These materials could be shipped back home to the mother country and converted into manufactured goods, which were resold to the colonists at high prices.

THE NAVIGATION ACTS

Immediately following the cessation of the French and Indian War, British Prime Minister George Grenville ordered the Royal Navy to begin enforcing the old Navigation Acts. Parliament had passed a major Navigation Act in 1651 to prevent other European powers (especially the Dutch) from encroaching on British colonial territories; the act required colonists to export certain key goods, such as tobacco, only to Britain. In addition, any European goods bound for the colonies had to be taxed in Britain. Although the law had existed for over one hundred years, it had never before been strictly enforced.

GRENVILLE AND THE SUGAR ACT

Because the French and Indian War had left Britain with an empty pocketbook, Parliament also desperately needed to restock the Treasury. Led by Grenville, Parliament levied heavier taxes on British subjects, especially the colonists. First, in 1764, Grenville's government passed the Sugar Act, which placed a tax on sugar imported from the West Indies. The Sugar Act represented a significant change in policy: whereas previous colonial taxes had been levied to support local British officials, the tax on sugar was enacted solely to refill Parliament's empty Treasury.

THE CURRENCY AND QUARTERING ACTS

The same year, Parliament also passed the Currency Act, which removed devalued paper currencies, many from the French and Indian War period, from circulation. In 1765, Parliament passed the Quartering Act, which required residents of some colonies to feed and house British soldiers serving in America. These acts outraged colonists, who believed the taxes and regulations were unfair. Many also questioned why the British army needed to remain in North America when the French and Pontiac had already been defeated.

THE STAMP ACT

Though the colonists disliked all of these acts, they particularly took offense to the 1765 Stamp Act. This tax required certain goods to bear an official stamp showing that the owner had paid his or her tax. Many of these items were paper goods, such as legal documents and licenses, newspapers, leaflets, and even playing cards. Furthermore, the act declared that those who failed to pay the tax would be punished by the vice-admiralty courts without a trial by jury.

Colonists were particularly incensed because the Stamp Act was passed in order to pay for the increased British troop presence in the colonies. Not only did the colonists feel that the troop presence was no longer necessary, they also feared that the troops were there to control them. This military presence, combined with the vice-admiralty courts and Quartering Act, made the Americans very suspicious of Grenville's intentions.

TAXATION WITHOUT REPRESENTATION

In protest, the American public began to cry out against "taxation without representation." In reality, most colonists weren't seriously calling for representation in Parliament; a few minor representatives in Parliament likely would have been too politically weak to accomplish anything substantive for the colonies. Rather, the slogan was symbolic and voiced the colonists' distaste for paying taxes they hadn't themselves legislated.

VIRTUAL REPRESENTATION

In defense, Grenville claimed that the colonists were subject to "virtual representation." He and his supporters argued that all members of Parliament—no matter where they were originally elected—virtually represented all British citizens in England, North America, or anywhere else. To the colonists, the idea of virtual representation was a joke.

THE STAMP ACT CONGRESS

Unwilling to accept the notion of virtual representation, colonists protested the new taxes—the Stamp Act in particular—using more direct methods. In 1765, delegates from nine colonies met in New York at the Stamp Act Congress, where they drafted a plea to King George III and Parliament to repeal the Stamp Act.

THE SONS AND DAUGHTERS OF LIBERTY

Other colonists took their protests to the streets. In Boston, a patriot group called the Sons of Liberty erected "liberty poles" to hang images of tax collectors and even tarred and feathered one minor royal official. People throughout the colonies also refused to import British goods. Homespun clothing became popular as colonial wives, or Daughters of Liberty, refused to purchase British cloth.

THE DECLARATORY ACT

Parliament eventually conceded and repealed the Stamp Act in 1766, which overjoyed the colonists. Quietly, however, Parliament also passed the Declaratory Act to reserve Britain's right to govern and "bind" the colonies whenever and however it deemed necessary.

The Declaratory Act proved far more damaging than the Stamp Act had ever been, because it emboldened Britain to feel that it could pass strict legislation freely, with few repercussions. It was during the aftermath of the Declaratory Act, from 1766 to 1773, that colonial resistance to the Crown intensified and became quite violent.

THE BOSTON MASSACRE AND TEA PARTY: 1767–1774

- 1767 - Townshend Acts impose duties on goods, suspend the New York assembly

- 1768 - British troops occupy Boston

- 1770 - Parliament repeals all duties under the Townshend Acts except tax on tea Boston Massacre occurs

- 1773 - Boston Tea Party occurs

- 1774 - Parliament passes Coercive, or Intolerable, Acts Parliament passes Quebec Act

- Thomas Hutchinson - Governor of Massachusetts during early 1770s; instituted policies that prompted the Boston Tea Party

- Charles Townshend - British member of Parliament who crafted the 1767 Townshend Acts

THE TOWNSHEND ACTS

Parliament wasted little time invoking its right to "bind" the colonies under the Declaratory Act. The very next year, in 1767, it passed the Townshend Acts. Named after Parliamentarian Charles Townshend, these acts included small duties on all imported glass, paper, lead, paint, and, most significant, tea. Hundreds of thousands of colonists drank tea daily and were therefore outraged at Parliament's new tax.

IMPACT OF THE TOWNSHEND ACTS

Fueled by their success in protesting the Stamp Act, colonists took to the streets again. Nonimportation agreements were strengthened, and many shippers, particularly in Boston, began to import smuggled tea. Although initial opposition to the Townshend Acts was less extreme than the initial reaction to the Stamp Act, it eventually became far greater. The nonimportation agreements, for example, proved to be far more effective this time at hurting British merchants. Within a few years' time, colonial resistance became more violent and destructive.

THE BOSTON MASSACRE

To prevent serious disorder, Britain dispatched 4,000 troops to Boston in 1768—a rather extreme move, considering that Boston had only about 20,000 residents at the time. Indeed, the troop deployment quickly proved a mistake, as the soldiers' presence in the city only made the situation worse. Bostonians, required to house the soldiers in their own homes, resented their presence greatly.

Tensions mounted until March 5, 1770, when a protesting mob clashed violently with British regulars, resulting in the death of five Bostonians. Although most historians actually blame the rock-throwing mob for picking the fight, Americans throughout the colonies quickly dubbed the event the Boston Massacre. This incident, along with domestic pressures from British merchants suffering from colonial nonimportation agreements, convinced Parliament to repeal the Townshend Acts. The tax on tea, however, remained in place as a matter of principle. This decision led to more violent incidents.

THE TEA ACT

In 1773, Parliament passed the Tea Act, granting the financially troubled British East India Company an exclusive monopoly on tea exported to the American colonies. This act agitated colonists even further: although the new monopoly meant cheaper tea, many Americans believed that Britain was trying to dupe them into accepting the hated tax.

THE BOSTON TEA PARTY

In response to the unpopular act, tea agents in many American cities resigned or canceled orders, and merchants refused consignments. In Boston, however, Governor Thomas Hutchinson resolved to uphold the law and ordered that three ships arriving in Boston Harbor be allowed to despoit their cargoes and that appropriate payment be made for the goods. This policy prompted about sixty men, including some members of the Sons of Liberty, to board the ships on the night of December 16, 1773 (disguised as Native Americans) and dump the tea chests into the water. The event became known as the Boston Tea Party.

The dumping of the tea in the harbor was the most destructive act that the colonists had taken against Britain thus far. The previous rioting and looting of British officials' houses over the Stamp Act had been minor compared to the thousands of pounds in damages to the ships and tea. Governor Hutchinson, angered by the colonists' disregard for authority and disrespect for property, left for England. The "tea party" was a bold and daring step forward on the road to outright revolution.

THE INTOLERABLE ACTS

The Tea Party had mixed results: some Americans hailed the Bostonians as heroes, while others condemned them as radicals. Parliament, very displeased, passed the Coercive Acts in 1774 in a punitive effort to restore order. Colonists quickly renamed these acts the Intolerable Acts.

Numbered among these Intolerable Acts was the Boston Port Bill, which closed Boston Harbor to all ships until Bostonians had repaid the British East India Company for damages. The acts also restricted public assemblies and suspended many civil liberties. Strict new provisions were also made for housing British troops in American homes, reviving the indignation created by the earlier Quartering Act, which had been allowed to expire in 1770. Public sympathy for Boston erupted throughout the colonies, and many neighboring towns sent food and supplies to the blockaded city.

THE QUEBEC ACT

At the same time the Coercive Acts were put into effect, Parliament also passed the Quebec Act. This act granted more freedoms to Canadian Catholics and extended Quebec's territorial claims to meet the western frontier of the American colonies.

THE REVOLUTION BEGINS: 1772–1775

- 1772 - Samuel Adams creates first Committee of Correspondence
- 1774 - First Continental Congress convenes in Philadelphia Boycott of British goods begins

- 1775 - American forces win Battle of Lexington and Concord Second Continental Congress convenes in Philadelphia Second Continental Congress extends Olive Branch Petition King George III declares colonies in state of rebellion

- John Adams - Prominent Bostonian lawyer who opposed reconciliation with Britain during the Continental Congresses

- Samuel Adams - Second cousin to John Adams and ardent political activist

- George III - King of Great Britain; declared colonies in state of rebellion in 1775

- Patrick Henry - Fiery radical famous for his "Give me liberty or give me death" speech

- George Washington - Virginia planter and militia officer; took command of the Continental Army in 1775

COMMITTEES OF CORRESPONDENCE

In 1772, Samuel Adams of Boston created the first Committee of Correspondence, which was primarily an exchange of ideas in letters and pamphlets among members. Within a few years, this one committee led to dozens of similar discussion groups in towns throughout the colonies. Eventually, these isolated groups came together to facilitate the exchange of ideas and solidify opposition to the Crown. The Committees of Correspondence proved invaluable in uniting colonists, distributing information, and organizing colonial voices of opposition.

THE FIRST CONTINENTAL CONGRESS

In response to the Intolerable Acts, delegates from twelve of the thirteen colonies (Georgia chose not to attend) met at the First Continental Congress in Philadelphia in the autumn of 1774 to discuss a course of action. The delegates were all fairly prominent men in colonial political life but held different philosophical beliefs. Samuel Adams, John Adams, Patrick Henry, and George Washington were among the more famous men who attended.

Although rebellion against the Crown was at this point still far from certain, leaders believed grievances had to be redressed to Parliament and King George III. The delegates met for nearly two months and concluded with a written Declaration of Rights and requests to Parliament, George III, and the British people to repeal the Coercive Acts so that harmony could be restored.

NATURAL RIGHTS

The First Continental Congress marked an important turning point in colonial relations with Britain. Although some delegates still hoped for reconciliation, the decisions they made laid the foundations for revolt. Even though American colonial leaders had petitioned Parliament and King George III to repeal taxes in the past, never had they boldly denounced them until this point, when they claimed that Britain's actions had violated their natural rights and the principles of the English constitution.

This appeal to natural rights above the king or God was groundbreaking because it justified and even legalized colonial opposition to the Crown. It converted the riotous street mobs into people justly defending their freedoms. In other words, the Americans were not in the wrong for resisting British policy. Rather, Britain was to blame because it had attempted to strip Americans of their natural rights as human beings. Thomas Jefferson later extrapolated these legal appeals in the Declaration of Independence.

THE BOYCOTT

The Continental Congress delegates decided that until the Coercive Acts were repealed, a stronger system of nonimportation agreements, including a new boycott of all British goods, should be organized and administered throughout the colonies. Patriotic colonists argued that the purchase of any British-produced goods—especially those goods made from American raw materials—only perpetuated the servile relationship the colonies had to London under the system of mercantilism.

COMMITTEES OF OBSERVATION AND SAFETY

The Congress therefore created the Committees of Observation and Safety and gave them the task of making sure no citizens purchased British merchandise under the authority of the Continental Association. The Congress also attempted to define the exact relationship Britain had with America and the degree to which Parliament could legislate. Although the Congress did not request home rule, it did claim that colonial legislatures should be entrusted with more responsibilities.

The Committees of Observation and Safety had a profound effect on American colonial life. As British officials shut down or threatened to shut down town legislatures and councils throughout the colonies, the committees often became de facto governments. Many established their own court systems, raised militias, legislated against Loyalist demonstrations, and eventually coordinated efforts with other observation committees in nearby communities. Also, most of these committees were democratically elected by community members and were thus recognized by patriotic colonists as legitimate supervisory bodies. Their creation and coordination helped spread revolutionary ideas and fervor to the countryside and later smoothed the transition to democracy after independence.

THE BATTLE OF LEXINGTON AND CONCORD

By 1775, colonial resentment toward Britain had become a desire for rebellion. Many cities and towns organized volunteer militias of "minutemen"—named for their alleged ability to prepare for combat at the drop of a hat—who began to drill openly in public common areas.

On April 19, 1775, a British commander dispatched troops to seize an arsenal of colonial militia weapons stored in Concord, Massachusetts. Militiamen from nearby Lexington intercepted them and opened fire. Eight Americans died as the British sliced through them and moved on to Concord.

The British arrived in Concord only to be ambushed by the Concord militia. The "shot heard round the world"—or the first shot of many that defeated the British troops at Concord—sent a ripple throughout the colonies, Europe, and the rest of the world. The British retreated to Boston after more than 270 in their unit were killed, compared to fewer than 100 Americans. The conflict became known as the Battle of Lexington and Concord.

The minutemen's victory encouraged patriots to redouble their efforts and at the same time convinced King George III to commit military forces to crushing the rebellion. Almost immediately, thousands of colonial militiamen set up camp around Boston, laying siege to the British position. The battle initiated a chain of events, starting with the militia siege of Boston and the Second Continental Congress, that kicked the Revolutionary War into high gear.

THE SECOND CONTINENTAL CONGRESS

The Second Continental Congress was convened a few weeks after the Battle of Lexington and Concord to decide just how to handle the situation. Delegates from all thirteen colonies gathered once again in Philadelphia and discussed options. The desire to avoid a war was still strong, and in July 1775, delegate John Dickinson from Pennsylvania penned the Olive Branch Petition to send to Britain. All the delegates signed the petition, which professed loyalty to King George III and beseeched him to call off the troops in Boston so that peace between the colonies and Britain could be restored. George III eventually rejected the petition.

WASHINGTON AND THE CONTINENTAL ARMY

Despite their issuance of the Olive Branch Petition, the delegates nevertheless believed that the colonies should be put in a state of defense against any future possible British actions. Therefore, they set aside funds to organize an army and a small navy. After much debate, they also selected George Washington to command the militia surrounding Boston, renaming it the Continental Army. Washington was a highly respected Virginian plantation owner, and his leadership would further unite the northern and southern colonies in the Revolution.

THE BATTLE OF BUNKER HILL

The delegates' hopes for acknowledgment and reconciliation failed in June 1775, when the Battle of Bunker Hill was fought outside Boston. Although the British ultimately emerged victorious, they suffered over 1,000 casualties, prompting British officials to take the colonial unrest far more seriously than they had previously. The engagement led King George III to declare officially that the colonies were in a state of rebellion. Any hope of reconciliation and a return to the pre-1763 status quo had vanished.

AMERICAN SOCIETY IN REVOLT: 1776–1777

- 1776 - Thomas Paine writes Common Sense

- 1777 - Vermont adopts a state constitution prohibiting slavery Iroquois begin to raid colonial settlements in western New York and Pennsylvania

- George Washington - Commander of the Continental Army

- Nathanael Greene - Aide to Washington; one of the highest-ranking and most respected American generals in the war

- Baron von Steuben - German commander who helped George Washington and Nathanael Greene train the Continental army

- Thomas Paine - Radical philosopher who strongly supported republicanism; wrote 1776 pamphlet Common Sense, which was a best-seller in the American colonies

- Joseph Brant - Mohawk chief who advocated alliance with Britain against American forces in the Revolutionary War

TRAINING THE CONTINENTAL ARMY

As the colonies prepared themselves for war, new militias were formed throughout America, primarily to defend local communities from British aggression. Other units, however, rushed to join their comrades in Boston as soon as every man had a musket. Under the strict command of George Washington, Nathanael Greene, and the German Baron von Steuben, this ragtag collection of undisciplined militiamen eventually became the well-trained Continental Army.

POPULAR SUPPORT FOR THE WAR

When the Revolutionary War began, Britain made a costly and ultimately fatal error in assuming that opposition to British policies came only from a core group of rabble-rousing ringleaders such as Washington, Jefferson, and the Adams cousins. The British believed, incorrectly, that if they arrested these men, the revolt would collapse and the minutemen would return to their homes. They failed to understand that a significant majority of Americans disliked British rule and desired something better. Historians estimate that the majority of eligible American men served at some point in the Continental Army, the militias, or both.

PATRIOTIC WOMEN

Many American women supported the war effort as well. Some particularly daring women chose to serve as nurses, attendants, cooks, and even spies on the battlefields. Others, such as the famous "Molly Pitcher" (a woman named Mary Hays McCauly, who fought in her husband's place) and Deborah Sampson (who disguised herself as a man) saw action in battle. Most women, however, fought the war at home. As more and more husbands and fathers left home to fight, more and more wives and mothers took to managing the farms and businesses. A majority of women helped by making yarn and homespun necessities such as socks and underwear, both to send to militiamen and to support the boycott of British goods.

COMMON SENSE

The radical English author and philosopher Thomas Paine helped turn American public opinion against Britain and solidify the emerging colonial unity with his January 1776 pamphlet Common Sense, which denounced King George III as a tyrannical "brute." Paine, reasoning that it was unnatural for the smaller England to dominate the larger collection of American states, called on Americans to unite and overthrow British rule so that they could usher in an era of freedom for humanity. Inspiring and easy to read, Common Sense stirred the hearts of thousands of Americans and persuaded many would-be Loyalists and fence-sitters to fight for independence. The pamphlet caused a huge sensation throughout the colonies and sold over 100,000 copies within a few months of its first printing.

THE LOYALISTS

Although most Americans supported the decision to break away from Britain and declare independence, about one-third of the colonists did not. These Loyalists were heavily concentrated in the lower southern colonies but could also be found in concentrated pockets throughout other regions, including the North.

The Loyalists had several reasons for choosing to support Britain. Some, including many wealthy merchants, Anglican clergymen, and officials, disagreed with Parliament's policies but felt that it was not right to challenge British rule. Others were political conservatives who preferred the status quo. Many ethnic minorities, including blacks and Native Americans, also backed Britain, fearful that victorious white Americans would trample their rights.

One hundred thousand Loyalists fled to Canada, England, and the West Indies before and during the war. Those who stayed faced persecution, especially in the northern colonies. In the lower southern colonies, however, many pro-British colonial men formed Loyalist militias. Tens of thousands of Loyalists also joined the British army to fight for king and country.

NATIVE AMERICANS

Native Americans were particularly fearful of future American expansion into their lands, and the majority of tribes chose to support Britain. In particular, the influential Mohawk chief Joseph Brant worked tirelessly to convince the Iroquois tribes to support the British. As a result of his efforts and those of others like him, thousands of Iroquois, Creek, Cherokee, Choctaw, and other warriors joined forces with the British and coordinated independent raids on American arsenals and settlements along the western frontier.

The Native American decision to ally themselves with the British and raid American outposts and towns proved in the end to be a fatal one. Most believed that the British were a sure bet and that the rebellious colonies stood almost no chance of winning. The ultimate British surrender was a huge loss for Native Americans: white settlers were already pushing westward, and after the war, they felt justified in their taking of native lands.

AFRICAN AMERICANS

Blacks, too, generally supported the British because an American victory would only keep them in bondage. Although roughly 5,000 blacks did serve in militias for the United States, most who had the opportunity chose to flee to British and Loyalist areas that promised freedom from slavery. Consequently, colonies both north and south lost tens of thousands of slaves.

To some degree, blacks fared better after the war than before. Faced with the somewhat embarrassing predicament of supporting the premise that "all men are created equal," as stated in the Declaration of Independence, while at the same time practicing human bondage, many states, such as Vermont, eventually abolished slavery. Other states legislated more gradual forms of emancipation. As a result, the number of free blacks in the United States skyrocketed into the tens of thousands by the end of the century. Slavery was by no means a dead institution (as the early 1800s proved), but these liberal decisions made during the war were significant steps forward on the road to equality.

UNDECIDED COLONISTS

Finally, some men and women were neither patriots nor Loyalists and opted to take a wait-and-see approach. Civilian casualties remained low throughout the war, so such fence-sitting was an attractive alternative for some colonists. Some of the colonies, however, tried to curb the number of free riders by passing laws that essentially ordered citizens to choose sides. Able-bodied men who failed to join militias were prosecuted in some colonies for failing to show support for the patriotic cause.

THE DECLARATION OF INDEPENDENCE: 1776

- June 7 - Second Continental Congress begins to debate independence

- July 2 - Second Continental Congress votes to declare independence

- July 4 - Delegates sign Declaration of Independence

- Thomas Jefferson - Virginia statesman who drafted the Declaration of Independence

- John Adams - Massachusetts delegate at the Continental Congress; assisted Jefferson with revisions to the Declaration of Independence

- Benjamin Franklin - Pennsylvania delegate at the Continental Congress; assisted Jefferson with revisions to the Declaration of Independence

- George III - King of Great Britain throughout the American Revolution

VIRGINIA PROPOSES INDEPENDENCE

At a meeting of the Second Continental Congress in the summer of 1776, Richard Henry Lee, a delegate from Virginia, proposed that the American colonies should declare their independence from Britain. Delegates debated this proposal heavily for a few weeks, and many returned to their home states to discuss the idea in state conventions.

By this point—after the Battle of Lexington and Concord, the Battle of Bunker Hill, and George III's rejection of the Olive Branch Petition—the thought of independence appealed to a majority of colonists. By July 2, 1776, the Continental Congress, with the support of twelve states (New York did not vote), decided to declare independence.

JEFFERSON AND THE DECLARATION OF INDEPENDENCE

Congress then selected a few of its most gifted delegates, including Benjamin Franklin, John Adams, and Thomas Jefferson, to draft a written proclamation of independence. Jefferson was chosen to be the committee's scribe and principal author, so the resulting Declaration of Independence was a product primarily of his efforts.

Jefferson kept the Declaration relatively short and to the point: he wanted its meaning to be direct, clear, and forceful. In the brief document, he managed to express clearly the ideals of the American cause, level weighty accusations against George III, offer arguments to give the colonies' actions international legitimacy, and encapsulate the American spirit of freedom and unity. In his first draft, Jefferson also wrote against slavery, signifying that people were fundamentally equal regardless of race as well—but this portion was stricken from the final document. Nevertheless, Jefferson's words gave hope to blacks as well as landless whites, laborers, and women, then and for generations to come.

LIFE, LIBERTY, AND THE PURSUIT OF HAPPINESS

The Declaration's second paragraph begins the body of the text with the famous line, "We hold these truths to be self-evident, that all men are created equal, that they are endowed by their Creator with certain unalienable Rights, that among these are Life, Liberty, and the pursuit of Happiness." With these protections, any American, regardless of class, religion, gender, and eventually race, could always strive—and even sometimes succeed—at improving himself via wealth, education, or labor. With those seven final words, Jefferson succinctly codified the American Dream.

THE SOCIAL CONTRACT

Jefferson argued that governments derived their power from the people—a line of reasoning that sprang from the writings of contemporary philosophers including Jean-Jacques Rousseau and Thomas Paine. Both had argued that people enter into a social contract with the body that governs them and that when the government violates that contract, the people have the right to establish a new government. These notions of a contract and accountability were radical for their time, because most Europeans believed that their monarchs' power was granted by God. The Declaration of Independence thus established a new precedent for holding monarchies accountable for their actions.

ABUSES BY GEORGE III

In the Declaration, Jefferson also detailed the tyrannical "abuses and usurpations" that George III committed against the American colonies. Jefferson claimed that the king had wrongly shut down representative colonial legislatures, refused to allow the colonies to legislate themselves, and convened legislatures at inconvenient locations. He also accused the king of illegally assuming judicial powers and manipulating judges and the court system. Finally, Jefferson claimed that George III had conspired with others (other nations and Native Americans) against the colonists, restricted trade, imposed unjust taxes, forced American sailors to work on British ships, and taken military actions against Americans. Jefferson noted that the colonists had repeatedly petitioned the king to try to restore friendly relations but that he had consistently ignored them. Americans had also appealed to the British people for help on several occasions, again to no avail.

Jefferson concluded that, in light of these facts, the colonists had no choice but to declare independence from Britain and establish a new government to protect their rights. He stated that in order to achieve this goal, the independent states would come together to become the United States of America.

SIGNING OF THE DECLARATION

Jefferson's bold document was revised in the drafting committee and then presented to the Congress on July 4, 1776. The Congress's members felt that Jefferson's case was strong enough that it would convince other nations that America was justified in its rebellion. The thirteen states unanimously approved of the Declaration of Independence, and the United States was born.

THE REVOLUTIONARY WAR: 1775–1783

- 1775 - Battle of Lexington and Concord Second Continental Congress convenes

- 1776 - Jefferson writes Declaration of Independence

- 1777 - Battle of Saratoga

- 1778 - France and United States form Franco-American Alliance

- 1779 - Spain enters war against Britain

- 1781 - British forces under Cornwallis surrender to Washington at Yorktown

- 1783 - Peace of Paris signed to end war

- George Washington - Commander of the Continental army

- Lord Charles Cornwallis - Commander of British forces that surrendered at Yorktown

BRITISH STRENGTHS

When war erupted in 1775, it seemed clear that Britain would win. It had a large, well-organized land army, and the Royal Navy was unmatched on the sea. Many of the British troops in the Revolutionary War were veterans who had fought in the French and Indian War. On the other hand, the Americans had only a collection of undisciplined militiamen who had never fought before. The American navy was small and no match for the thousand ships in the royal fleet. The state of the army did improve after George Washington whipped the Continental Army into a professional fighting force, but the odds still seemed heavily stacked in Britain's favor.

AMERICAN STRENGTHS

Nonetheless, the Americans believed that they did have a strong chance of success. They had a lot at stake: unlike the British, they were fighting on their home turf to protect their own homes and families. Perhaps most important, they were also fighting a popular war—a majority of the colonists were patriots who strongly supported the fight for independence. Finally, though most Americans had no previous military experience, their militia units were usually close-knit bands of men, often neighbors, who served together in defense of their own homes. They elected their own officers—usually men who did have some military training but who also knew the territory well. This native officer corps was a great source of strength, and as a result, American morale was generally higher than morale in the Royal Army.

GEOGRAPHY IN THE WAR

Geography also gave the Americans an advantage that proved to be a major factor in the war's outcome. To the British forces, the North American terrain was unusually rugged: New England was rocky and cold in winter, the South was boggy and humid in the summer, and the western frontier was almost impenetrable because of muddy roads and thick forests. In addition, because American settlements were spread out across a vast range of territory, the British had difficulty mounting a concentrated fight and transporting men and supplies. American troops, on the other hand, were used to the terrain and had little trouble. Finally, the distance between England and the United States put a great strain on Britain, which spent a great deal of time, energy, and money ferrying soldiers and munitions back and forth across the Atlantic.

THE BATTLE OF SARATOGA

After numerous battles, the turning point in the war came in 1777 at the Battle of Saratoga in upstate New York. When American forces won, their victory encouraged France to pledge its support for the United States in the Franco-American Alliance of 1778. A year later, Spain followed suit and also entered the war against Britain.

Spain, hoping to see Britain driven out of North America, had tacitly supported the Americans by providing them with munitions and supplies since the beginning of the war. Their entry as combatants took pressure off the Americans, as Britain was forced to divert troops to fight the Spanish elsewhere. Finally, the Netherlands entered the war against Britain in 1780.

CONTINUING POPULAR SUPPORT

Though the war went on for several years, American popular support for it, especially after France and Spain entered the fray, remained high. The motivation for rebellion remained strong at all levels of society, not merely among American military and political leaders. Many historians believe that it was this lasting popular support that ultimately enabled the United States to fight as long as it did. Although the United States did not really "win" the war—there were no clearly decisive battles either way—it was able to survive long enough against the British to come to an impasse. French and Spanish assistance certainly helped the Americans, but without the grassroots support of average Americans, the rebellion would have quickly collapsed.

WHIGS IN ENGLAND AGAINST THE WAR

Meanwhile, support in England for the war was low. In Parliament, many Whigs (a group of British politicians representing the interests of religious dissenters, industrialists, and others who sought reform) denounced the war as unjust. Eight years of their carping, combined with the Royal Army's inability to win a decisive victory, fatigued the British cause and helped bring the Revolutionary War to an end.

THE SURRENDER AT YORKTOWN

Fortified by the Franco-American Alliance, the Americans maintained an impasse with the British until 1781, when the Americans laid siege to a large encampment of British forces under Lord Charles Cornwallis at Yorktown, Virginia. Scattered battles persisted until 1783, but the British, weary of the stalemate, decided to negotiate peace.

THE PEACE OF PARIS

The war came to an official close in September 1783, when Britain, the United States, France, and Spain negotiated the Peace of Paris. The treaty granted vast tracts of western lands to the Americans and recognized the United States as a new and independent country. The last British forces departed New York in November 1783, leaving the American government in full control of the new nation.

THE DECLARATION OF INDEPENDENCE (1776)

The Declaration of Independence, completed and signed in July of 1776, marked the official separation between the 13 colonies and Great Britain. An armed struggle between the colonies and Britain had begun just over a year before, with the Battles of Lexington and Concord. The formal declaration of independence established the new American revolutionary government and officially declared war against Great Britain. The primary purpose of the declaration was to assist the Second Continental Congress in obtaining aid from foreign countries. The document also clearly outlines the history of abuses the colonists had suffered under British rule since the end of the French and Indian war in 1763.

Prior to the French and Indian war, the colonists had enjoyed over a hundred years of "salutary neglect." In other words, although laws were in place to maintain the subordinate status of the colonies to Great Britain, they were usually not enforced. After the French and Indian war, which increased Britain's share of North America, King George III and Parliament sought to establish firm control over the land newly obtained from France, and to help pay war debts by taxing the colonies. They did this by enacting a number of acts that either taxed the colonists or placed stricter controls on trade. These laws included the Sugar Act (1764), the Stamp Tax (1765), the Townshend Acts (1767), and the Tea Act (1773). Additionally, Parliament enacted the Quartering Act (1765) which forced colonists to help pay for the British military stationed in the colonies.

Colonists initially protested these acts through peaceful means such as petition, boycott, and committees. They argued that since they had no representation in Parliament, they could not be rightfully taxed by Parliament. As their petitions were repeatedly ignored, and taxes continually added, colonists turned to increasingly more destructive actions, like the Boston Tea Party of 1774. In response to this rebellious action by the Massachusetts Colony, the King and Parliament exacted punishment through legislation referred to by colonists as the "Intolerable Acts."

The Intolerable Acts sparked the colonies to call an inter-colonial congress for the purpose of discussing a unified response to the King and Parliament. This First Continental Congress, as it was called, met in September 1774 in Philadelphia. All 13 colonies were present except for Georgia. The Congress drafted a declaration claiming that the Intolerable Acts were unconstitutional, that the colonists retained the same civil rights as English citizens, and that they would boycott all English goods until reconciliation was reached. The negotiations never happened. Instead, tensions continued to mount between the colonists and Great Britain. The First Continental Congress agreed to meet again in May 1775 if no reconciliation had been reached. At this Second Continental Congress, all thirteen colonies were present.

It took 14 months, military mobilization, persuasive pamphleteering, and the further abuse of colonial rights before all 13 colonies agreed to pursue independence. At issue were political as well as practical concerns. Upper class colonists tended to fear the lower class gaining too much power through revolution. Middle class colonists could not afford to see their businesses continue to decline due to trade restrictions. All colonists resented that the King and Parliament denied them representative government and their civil rights. However, they also doubted whether they would be strong enough to resist the British military.

Early in 1776, Thomas Paine published his pamphlet Common Sense, which won over many colonists to the cause of independence. Meanwhile, the congress had sent the King an Olive-Branch Petition as a last effort towards reconciliation. Not only did he refuse to respond to the colonists' plea, he sent an additional 20,000 troops to North America and hired mercenaries from Germany to bolster his military force. An all-out war seemed imminent and even moderate delegates realized that in order to obtain much-needed military support from France, they would have to declare themselves wholly independent from Great Britain. Richard Henry Lee of Virginia proposed a resolution for independence in June of 1776. The Congress appointed a committee to draft a declaration of independence that consisted of John Adams (MA), Benjamin Franklin (PA), Thomas Jefferson (VA), Robert Livingston (NY) and Roger Sherman (CT).

The job of drafting the Declaration of Independence fell to the youngest member of the committee, Thomas Jefferson. In composing the declaration, Jefferson drew on ideas from the Enlightenment, especially those of John Locke. Not only did the declaration represent a milestone in the history of the United States, it also turned the political philosophies of 18th century Europe into real political practice.

The Declaration of Independence, written by Thomas Jefferson and adopted by the Second Continental Congress, states the reasons the British colonies of North America sought independence in July of 1776.

The declaration opens with a preamble describing the document's necessity in explaining why the colonies have overthrown their ruler and chosen to take their place as a separate nation in the world.

All men are created equal and there are certain unalienable rights that governments should never violate. These rights include the right to life, liberty and the pursuit of happiness. When a government fails to protect those rights, it is not only the right, but also the duty of the people to overthrow that government. In its place, the people should establish a government that is designed to protect those rights. Governments are rarely overthrown, and should not be overthrown for trivial reasons. In this case, a long history of abuses has led the colonists to overthrow a tyrannical government.

The King of Great Britain, George III, is guilty of 27 specific abuses. The King interfered with the colonists' right to self-government and for a fair judicial system. Acting with Parliament, the King also instituted legislation that affected the colonies without their consent. This legislation levied taxes on the colonists. It also required them to quarter British soldiers, removed their right to trial by jury, and prevented them from trading freely. Additionally, the King and Parliament are guilty of outright destruction of American life and property by their refusal to protect the colonies' borders, their confiscation of American ships at sea, and their intent to hire foreign mercenaries to fight against the colonists.

The colonial governments tried to reach a peaceful reconciliation of these differences with Great Britain, but were continually ignored. Colonists who appealed to British citizens were similarly ignored, despite their shared common heritage and their just cause. After many peaceful attempts, the colonists have no choice but to declare independence from Great Britain.

The new nation will be called the United States of America and will have no further connections with Great Britain. The new government will reserve the right to levy war, make peace, make alliances with foreign nations, conduct trade, and do anything else that nations do.

KEY HISTORICAL FIGURES

Colonies - The 13 colonies of British North America included New Hampshire, Massachusetts, Connecticut, Rhode Island, New York, New Jersey, Pennsylvania, Delaware, Maryland, Virginia, North Carolina, South Carolina, and Georgia. A representative from each colony was sent to the Second Continental Congress in May of 1775 to debate the topic of independence. Although initial disagreement seemed to stall the drive towards independence, by July 2nd, 1776 all 13 colonies committed to fighting in the war for independence.

Thomas Jefferson - A plantation owner and a lawyer, Thomas Jefferson was a delegate from Virginia to the Second Continental Congress. After Richard Henry Lee called for independence in June of 1776, Thomas Jefferson was appointed to a committee to draft the Declaration of Independence. Thomas Jefferson is known as the author of the Declaration of Independence, although his draft was heavily edited by the delegates of the Second Continental Congress. Thomas Jefferson continued as an important figure in early American politics by serving as diplomat to France, Secretary of State, and as the third President of the United States.

King of Great Britain - King George III reigned over Great Britain and Ireland from 1760 to 1820. King George III was a descendent of the house of Hanover, a German royal family, but the first of his family to be born and educated as an Englishman. Unlike his predecessors, he aimed to rule strongly over British concerns abroad (such as the colonies) and did so by revoking the policy of salutary neglect that had dominated colonial policy until then. He also attempted to diminish the powers of parliament by frequently appointing new ministers to carry out his policy. This led to political chaos throughout Great Britain, and also contributed to the strict laws imposed on the colonies after 1763.

John Locke - John Locke was an English Philosopher who influenced the thoughts and actions of American leaders in the revolutionary era. The author of Two Treatises of Government (1690), Locke attacked the theory of divine right of kings, arguing that the power of the state rested on the power of the people. Locke believed that governments were formed to protect the natural rights of men, and that overthrowing a government that did not protect these rights was not only a right, but also an obligation. His thoughts influenced many revolutionary pamphlets and documents, including the Virginia Constitution of 1776, and the Declaration of Independence.

Additionally, his ideas about checks and balances and the division of church and state were later embodied in the U.S. Constitution.

Second Continental Congress - The Second Continental Congress met in Philadelphia in May of 1775 because the First Continental Congress had vowed to meet again if its attempts at peace with Great Britain failed. In April 1775, it became clear that the colonies were already in an undeclared war against Great Britain, evidenced by the Battles at Lexington and Concord. The Second Continental Congress had the dual responsibility of coordinating the ongoing defensive war effort in the colonies and debating the question of independence.

Salutary Neglect - An unwritten though longstanding British policy of letting slide the many British laws meant to maintain the colonies as economically and politically subordinate to England. King George III wanted to more strongly govern the colonies and put an end to salutary neglect.

PREAMBLE

It has become necessary for the 13 colonies to separate from Great Britain. These 13 colonies have the right to become a nation as legitimate as any other nation. Additionally, it is important to explain to the public, including those in other nations, why this declaration of independence is being made.

This declaration is based on certain truths. All men are meant to be equal and to have certain rights ("unalienable rights") that the government should never take away. These rights include "life, liberty and the pursuit of happiness."

Governments exist to support the rights of men. Governments exist only through the power of the people that they represent. When a government fails to grant rights to the people and removes the involvement of the people, the people have the right to change their government in a way that will allow for their unalienable rights to be protected. Governments should not be overthrown for trivial reasons; it is not typical for people to change a system that they are accustomed to. However, when the people have suffered many abuses under the control of a totalitarian leader, they not only have the right but the duty to overthrow that government.

The Declaration of Independence is important because it inspired many revolutionary efforts throughout the world and contributed to Americans' understanding of their values as a new nation. The introduction, called the preamble, to the Declaration of Independence is especially important because it builds connections between philosophical theory and practical politics, expresses the fundamental values of the new American government, and also appeals to other nations to accept the new nation.

The introduction relies heavily on the philosophical and political ideas of the Enlightenment period of 18th century Europe, including the ideas of Thomas Hobbes, Jean Jacques Rousseau, and, most particularly, John Locke. Locke believed that humans, by nature, had the right to protection of life, health, liberty and possessions. Jefferson altered this slightly when he claims the unalienable rights include "life, liberty and the pursuit of happiness." Locke also strongly opposed the divine right of kings--which held that kings held absolute power because they were placed on their throne by God--and insisted that the people had the right to consent to their government and that the power of law making resides with the people. Jefferson included this theory when he writes "to secure these rights, governments are instituted among men deriving their just powers from the consent of the governed." Jefferson's declaration helped to put Locke's philosophies into the realm of real-world politics. Many revolutions that occurred after the American Revolution cited Jefferson's Declaration of Independence as justification in overthrowing a corrupt and dictatorial power.

The introduction to the Declaration of Independence also is important for the ways it contributed to Americans' understanding of their rights as citizens. Americans continue to believe that the phrase "all men are created equal" is a fundamental "law" in the country. While this phrase was included in the introduction to the declaration, it appears nowhere else in official documents defining rights granted under the U.S. Government. The Declaration of Independence holds no legal authority in our country, yet it continues to be cited as the foundation for American equality. Various groups throughout history have criticized American "equality", referring to the introduction of the declaration for support. Critics point to Jefferson's contradictory message regarding equality in reference to slavery. Although Jefferson stated that all men are created equal and have the right to liberty, he ran a large plantation and was a slaveholder. Other critics point to the use of the word "men" as excluding women citizens. The 1848 Seneca Falls Convention used Jefferson's format and style to draft The Declaration of Sentiments, a document declaring women's unfair treatment by the U.S. government and by society. Both as a source for debate about equality and as a definition of the ideological foundation of the new nation, the introduction to the Declaration played a crucial role in defining American values and laws.

The introduction is also significant because Jefferson insisted on the importance of explaining the rebellious actions of the 13 colonies to the nations and statesmen of the world. The most powerful nations of the world in the 18th century were monarchies. The ideas of Jefferson could serve not only to threaten Great Britain's colonial empire, but the colonial empires of other nations in Europe. Recognizing the importance of maintaining good diplomatic relations with European nations, Jefferson sought to explain the actions of the 13 colonies in rational terms. Anticipating that this document would influence rebellions elsewhere, Jefferson clarified that governments should not be overthrown for trivial causes. Instead, Jefferson explained that only "despotic" or totalitarian governments should be overthrown.

LIST OF ABUSES AND USURPATIONS

The colonies have suffered 27 at the hands of the King George III. Each of these abuses has been directed at the colonies for the purpose of establishing a tyrannical government in North America. Jefferson claims that the colonists have patiently suffered these abuses and that it is now time to expose these abuses to the nations of the world.

The first 12 abuses involve King George III's establishment of a tyrannical authority in place of representative government. The foundation of representative government is the power of the people to make laws for the public good. King George III interfered with that process by rejecting legislation proposed by the colonies, dissolving colonial bodies of representation, replacing colonial governments with his appointed ministers, and interfering with the naturalization of citizens in new regions. King George III extended his tyrannical control by interfering with the objective judicial processes and the civil rights of the colonists. King George III prevented the establishment of judicial powers in the colonies and made judges dependent on him for their jobs and salaries. King George III further established tyrannical control by maintaining a strong military presence under his direct command. The King is a tyrant, because he keeps standing armies in the colonies during a time of peace, makes the military power superior to the civil government, and forces the colonists to support the military presence through increased taxes.

Abuses 13 through 22 describe the involvement of parliament in destroying the colonists' right to self-rule. The king has "combined with others" to subject the colonists to legislation passed without colonial input or consent. Legislation has been passed to quarter troops in the colonies, to shut off trade with other parts of the world, to levy taxes without the consent of colonial legislatures, to take away the right to trial by jury, and to force colonists to be tried in England. Additionally, legislation has established absolute rule in a nearby area, taken away the authority of colonial governments, and forbidden further legislation by colonial governments.

The last 5 abuses, 23 through 27, refer to specific actions that the King of Great Britain took to abandon the colonies and to wage war against them. The King has attempted to suppress the colonial rebellion through violence and military means. He sent the British military to attack colonists, burn their towns, attack their ships at sea, and destroy the lives of the people. He hired foreign mercenaries to fight against the colonies. He kidnapped American sailors to force them into British military service, refused to protect the colonies from Native American attack, and has caused colonists to fight against each other.

The list of abuses reflects the colonists' belief that their rights as British Citizens had been slowly eroded ever since the French and Indian War ended in 1763. Although the Declaration does not name the specific legislation passed by Parliament, its listing of the abuses and usurpation effectively covers the history of the King and Parliament's attempts to gain more power and control over the colonies. The list crescendos with the most offensive actions, aimed at total suppression of the colonies, that were put into effect just prior to the signing of the Declaration.

Many of the acts that the Declaration criticizes were intended to tighten royal control over the colonies. The history of Parliament's acts unfolded over a period of 13 years during which royal attempts to squash the civil liberties of colonists met with heightened colonial resistance. Beginning with The Proclamation of 1763, Parliament stripped colonists of the right to settle in the land between the Appalachian Mountains and the Mississippi River. This meant that although many colonists had given their lives to defend that land from the French, they would not be permitted to reap the benefits. Shortly after the proclamation, Parliament decided that the colonies would help repay the war debts, and enacted laws such as the Sugar Act (1764), the Stamp Tax (1765), the Townshend Acts (1767) and the Tea Act (1773). When the colonists protested against these acts, the King and Parliament responded by further suppressing the rights of colonists. Legislation in 1774 referred to by colonists as the "Intolerable Acts" struck especially hard at the civil rights of the colony of Massachusetts.

The Intolerable Acts differed from previous legislation. These acts struck not only at the economic freedom of the colonies, but at their political rights and legislative independence as well. Not only was the port of Boston closed to all trade, but a military governor was also appointed and the people of Massachusetts no longer had the right to elect their representatives, select jurors, or hold town meetings. Additionally, British soldiers accused of crimes would be tried in England, not in the colony, and a new Quartering Act forced colonists in Massachusetts to feed and house British soldiers. The passage of the Intolerable Acts indicated to many colonists, even those not living in Massachusetts, that the King and Parliament were more interested in asserting unconditional control than in preserving the civil liberties of the colonists.

The basic principle upon which the Declaration rests is that colonists, as British citizens, believed they were entitled to the rights and privileges granted by the Magna Carta, and the British Bill of Rights of 1689. Among other things, these documents established that the King was not above the law, that the people, represented in parliament, had a right to endorse or reject taxation, and that citizens were entitled to a trial by jury of their peers. Additionally, the Declaration relied on precedent: most British colonies had enjoyed self-rule and had been governed through their own legislative bodies since their founding. By 1774, most of the colonists that had once protested "no taxation without representation" found themselves without any representation whatsoever, neither in Parliament nor in any colonial house of representation.

Towards the end of the list of abuses, the Declaration focuses attention on a few specific incidents that demonstrate the King's disregard for colonial life and liberty, the danger of colonists remaining divided on the issue of independence, and the preparations being made by Great Britain for an all-out war. These statements served, in many cases, to convince moderates in the Second Continental Congress to see that reconciliation was not a possibility and to cast their vote in favor of independence.

The British attack on colonists and the loss of American lives at the Battles of Lexington and Concord in April of 1775 and the Battle of Bunker Hill in June of 1775 demonstrated the King's "waging war against us" and his disregard for American lives. In December of 1775, Parliament withdrew British military protection from the colonies and enacted a policy of seizure and confiscation of American ships and sailors ("...[King George] has plundered our seas...he has constrained our fellow-citizens, taken captive on the high seas..."). This action also left colonists living on the frontier, especially those in Georgia, with no military protection from Native American attacks ("...he has endeavored to bring on the inhabitants of our frontiers the merciless Indian savages..."). Furthermore, the heightened tension between colonists and the King began to overflow into hostile relations between those colonists loyal to the king (Tories) and those seeking independence (Whigs). This tension actually erupted into an armed battle between colonists in early 1776 in the Battle at Moore's Creek Bridge ("He has excited domestic insurrections among us...").

It is interesting to note that the Declaration reserved his most scathing language to describe the King's use of mercenaries. Accusing George III's mercenaries of cruelty "scarcely paralleled in the most barbarous ages, and totally unworthy the head of a civilized nation, "the Declaration aims to evoke support from moderates within the colonies by revealing that the British civilization in which they took pride was no more than a cruel and tyrannical monarchy.

Interestingly, Jefferson devoted approximately one-fourth of the abuses in his original draft of the Declaration of Independence to the topic of slavery. Jefferson held the King accountable for maintaining and protecting slavery as an institution in the colonies. Not surprisingly, the moderate congress, already fearful of being too radical, removed all references to slavery from the document. It remains a source of historical debate why a slave-owning man like Jefferson would have devoted so much intellectual energy to criticizing slavery and to attempting to remove it from the colonies.

PAST ACTIONS OF COLONISTS

Up until this declaration, colonists have used non-violent means, such as petitions, to protest the abuses of King George III. Each attempt to request peaceful negotiations was met by neglect and more abuse.

Additionally, colonists tried to appeal to Parliament and other British citizens for help. These attempts were ignored. Colonists appealed to British citizens' sense of justice, to their shared heritage and culture, and to their economic connection. These attempts failed, however, and the colonies have no other choice but to declare separation. In doing so, the new separate nation will view British citizens as enemies during wartime, and as friends in peacetime.

Between 1763 and 1776, American colonists made many attempts to organize in protest against the acts of Parliament. The Declaration of Independence represents the last in a long chain of declarations that began with the declaration of the Stamp Act Congress of 1765, which stated colonists were entitled to the same rights as Englishmen. This document also affirmed that taxing the colonists without their consent was a violation of their rights as British Citizens and that Parliament had no right to tax colonists. In 1774, after the passage of the Intolerable Acts, these themes would surface again in a document written by the First Continental Congress called the Declaration of Rights and Grievances. This document clarified the Stampt Act Congress declaration by stating only colonial legislatures had the right to tax the colonists. Additionally, this document declared the Intolerable Acts unconstitutional and criticized the King and Parliament for dissolving colonial assemblies, maintaining a standing army in peacetime, and for enforcing heavy taxation. Meeting again as the Second Continental Congress in May of 1775, the delegates understood that things had only worsened between the colonists and the British government. Although fighting had already broken out between minutemen and British troops, many delegates still pressed for a peaceful reconciliation. This congress issued a Declaration of Causes of Taking-up Arms and sent an Olive-Branch Petition to the King to humbly request that he negotiate a peaceful reconciliation. Once again, the King ignored the requests of the colonists and responded instead by sending an additional 20,000 troops to the colonies.

Throughout the struggle to assert their rights, colonial leaders understood the importance of maintaining unity between the 13 colonies. Samuel Adams knew that the people would have to be persuaded to view an attack on one colony as an attack on all colonies. To help maintain a unified protest, Samuel Adams organized Committees of Correspondence in 1772 to ensure that colonies could stay informed about new developments regarding the

British King and Parliament. This information network proved crucial when the First Continental Congress agreed to boycott trade with Great Britain and to refuse to use British goods until a resolution was reached. During the Second Continental Congress, patriot leaders carefully waited to declare independence until all delegations unanimously supported it. Although the colonies were technically at war with Great Britain for most of the time the congress met, it took them 14 months to write the formal declaration of war. After the rejection of the Olive Branch Petition, the publication of Thomas Paine's Common Sense, and the hiring of German mercenaries, all of which took place in early 1776, the themes stated in earlier declarations were finally put to use to justify separation rather than reconciliation.

The Declaration of Independence relied on the content and claims of earlier declarations, but firmly stated that ten years of peaceful political and economic actions had failed to reach the desired effect. Therefore, as concluded in this section, the King and Parliament left the colonists no other choice but to seek separation through military means.

CONCLUSION AND DEFINITION OF A NEW GOVERNMENT

The Second Continental Congress represents the people of the new nation called the United States of America. This declaration informs all the people of the world that the 13 united colonies are free from British rule and any political connections with Great Britain. The declaration also serves to appeal to the people of the world to understand the reasons why this separation is justifiable.

The independent states claim the power to levy war, make peace, make alliances with foreign nations, conduct trade, and to do anything else that independent states have the right to do.

The newly independent states believe that God will protect them in their venture to establish a just government. The citizens of each colony have pledged their loyalty and lives to the cause of the newly independent nation.

The conclusion is important in clarifying the identity of the new nation, as well as defining the powers granted to the new government. Many of the delegates to the Second Continental Convention saw the Declaration of Independence as important because of the message it would send to foreign nations. They were especially concerned with enlisting the military help of the French in their war against Great Britain. They therefore thought it necessary to assert clearly that they had no allegiance or connection to Great Britain.

The new nation is not only named in this conclusion as the United States of America, but its authority is defined as well. The conclusion serves to establish the authority of the Second Continental Congress over issues of international affairs, war and peace, and trade. With these powers in hand, the Congress is empowered to run the affairs of government related to the declared war.

However, the conclusion is unclear regarding the individual states' responsibilities to each other. The Declaration describes itself as a union of colonies, each of which is a free and independent state. This is problematic because the statement indicates that the colonies are one united whole, while simultaneously stating that each state is free and independent. A few sentences later, the Declaration states that the former colonies, " as free and independent states, ... have full power to levy war," thereby indicating that each state, individually, has the right to levy war, make peace, etc. This inconsistency would later turn into a debate about the nature of the government of the United States. Was the United States a loose confederation of independent states, each of which could act on behalf of its own interest? Or, was the United States a strong centralized nation in which the powers of the whole were stronger than the powers of each individual state? The Declaration states that the colonists have pledged mutual allegiance, but does that mean the pledge will continue beyond the war effort?

Another problem with the Declaration is that while the free and independent states are granted the right to make war and peace, the document gives no specific provisions explaining how the war will be paid for. This problem plagued Congress during the Revolutionary War and for many years afterwards. Without the power to tax, Congress could only request money from colonial governments, which had debts of their own to pay. The vague reference to these issues served to keep the statement of independence from being further bogged down in political debate.

CHAPTER 4 - BUILDING THE STATE (1781-1797)

After the United States declared its Independence from Britain on July 4, 1776, the long process of building the state began. This era started with the individual state constitutions, which blended the traditions of British and colonial rule with the new, more radical republicanism that infused the nation during the Revolutionary War. State governments established, Americans realized the need for a national government to take on responsibility for diplomatic representation and military control. The first attempt at national government was laid out in the Articles of Confederation. The Articles established a loose federation of states that all essentially acted as individual republics; the balance of power lay heavily in the states favor and the national government was far too weak to perform even its basic duties.

During the mid 1780s, the government under the Articles of Confederation proved unable to successfully levy and collect taxes, and unable to carry out the basic requirements of diplomacy. The nation was in danger of breaking apart. After Shays' Rebellion alerted many Americans to the weakness of the current national government, political leaders decided to alter the framework of government under which the United States operated.

The Constitutional Convention met in Philadelphia and determined that it was in the nation's best interest to create an entirely new framework of government. For nearly four months, the delegates at the convention deliberated on how best to accomplish this rebuilding effort. The Constitution, the result of these proceedings, sets out the tripartite system of government that is still in place in the US today. It created a bicameral legislature consisting of the House of Representatives and the Senate, an executive branch headed by the president and staffed by the cabinet, and provided for the establishment of a judicial branch, consisting of a federal-court system headed by the Supreme Court.

Although the Constitution established the basic framework of government, its wording was vague in regard to the details. Thus, the first Congress under the Constitution and the first President, George Washington, were responsible for working out the details of governance. In the first years of the new United States, Washington and the Congress created, among other things, the now accepted traditions of the cabinet and the judicial system. The precedents they set established the standard operating procedure of the national government for years to come.

During the fight to ratify the Constitution, a division sprang up between those who wanted to grant the central government broad powers, the Federalists, and those who feared that a national government which was too strong would prove despotic, the Anti-federalists. This debate continued into the Washington administration, as Secretary of State Alexander Hamilton set forth a program of economic Federalism which included the assumption of state debts by the national government, and the creation of the Bank of the United States. His efforts paid off for the US on a general scale, but Hamilton's actions turned many away from Federalism, since they believed Hamilton had overstepped the bounds of the national government.

Added to the growing internal turmoil was the threat of war with Britain, Spain, and the Native Americans over the control of the American West (which at this point was the area around Ohio). On the brink of war with all three parties, Washington sent successful diplomatic missions to achieve peace. However, international relations proved to be yet another area where passions ran high and the American population was divided. Washington left office in 1797 pleading for an end to political division and embroilment in foreign affairs. Yet despite his best efforts, the American public was far more sharply divided in 1797 than it had been at the outset of his presidency. Even so, upon Washington's departure from office, America itself was a far more powerfully established nation.

During the seventeenth and eighteenth centuries, the American colonies developed, for the most part, independently of each other. Each of the colonies had a distinctive character, distinctive customs and traditions, and a different style of government. Though geographically united and all colonies of Great Britain, they existed in isolation, the majority ignorant of the needs and desires specific to other colonies. However, as the colonies underwent similar experiences subjected to British oppression, they began to see the need for unity. Communication between the political leaders of the separate colonies increased and, gradually, political interaction followed. The First Continental Congress convened in 1774, uniting the colonies in political resistance to the British, and symbolizing the first step toward unified national government. Still, political leaders and common colonists alike found it difficult to define their citizenship and interests beyond the borders of their towns and colonies.

On July 4, 1776 the American colonies declared their independence from Great Britain and began in earnest the Revolutionary War, which would win them that independence. Primary among the many concerns facing the new nation was the creation of a united national government out of the thirteen disparate governments of the states. This was officially accomplished by the adoption of the Articles of Confederation in 1777. However, during the war there was little time to devote to establishing the institutions and functions of government and the Second Continental Congress ruled under an uncertain set of rules, basically concerning itself with matters of diplomatic and military concern on an as-needed basis.

Once the war ended, however, the need for a well-defined national government was clear. The government organized according to the Articles of Confederation and the nation began the effort of defining its government, a process that took many twists and turns during the early years of American history. This early founding period resulted in the ultimate failure of the Articles and left the nation with a new document that has served as the framework of US government for more than 200 years since its drafting, the Constitution. The period also ended with the details of many of the functions of the national government solidified through precedent. In fact, many of the precedents set by the first Congress, the newly established Supreme Court, and by the nation's first president, George Washington, still endure as standard operating procedure for the national government.

During this period, some of the nation's most prominent future leaders first made their mark on the national government. John Adams, Thomas Jefferson, James Madison, and James Monroe, all future Presidents of the United States, played active roles in the framing of the Constitution and the exploration of national politics that followed during Washington's administration. All of these men formed the political values that would shape their presidencies during the period of state-building.

More than anything, the period that saw the building of the state left much room for the nation to grow and evolve, and established the conditions under which this evolution would take place. Washington left office with the international situation uncertain, the fate of westward expansion unknown, and the powers of the national government still contested. Perhaps the greatest legacy of the party emerged from the conflicts arising from the central issues of building the state, the evolution of the government into two major political parties, a system which still prevails today. The existence of both a majority and opposition party determined the course of the United States as it grew into what it is today. Additionally, the problems faced by the early national government of reconciling the interests of geographically and ideologically varied states hinted at the emergence of sectionalism, the defining political reality of the first half of the nineteenth century.

IMPORTANT TERMS, PEOPLE, AND EVENTS

Terms

- **Anti-Federalists** - Anti-federalists rose up as the opponents of the Constitution during the period of ratification. They advocated a governmental structure that granted power to the states.

- **Antidisestablishmentarianism** - The movement in opposition to the disbanding of formal ties between government and religion. Antidisestablishmentarianism proved especially formidable in New England. Whereas most states broke all government ties with religion shortly after the Declaration of

Independence, the Congregational Church continued collecting tithes (taxes) in New Hampshire, Connecticut, and Massachusetts well into the nineteenth century.

- Articles of Confederation - Adopted in 1777 during the Revolutionary War, the Articles were the document that established the United States of America. The Articles granted few powers to the central government and left most powers up to the individual states. The result was a weak, rather ill-defined state. The Articles were replaced by the Constitution in 1789. SparkNote on the Articles of Confederation.

- Bicameral - Name for a legislative system composed of two complementary houses. Congress, like its model the British Parliament, is bicameral; the Senate and the House of Representatives make up its two houses.

- Bill of Rights - Though the Anti-federalists were not able to block the ratification of the Constitution, they did make progress in ensuring that the Bill of Rights would be created. The Bill of Rights, drafted by a group led by James Madison, was the collection of the first ten amendments to the Constitution, which guaranteed the civil rights of American citizens.

- Checks and Balances - The Constitution set forth a government composed of 3 branches: the legislative, executive, and judicial. Each branch was given certain powers over the others to ensure that no one branch usurped a dangerous amount of power. This system, known as checks and balances, represented the solution to the problem of how to empower the central government, yet protect against corruption and despotism.

- Congress - The bicameral legislative body set up by the Connecticut Compromise. The two houses of Congress, the Senate and the House of Representatives, accorded to both the Virginia Plan and the New Jersey Plan, in that membership numbers in the House were determined by state population, and representatives in the Senate were fixed at two per state.

- Connecticut Compromise - Ending weeks of stalemate, the Connecticut Compromise reconciled the Virginia Plan and the New Jersey Plan for determining legislative representation in Congress. The Connecticut Compromise established equal representation for all states in the Senate and proportional representation by population in the House of Representatives.

- Constitution - The document produced by the Constitutional Convention, and ratified by the states in 1789. As opposed to the Articles of Confederation, the document the Constitution replaced, the Constitution created a strong central government with broad judicial, legislative, and executive powers, though the extent of these powers were purposely reined in by the Constitution itself. SparkNote on the Constitution.

- Elastic Clause - Article I, Section VIII of the Constitution states that Congress shall have the power "to make all laws which shall be necessary and proper for carrying into execution...powers vested by this Constitution in the government of the United States." This clause, known as the elastic clause, was the point of much contention between those who favored a loose reading of the Constitution and those who favored a strict reading.

- The Federalist Papers - The Federalist Papers contain a series of newspaper articles written by John Jay, James Madison, and Alexander Hamilton which enumerate the arguments in favor of the Constitution and against the Anti-federalists. SparkNote on the Federalist Papers

- Federalists - First rising to national attention during the process of ratification, Federalists remained an important influence on the government throughout the Washington administration. Led by Alexander Hamilton, the Federalists believed in a strong central government at the expense of state powers.

- Jay's Treaty - Jay's Treaty provided for the removal of British troops from American land, and avoided the outbreak of war with Britain. While seen as unsuccessful by the majority of the American public, Jay's Treaty may have been the greatest diplomatic feat of the Washington administration, avoiding the outbreak of war.

- New Jersey Plan - The New Jersey Plan was presented at the Constitutional Convention as an alternative to the Virginia Plan. The New Jersey Plan favored small states in that it proposed a unicameral Congress with equal representation for each state.

- Northwest Ordinance - The 1787 Northwest Ordinance defined the process by which new states could be admitted into the Union from the Northwest Territory. It forbade slavery in the territory, but allowed citizens to vote on the legality of slavery once statehood had been established. The Northwest Ordinance was the most lasting measure of the national government under the Articles of Confederation, in that it established the model which would be used for admission of new states well into the future.

- Republicans - Rising up as the opposition party to the dominant Federalists during the Washington administration, Republicans claimed that liberty could only be protected if political power were rested firmly in the hands of the people and those government officials closest and most responsive to the people. They fought to overturn Alexander Hamilton's measures and distribute greater power to the states.

- Society of Cincinnati - The Society of Cincinnati was a fraternal order of Continental Army officers, which instated a system of hereditary membership. Despite the fact that many political luminaries, such as George Washington, were members, republicans often clashed with the society, fearing that it would eventually become a hereditary aristocracy akin to the British nobility.

- Strict Constructionists - Strict constructionists favored a strict reading of the Constitution and especially of the elastic clause, in order to limit the powers of the central government. Led Thomas Jefferson, strict constructionists embodied the ideological core of the Republican Party.

- Supreme Court - The highest judicial body in the land, as created by the Constitution.

- Three-fifths Clause - During the framing of the Constitution, Southern delegates argued that slaves should count toward representative seats, while the delegates of northern states, most of which had or would soon abolish slavery, argued that to count slaves as members of the population would grant an unfair advantage to the southern states. The result of this debate was the adoption of the Three-fifths Clause, which allowed three-fifths of all slaves to be counted as people.

- Virginia Plan - The Virginia Plan was the first major proposal covering representation presented to the Constitutional Convention. It proposed the creation of a bicameral legislature with representation in both houses proportional to population. The Virginia Plan favored the large states, who would have a much weightier voice than the small states under this plan. The small states proposed the New Jersey Plan in opposition.

People

- Chief Joseph Brant - A Mohawk Chief who had distinguished himself during the Revolutionary War, Joseph Brant organized a military alliance of Native American tribes in the northwest, which, while it faltered because of limited support from certain portions of the Iroquois, presented the government under the Articles of Confederation with a challenge in the west.

- Benjamin Franklin - An inventor, a writer, and former ambassador to France, Benjamin Franklin was the oldest delegate to the Constitutional Convention. The other delegates admired his wisdom, and his advice was crucial in the drafting of the Constitution.

- Alexander Hamilton - The outspoken leader of the Federalists, Hamilton emerged as a major political figure during the Constitutional Convention, and during the period of ratification, as one of the authors of The Federalist Papers. As Secretary of Treasury under Washington, Alexander Hamilton spearheaded the government's Federalist initiatives, most notably through his proposals on the subject of public credit and the creation of the Bank of the United States.

- John Jay - John Jay played an important role in the establishment of the new government under the Constitution. One of the authors of The Federalist Papers, he was involved in the drafting of the Constitution, became the first Chief Justice of the Supreme Court under Washington, and went on to negotiate Jay's Treaty with Britain to head off war in 1795.

- Thomas Jefferson - Jefferson attained political fame originally as the author of the Declaration of Independence. A prominent statesman from Virginia, Jefferson became Washington's first Secretary of State. However, in 1793, Jefferson resigned from that post in opposition to Alexander Hamilton's continued efforts to garner power for the national government. With James Madison, Jefferson took up the cause of the strict constructionists and the Republican Party, advocating the limitation of the national government.

- Henry Knox - Washington appointed Henry Knox his first Secretary of War. Knox played a valuable role in the development of the executive branch. His most notable actions came in relation to the struggle with the Native Americans on the frontier, where he declared the Indian title to the land officially recognized by the US in the early 1790s.

- James Madison - Madison joined forces with Alexander Hamilton and John Jay as a Federalist leader during the Constitutional Convention and beyond. He was one of the authors of The Federalist Papers and, as a member of the first Congress, a staunch advocate of strong central government. However, after a string of Federalist measures that asserted the power of the national government over the state in questionable areas, Madison defected from the Federalist cause and became a critic of excessive central power. He joined Thomas Jefferson in leading the rising Republican Party.

- George Washington - Washington, as the general of the Continental Army during the Revolutionary War, was the obvious choice to be the first President of the United States. Washington took on the task of defining the presidency, attempting to establish the role through precedent. He intervened little in legislative affairs, and concentrated mostly on diplomacy and finance. A Federalist, he granted Alexander Hamilton a great deal of support, despite frequent misgivings.

Events

- Annapolis Convention - Originally planning to discuss the promotion of interstate commerce, delegates from five states met at Annapolis in September 1786 and ended up suggesting a convention to amend the Articles of Confederation.

- Constitutional Convention - In response to the Annapolis Convention's suggestion, Congress called for the states to send delegates to Philadelphia to amend the Articles of Confederation. Delegates came to the convention from every state but Rhode Island on May 25, 1787, and decided to draft an entirely new framework of government, which would give greater powers to the central government. This document became the Constitution.

- Proclamation of American Neutrality - In the early 1790s, Britain and France went to war with one another. The American public was torn over the issue of which nation to support, the South pulling for a pro-French foreign policy, and the North advocating a pro-British policy. Issued on April 22, 1793, the Proclamation of American Neutrality was Washington's response to the division of the nation, stating that the US would stay out of the war.

- Shays' Rebellion - As economic depression struck Massachusetts, farmers were increasingly burdened by debt, a problem exacerbated by an increase in taxes. In August 1786, Western Massachusetts farmers organized in an attempt to shut down three county courthouses through violent means in order to prevent foreclosure proceedings. The rebellion was easily put down, but it alerted many to the weaknesses of the government under the Articles of Confederation.

- Whiskey Rebellion - Alexander Hamilton had pushed a high excise tax through Congress as part of his economic policy efforts. However, the tax affected western Pennsylvania distillers almost exclusively, and was administered by federal officials with little knowledge of or compassion for the situation of the small farmers. Violence broke out in July 1794. In a short period of time over one hundred men attacked a US Marshall, the chief revenue officer for Allegheny County saw his house and stables burned to the ground, and organized, militant farmers threatened to form a separate country. In a show of strength, George Washington himself, led a force of militiamen to crush the rebellion.

- Washington's Farewell Address - Published on September 19, 1796, George Washington officially resigned the presidency after two terms, setting a precedent that would remain in place until FDR in the 1930s. The focus of the address was a warning that Americans should avoid the rise of political parties that the previous years had seen. He further advised future generations to maintain a policy of isolationism in foreign affairs.

TIMELINE

July 4, 1776: Declaration of Independence is Approved by Congress Independence is proposed on June 9 by Richard Henry Lee. Less than a month later, on the most celebrated day in the nation's history, Thomas Jefferson's Declaration of Independence is adopted by Congress.

November 17, 1777: The Articles of Confederation are Adopted by Congress The Articles of Confederation, brought to Congress on July 12, 1776, are officially adopted and sent to the states for ratification.

March 1, 1781: The Articles of Confederation Become Law Maryland is the last state to ratify the Articles of Confederation and they become the law of the land.

September 3, 1783: The Treaty of Paris is Signed After nearly a year of peace talks, the Treaty of Paris is finally signed, officially granting the US its independence.

May 20, 1785: The Ordinance of 1785 is Passed The Ordinance of 1785 establishes the protocol for settlement of western lands.

1786: Chief Joseph Brant Organizes an Alliance of the Northwest Tribes Chief Joseph Brant allies the tribes of the northwest wilderness in an effort to resist white settlement on Indian lands.

August 1786: Outbreak of Shays' Rebellion Western Massachusetts farmers, under the pressures of economic depression, organize in an attempt to shut down three county courthouses through violent means. The rebellion is put down, but highlight the weaknesses of the Articles of Confederation.

September 11 - 14, 1786: The Annapolis Convention Originally planning to discuss the promotion of interstate commerce, delegates from five states meet at Annapolis and end up suggesting a convention to amend the Articles of Confederation.

May 25 - September 27, 1787: The Constitutional Convention Delegates of every state but Rhode Island meet in Philadelphia to discuss the amendment of the Articles of Confederation. Though it was not their original intent they decide to scrap the Articles, and produce the Constitution, laying out a new framework of government.

July 13, 1787: The Northwest Ordinance is Passed The Northwest Ordinance defines the process by which new states could be admitted into the Union from the Northwest Territory.

July 17, 1787: The Connecticut Compromise is Approved by the Constitutional Convention Ending weeks of stalemate, the Connecticut Compromise reconciles the Virginia Plan and the New Jersey Plan for determining legislative representation in Congress. The Connecticut Compromise establishes equal representation for all states in the Senate and proportional representation by population in the House of Representatives.

September 17, 1787: The Constitution, in its Final Form, is Approved by the Constitutional Convention The Constitutional Convention officially endorses the Constitution and sends it to the states for ratification.

June 21, 1788: New Hampshire Becomes the Ninth State To Ratify the Constitution Having been ratified by two-thirds of the states, the Constitution becomes the law of the land.

June 25, 1788: Virginia Ratifies the Constitution Following nearly a year of intense debate, Federalists win out in Virginia, which ratifies the Constitution.

July 26, 1788: New York Ratifies the Constitution Following Virginia's lead, New York ratifies the Constitution. The two states represent the most crucial states to the functioning of the Union; their ratification ensures the success of the Constitution.

March 4, 1789: The First Congress Under the Constitution Convenes in New York The first Congress convenes, symbolizing the beginning of a long period of working out the details of the new government.

April 30, 1789: George Washington is Inaugurated Washington, the nation's first president, takes the Oath of Office.

January 1790: Alexander Hamilton presents his Report on Public Credit to Congress Hamilton suggests the national assumption of state debt, the sale of US government bonds, and the establishment of a permanent national debt. Though met with opposition, his measures pass in Congress.

December 1790: Alexander Hamilton presents his Report on a National Bank to Congress Hamilton's most controversial proposal, he suggests the creation of the Bank of the United States as a depository for federal revenue and a source of federal loans. The bank is granted a twenty-year charter in February 1791.

December 1791: Alexander Hamilton presents his Report on Manufacturers to Congress Hamilton's report on Manufactures suggests a policy of protectionism, levying high tariffs on imports and providing incentives for goods to be imported on American ships. The high tariffs do not pass Congress, but a number of protectionist proposals do.

June 1, 1792: Kentucky admitted to the Union As the US expands into the Southwest, Kentucky becomes the first new state in that region. It is followed on June 1, 1796 by Tennessee.

April 22, 1793: Washington issues the Proclamation of American Neutrality The Proclamation of American Neutrality is Washington's response to the division of the nation between those advocating support of the French and those in favor of the British; those two nations had gone to war with one another as part of the fallout of the French Revolution.

February 1794: Canada's Royal Governor Denies US Claims to Land in the Northwest Territory Canada's royal government, speaking to a Native American audience, denies US claims to land north of the Ohio River as granted by the Treaty of Paris. He encourages Indian tribes to resist white settlement of the land, and the British begin construction of Fort Miami on US territory.

July 1794: The Whiskey Rebellion Distillers in western Pennsylvania, angry at the imposition of a heavy excise tax on Whiskey rebel, attack a tax collector, lay siege to the house of the chief revenue officer's house, and threaten to secede. George Washington himself led troops into Pennsylvania to crush the rebellion.

June 25, 1795: Jay's Treaty is Signed Jay's Treaty provides for the removal of British troops from American land, and avoids the outbreak of war with Britain.

August 3, 1795: The Treaty of Greenville is Signed General Anthony Wayne concludes his military campaign against the Indians of the northwest with this treaty, which ends hostilities and opens the land that is now Ohio to settlement.

October 27, 1795: The Treaty of San Lorenzo is Signed The Treaty of San Lorenzo heads off war with Spain, removes Spanish troops from American land, and opens the Mississippi to US commerce.

September 19, 1796: Washington's Farewell Address After two terms, George Washington officially resigns the presidency, exhorting future generations to avoid the division of the nation into political parties and to maintain an isolationist foreign policy.

THE BEGINNING OF SELF-GOVERNMENT: THE STATES

After the Declaration of Independence was adopted, the citizens of the thirteen states of the new United States of America began the process of creating state governments, even as the states battled for their lives in the fighting of Revolutionary War. These governments varied widely in their framework, some drawing more upon the traditions established during the colonial period and some drawing more upon the rising tide of Revolution era radical democratic republican ideology. The signs of traditional influences included bicameral legislatures with an upper and lower house, property requirements for voters, the notion that representatives should exercise independent judgment rather than directly respond to popular sentiments, and the equal division of legislative seats between towns and counties without regard for population. The framing of new state governments reflected the tension between these traditions and the more radical ideology of the revolution.

The process of forming state governments reflected the political identity crisis of the new nation. Eleven of thirteen state constitutions maintained bicameral legislatures. In further adherence to tradition, in most states, the majority of political officials were appointed rather than elected. However, nine of thirteen states reduced property requirements for voting in a show of democratically leaning ideology, but no states fully abolished them. British government had held a constitution to be a body of unwritten customs and practices. State constitutions varied from traditional British constitutions in that they were written documents which were ratified by the people and could be amended by popular vote. These documents clearly enumerated the powers granted and denied to the government. Also, by 1784, every state constitution contained a bill of rights that outlined the civil rights and freedoms accorded citizens.

The trend toward less powerful executive branches and more responsive legislatures emerged clearly throughout the states. The powers of the executive office of the governor were drastically limited by every state constitution. The governor became an elected official and elections were held annually in every state but South Carolina, where they were biannual. Governors had very few powers of appointment and were left only to make some financial decisions and control the militia. Pennsylvania abolished governors altogether. State constitutions also made the legislature more responsive to public feelings and opinions. Of the constitutions written before 1780, eight had both chambers elected by popular vote, one had an electoral college elect the upper chamber, two had the lower house choose the members of the upper house, and two more, Pennsylvania and Georgia, created popularly elected unicameral legislatures.

Other changes wrought by the state constitutions included an increase in social equality and the disestablishment of state religions. Between 1776 and 1780, for instance, Thomas Jefferson drafted a series of bills that broke down the legal reinforcements for division by wealth. Virginia ended the practice of primogeniture, which required the eldest son of a family to inherit all of a family's land in the absence of a will, and took other steps to prevent the rise of a ruling aristocracy. The years of the American Revolution also saw the end of state-established religious organizations in many states, seen as detrimental to democratic government.

The reforms instituted by state constitutions were met with a combination of acceptance and resistance. While the radical thinking of the revolution informed many of the decisions of the framers of state government, as time went by a conservative backlash rose and challenged the new ideals. In Massachusetts, the constitution was revised in 1780 to place more emphasis on wealth, and Pennsylvania and Georgia eventually recreated upper legislative houses. Initiatives to foster equality met with resistance in many areas of the new nation from individuals and groups such as the Society of Cincinnati, which saw the values of heredity and aristocratic privilege to be in their best interests.

For political leaders of most states, the traditions of British and colonial governments exerted a strong pull, both for reasons of habit and because of the fact that the new governments required some system upon which to base their structure. The tradition of bicameral legislatures stemmed from the House of Lords and House of Commons in British Parliament, which in turn had given way to the common practice of colonial assemblies paired with higher bodies appointed by the colonies' royal governors or the lower assemblies themselves. This tradition claiming that commoners and aristocrats should be represented by separate bodies represented a powerful ideal, which, try as they might, the supporters of radical change could not break down in most states. The principle of property requirements for voters had its root in a more logical argument (to say nothing of its validity), which stated that if tenant farmers and poor hired laborers were allowed to vote, they might sell their votes to the highest bidder or be pressured to vote as their landlord dictated. Most political leaders recognized the basic flaws in this argument and advocated some extension of the franchise of voting, but only small gains were made in this area.

The notion that representatives should exercise independent judgment rather than carry out the explicit will of their constituents sprung from an ancient distrust of the common masses and a distrust of party politics as the politics of selfish factions out for their own good at the expense of the nation. Many thought that the public should elect officials based upon their reputation and merit rather than upon differing policy preferences. This idea prevailed in many areas, especially the north, and would continue to do so for years, despite the constant efforts of its opponents to increase responsiveness of the government to public desires. The tradition of equal division of legislative seats between towns and counties regardless of population was based purely on historical habit, and presented a serious ideological challenge to the framers of state governments and, later, the national government.

The major changes made in the writing of state Constitutions were the direct result of the colonial experience. Having haggled with British authorities over the constitutionality of many Acts and actions, it was crucial to the new governments that constitutions clearly enumerated and limited the powers of government, as well as including bills of rights, which enumerated the rights of the people upon which the government could not infringe. The creation of written state constitutions, which contained these elements, meant that governments were no longer the sole judges of the constitutionality of their actions. The constitution was written in black and white for all observers to read and see clearly what the government was within its bounds to do.

The assault on the executive branch sprang from the experience of the colonists under the arbitrary, and often cruel, rule of the royal governors. The American colonists feared the despotism of executive officeholders, and sought, through the state constitutions, to limit their power. Revolutionary leaders advocated strengthening legislatures at the expense of state governors. The balance between executive and legislative power was a principle concern of the republican thinkers as they set about designing the state governments.

At first, elites had to cope with state governments dominated by popularly elected officials. However, eventually these elites united in efforts to reassert political control and privilege. In Massachussets, a 1780 convention passed a constitution with stricter property requirements for voting and holding office, senate districts defined by property value, and a stronger governor. Many states followed Massachusetts' lead by increasing property requirements for senators. This conservative backlash swept the nation and prompted resistance to many of the initiatives of the new governments.

The Society of Cincinnati was a fraternal order of Continental Army officers, which instated a system of hereditary membership. Despite the fact that many political luminaries, such as George Washington, were members, republicans often clashed with the society, fearing that it would eventually become a hereditary aristocracy akin to the British nobility. The efforts of the republicans to end the ties between church and state met with some resistance as well, most prominently in New England where the strength of antidisestablishmentarianism kept the Congregational Church collecting tithes well into the nineteenth century in Connecticut, New Hampshire, and Massachusetts.

THE ARTICLES OF CONFEDERATION AS LAW OF THE LAND

Once the colonies had declared their independence, their first task was to create a unified national government. John Dickinson, a congressman from Pennsylvania, drafted the Articles of Confederation and brought them to Congress on July 12, 1776. Congress adopted the Articles on November 17, 1777, and began the process of ratification, sending copies of the Articles for review by state legislatures. The Articles of Confederation reserved to each state "its sovereignty, freedom, and independence" within the national structure. The central government consisted of the Congress alone, which was elected by state legislatures. Congress could request funds from the states, but had no power of taxation. Similarly, Congress lacked the power to regulate interstate or international commerce. With no executive branch, Congressional committees would be assigned to direct matters of finance, diplomacy, and the military. The Articles did not provide for a judicial system.

 The Articles of Confederation became law after Maryland, the last abstaining state, finally ratified them on March 1, 1781. Almost immediately, a host of challenges arose for the new government to cope with. The first challenge was to put the nation on sound financial ground. The war cost the 600,000 taxpayers in America a total of $160 million. To finance the war effort, the Continental Congress borrowed from foreign nations and wealthy Americans, and printed up its own paper money, called the Continental. Due to a lack of faith in the survival of the American government both at home and abroad, the value of the Continental fell 98 percent between 1776 and 1781, leading to rampant inflation.

In an attempt to rectify the situation, Congress made Robert Morris, a wealthy merchant, the nation's superintendent of finance in 1781. He proposed an import duty of five percent to finance the national budget and guarantee the payment of war debts. However, under the Articles of Confederation taxation required the agreement of every state in the Union, and Rhode Island, acting alone, rejected Morris' proposal. After the Revolutionary War came to an end in 1783, Congress proposed yet another tax to finance the budget, but this time New York stood in the way of its passage. Furthermore, throughout the 1780s states continually reduced the amount of financial support they granted to Congress. Additionally, the US economy suffered from British restrictions on trade with the Empire, including the British Isles and the West Indies, two important markets for US merchants. British ports often only accepted American goods if they were carried aboard British ships. Thus American trade declined, and was one of the leading causes of the economic depression which struck in 1784.

America's first national government under the Articles of Confederation incorporated, more than anything else, the widespread fear and distrust of centralized government. Having experienced the oppression of British government, in which the central government had seemed to act without concern for its constituents, early American political leaders advocated a governmental system in which the primary power of the government was distributed to the states, which could be more responsive to the specific needs of the people. Under the Articles of Confederation, the States took primacy over the Union as a whole to the extent that the national government was limited to only those actions that the states saw fit to permit.

With the Confederation in place, the US had taken a crucial step in defining the role of the national government. The Continental Congress had directed the war effort without clearly defined powers. Rather, it had assumed specific powers on an as-needed basis. Now, however, the new nation had a clearly organized government. The only problem was that the national government had been given so little power that it could not be truly effective. Subject to the veto power of any single state, the national government found it nearly impossible to pass measures even within the limited scope of its powers.

In no area was this more apparent than in regard to taxation and finance. While the Congress could ask the states for financial contributions, there was no guarantee that the states would comply, and taxes could only be levied at the national level with the agreement of all states, a feat of near impossibility. Almost every state raised taxes within their boundaries during and after the war, in order to finance their own internal military operations, reconstruction, and war debt. Pressured by these financial burdens, few states were likely to approve of new national taxes, or import tariffs that would raise the prices of all goods. Faced with the disapproval of the states, and declining voluntary contributions to the national cause, the central government was left with no recourse.

The increasing British restrictions on trade may be viewed as a side effect of the weakness of the American national government. Seeing that the Second Continental Congress was unable to control commerce even within the united States, Britain doubted that Congress would be able to muster any challenge to British trade policies. The restrictions on trade in the British Isles and the West Indies represented a blatant show of disrespect to the American government. Unable to control finance within the US and too weak to command the respect of foreign powers, the national government under the Articles of Confederation showed its first signs of crumbling almost immediately.

SETTLING THE WEST

Another challenge for the national government under the Articles of Confederation lay in overseeing the expansion of the United States westward. Settlers, speculators, and state governments all pressed for expansion into the wilderness lands granted to the US under the 1783 Treaty of Paris. The Ordinance of 1785 was the government's first attempt to control western expansion. It outlined the protocol for settlement, and established the basic geography of a township as a parcel of land six miles square. Each township was then divided into subsections to be occupied by settlers. After two successful years of settlement, the Northwest Ordinance, passed July 13, 1787, defined the process of the creation and admission of new states into the union from the area north of the Ohio River, designated the Northwest Territory. The Northwest Ordinance forbade slavery in the area as long as it was merely a territory, but allowed citizens to vote on the legality of slavery upon achieving statehood.

The major obstacles to Western expansion were the interests of foreign nations, most notably Britain and Spain, and the fact that Native Americans largely occupied the land to the west. Many political leaders advocated attempting to integrate the Natives into white American life. However, the Indians were not eager to give up their culture or their land. In postwar negotiations, many Indian tribes that had fought against the Continental Army had to accept treaties that deprived them of much of their land. The Iroquois, Delawares, and Shawnees, all wartime enemies of the US, were forced to give up nearly all of their land. However, most Indians rejected the validity of these treaties and refused to leave their traditional homes.

Mohawk Chief Joseph Brant, the commander of the most successful of all Indian forces during the Revolutionary War, led the Indian resistance. In 1786, Brant organized the northwestern Indian tribes into a military alliance to resist the movement of white settlers into the Northwest Territory. The alliance faltered because of a lack of support from certain portions of the Iroquois tribe, but nevertheless, it caused problems for settlers, and was a major concern for the national government. In the South, Spain and its Indian allies mobilized to prevent westward expansion by US settlers. The Creek Indians, under Alexander McGillivray, offered staunch military resistance to the seizure of Indian homelands, most notably in and around Georgia. Spain, for its part, restricted American access to the Mississippi River that had been granted to the US by the Treaty of Paris. Spain had not signed the treaty, and denied its validity with regard to the Mississippi, which it claimed as its own. In a move to further discourage westward settlement, the Spanish closed the port of New Orleans altogether to American commerce in 1784, a fierce blow to the US economy.

The early initiatives of the national government in regard to the settling of the West were the Confederation's only successful and lasting contributions. Both the Ordinance of 1785 and the Northwest Ordinance were effective in outlining the procedures by which the West was settled. Both measures served as models for later legislation outlining the process of creating and admitting states throughout the West. However, the Ordinances had very little immediate effect because of the Indian occupation of the Northwest Territory. The battle against the Indians for land went back to the seventeenth century and the original colonists. For as long as North America had been an area of interest for European powers, the Natives had been harassed and pushed westward, forced out of their traditional homes. In postwar negotiations, many American leaders had taken the stance that the Indians were a vanquished people and that their land, in full, belonged to the United States.

Therefore, it was not surprising that the Indians would have built up such hatred toward the white settlers, and as a result, provided the major obstacle to settling the West during the years of the Confederation. Indian resistance in the northwest stemmed from efforts to maintain control of Native American homeland and the hope that the British would provide support in the form of arms and ammunition should the struggle escalate to the point of military action. During the Revolutionary War the Indians had largely supported the British, fearing an expansionist independent America. Now as their fears were realized, they hoped the British would return the favor, and thought that perhaps they could defeat the forces of the weak and disorganized central government with British help. However, unable to unify the tribes, and receiving far less British support than had been hoped for, the Indian tribes, while not totally defeated and driven out of the Northwest Territory, certainly were not victorious in their attempts at resistance.

Indian resistance in the South was more successful due to both the leadership of Alexander McGillivray and the support of the Spanish government. The Spanish equipped and aided the Indians in their raids of the frontier states that had occupied Indian land, leading a campaign of terror against those who did not evacuate the land the Creeks claimed as their own. Moreover, the efforts at constricting expansion in the South were successful largely because of the restrictions on trade and travel that the closing of the Mississippi imposed on settlers in the Mississippi Valley. The Spanish, like the British earlier in the case of the West Indies, saw the weakness of the US national government under the Articles of Confederation as a chance to protect their own interests. They closed the port of New Orleans without fear of facing repercussions from a weak central government unable to control commerce and unsuccessful in attempts to ward off Indian resistance.

THE DEMISE OF THE ARTICLES OF CONFEDERATION

As the evidence piled up to suggest that the Articles of Confederation were an ineffective framework of government, criticism poured in from all areas of the nation. The depression that struck in 1784 hit Massachusetts particularly hard. Despite financial hard times, the state legislature voted to pay off the state's war debts by 1789. This necessitated a huge tax hike, which further hindered the financial situation of the majority of Massachusetts' residents. Meanwhile, the continued inflation of paper money elicited private creditors to demand payment of all debts on a short-term basis, and in specie (gold and silver coinage). This was a drastic reversal of the common custom of small farmers and poor laborers, who traditionally repaid debts with goods and services, and were often given years to make good on their debts. For these people, the prospect of repaying debts with hard currency in these financially trying times was simply not possible.

Farmers began to hold public meetings to discuss what they termed "the suppressing of tyrannical government" in the state of Massachusetts. After months of discussion and passive resistance to the actions of the state, violence broke out in what became known as Shays' Rebellion. In August 1786, Daniel Shays led about 2,000 men in an attempt to close the courts in three western Massachusetts counties to prevent the legal proceedings that would lead to foreclosure on farm mortgages. Shays' men were beaten badly by state troops in a number of conflicts, most notably at Springfield on January 25, 1787, where Shays' men attempted to seize the federal arsenal. After the uprising was crushed, Shays was condemned to death and many of his men were arrested. Though Shays' Rebellion had no immediate effect on the policy of the state legislature, during 1787, a group of Shays sympathizers gained control of the legislature, cut taxes, and pardoned Shays and his men for their parts in the uprising.

Most of the nation was far more tranquil than western Massachusetts. The Mid-Atlantic and Southern states all experienced greater success emerging from the depression of the mid 1780s, and most small farmers throughout the nation lived in closed communities in relative isolation from the actions of the national government. Still, the vociferous critics of the Confederation were gaining strength during the mid 1780s. The political leaders of all of the states could not help but listen.

From September 11 to 14, 1786, shortly after the outbreak of Shays' Rebellion, delegates from Virginia, Delaware, Pennsylvania, New Jersey, and New York met at the Annapolis Convention. The originally proposed purpose of the meeting had been to establish and promote interstate commerce. However, in light of the mounting criticism of the Articles of Confederation, the delegates turned their focus to what could be done to alleviate the tension between the nation's citizens and their government. They ended up proposing a convention to consider the amendment of the Articles of Confederation. Congress agreed that the Articles were in need of review, and asked that the states appoint delegates to convene in Philadelphia in May 1787.

That Massachusetts would have been the hardest hit by economic depression is not surprising considering the economic basis of the state in relation to the international economic position of the United States under the Articles of Confederation. Massachusetts' main source of income was through its ports. A high population of craftsmen and merchants created products to export to the world. Until the 1780s, Massachusetts' major trading partners were the British Isles and the British West Indies. However, in response to the insufficient powers granted to the central government by the Articles of Confederation, Britain had taken measures to restrict American trade with the British Isles, and had closed the ports of the West Indies entirely to American trade. This was one of the major causes of the economic depression of 1784, and while other states were able to find ways to climb out of the depression, Massachusetts had few options. Many merchants blamed the weakness of the national government for the failure to open the restricted ports or otherwise retaliate against British actions.

The demand for hard currency in specie (coined money), which arose in Massachusetts during the economic depression, sprung up from fears of devaluation of paper money in the state. Foreign creditors, who doubted the ability of the state to climb out of the depression, and feared the instability of the government, first started to demand payments in specie. They were followed by the state, which began to collect taxes in specie only. Due to these developments, the demand for payment in specie became universal. The combination of continued economic depression due to the inability of the government to break down barriers to trade, high taxes, and the demand for all payments in specie, caused many to speak out against the state and national governments and ultimately led to the outbreak of violence in Shays' Rebellion.

Shays' Rebellion was never a real threat to the Massachusetts state government, but it alerted many observers to the shortcomings and fragility of the national government under the Articles of Confederation. Critics of the Confederation argued that the weak central government was vulnerable to "mobocracy" and could not sufficiently control its citizens or the individual states. The claim that the central government had only a weak hold on the states was furthered by rumors that the Spanish had offered exportation rights in New Orleans to western settlers if they would secede from the Union. With merchants and artisans calling for a strong central government to secure international trading rights, inhabitants of the frontier calling for a strong central government to combat the Native American resistance, and the signs of disorder and even secession prominent in their minds, delegates from each state traveled to Philadelphia to amend the Articles of Confederation. They did not know at that time just how much they would eventually change the framework of government.

THE CONSTITUTIONAL CONVENTION

On May 25, 1787, 55 delegates, representing every state but Rhode Island, met at the Pennsylvania State House in Philadelphia, which is now known as Independence Hall. Notable delegates included George Washington, Benjamin Franklin, Alexander Hamilton, and James Madison. At first, the convention was very secretive. No members of the press were allowed to observe, and no official journal of the proceedings were kept. In fact, chaperones were assigned to Ben Franklin at all times, the eldest of the delegates, who had a reputation for being talkative. The chaperones assumed the responsibility for making sure that Franklin did not publicize the details of the debates. 39 of the 55 delegates had served in the Continental Congress, and were well aware of the restrictions placed on the national government by the Articles of Confederation. They were convinced of the need for a stronger national government. The vast majority of delegates entered the proceedings similarly convinced by their experiences under the Articles.

The first question facing the delegates was whether to attempt to amend the Articles of Confederation or to throw out the Articles and create a new framework of government. The decision was made early on to create a new framework embodied in a new national constitution. At this point, the convention became known as the Constitutional Convention. Once the drafting of the Constitution had begun, it became clear that the major stumbling block to agreement on a governmental system would be achieving a balance between the needs of large and small states.

James Madison presented the first suggested framework of government which contained a solution to this conflict of interests in the Virginia Plan. The Virginia Plan called for a strong, unified national government rather than a loose confederation of states. The Plan gave Congress unbridled powers of legislation and taxation, and allowed Congress to veto state laws and use military force against the states. The Plan further called for a bicameral legislature with representation in both houses based on state population. The lower house would choose the members of the upper house from a pool selected by the state legislatures. These houses would jointly name the president and federal judges.

The Virginia Plan met with staunch opposition, especially in regard to the scheme for representation as proportional to population. William Patterson, a delegate from New Jersey, presented an alternative to the Virginia Plan, called the New Jersey Plan, to counter Madison's proposal. The New Jersey Plan called for a unicameral congress in which each state would have an equal number of seats. This was the only main difference between the plans, as both would strengthen the national government at the expense of state power.

The debate over representation resulted in a long impasse that held up the proceedings of the convention for weeks. Finally, the delegates from each state agreed to assign one member to a "grand committee," which would decide the issue once and for all. On July 17, 1787 the committee approved the Connecticut Compromise, which gave each state an equal vote in the upper house, and made representation in the lower house proportional to population. The remaining debates went far more smoothly, and the decisions regarding the executive and judicial branches were fairly unanimous. On September 17, 1787, the new Constitution was approved by the convention and sent to the states for ratification.

The members of the Constitutional Convention arrived uncertain of just how large the changes they made to the Articles of Confederation would be. However, they knew that their actions would have dramatic ramifications for the national government. The commitment to secrecy at the outset of the convention opened the convention up to accusations of undemocratic behavior and conspiracy, but the delegates agreed that a policy of non-disclosure would allow them to debate the issues of national government free from the restrictions arising from public criticism.

All of the delegates agreed on the need for a stronger central government. However, it was not until after substantial debate that they decided the Articles of Confederation so lacked the structure of effective government that the only way to rectify the errors of the Articles was to scrap them altogether in favor of a new framework. The clean slate of a new document gave the delegates the freedom to break from tradition and plan an entirely new form of government, but it also opened the door to debate over many aspects of the government, including representation, which were previously settled by the Articles of Confederation.

Legislative representation is the cornerstone of democratic republican government, and assumed a primary role in the Constitutional Convention. One reason for this was the focus of the founders on the powers of the Congress, where they envisioned the majority of the power of the national government would lie. Additionally, as states gave up power to the national governments, delegates wanted to ensure that the representatives of the state would have a weighty vote in the national Congress. This desire brought into focus the conflicting interests of small and large states. Large states naturally preferred that representation in Congress be proportional to state population, ensuring that large states would have the largest number of votes. Such is the rational behind the Virginia Plan, presented by Madison. Small states naturally resisted the Virginia Plan, since under its auspices they would be dominated by the large states.

The Virginia Plan would have granted the four largest states a majority in Congress, leaving the 9 smallest states as a minority. On the other hand, under the New Jersey Plan, the smallest seven states would constitute a majority in Congress while those states held only 25 percent of the nation's citizens. The question of representation proved to be the most significant obstacle to the drafting of the Constitution. In fact, passions ran so strongly in favor of each of the alternate Plans that the Connecticut Compromise, which seems, in retrospect, the logical solution to the debate, was not even entertained for weeks after the subject of representation came up.

Despite the roadblock presented by the issue of representation, the Constitution was drafted in an impressively short amount of time, less than three months. This suggests that the delegates from every state, though they came from different geographical, economic, and ideological backgrounds, had experienced the period of government under the Articles of Confederation similarly, and thus were able to agree upon the most appropriate way in which to rectify the errors of the Articles.

THE CONSTITUTION AND A NEW GOVERNMENT

Finally approved on September 17, 1787, the Constitution laid out the framework for the new United States government. It reconciled the differences between the states on the subject of representation, and represented, ultimately, a balance between the delegates' knowledge that the national government had to be strengthened and their fear of despotism and tyranny. Congress was granted the power to lay and collect taxes, to regulate interstate commerce, and to conduct diplomacy as the single voice of the people in international affairs. States were thus disallowed to coin money and tax interstate commerce, and the national government had the power to invoke military action against the states. The Constitution declared all acts and treaties made by Congress to be binding on the states.

The Constitution set forth a government composed of 3 branches: the legislative, executive, and judicial. Each branch was given certain powers over the others to ensure that no one branch usurped a dangerous amount of power. This system, known as checks and balances, was the cornerstone of the new framework of government. The system of checks and balances represented the solution to the problem of how to empower the central government, yet protect against corruption and despotism.

The President was granted the power to veto acts of Congress deemed unnecessary or unjust, and would be responsible for appointing federal and Supreme Court judges. The Senate had to ratify treaties proposed by the President, and had to approve the President's cabinet appointments. Congress as a joint body was given the power to impeach, try, and remove the President from office, as well as Supreme Court justices, should it become necessary. The judicial branch, headed by the Supreme Court, had the responsibility and power to interpret the laws passed by Congress.

The Constitution set forth a form of federalism that balanced the authority of the state and national governments. The state legislatures would elect the members of the Senate, as well as select delegates to the Electoral College, which selected the President. Furthermore, the Constitution could be amended by a vote in favor of amendment by three-fourths of the state legislatures. The writers of the Constitution intended to increase the power of the national government, but they were wary of taking too much power from the states.

One debate that was resolved by the Constitution was that of whether slaves should be considered persons or property for reasons of representation. Southern delegates argued that slaves should count toward representative seats, whereas the representatives of northern states, most of which had already or would soon abolish slavery, argued that to count slaves as members of the population would grant an unfair advantage to the southern states. The result of this debate was the adoption of the Three-fifths Clause, which allowed three-fifths of all slaves to be counted as people. The Constitution further forbade any state to refuse to return run-away slaves to the states from which they came. Under the Constitution, Congress was permitted to ban the importation of slaves after 1808, but there was no explicit mention of the framers feelings about the legality of slavery.

Once approved by the Constitutional Convention in 1787, the Constitution was sent to the states for ratification.

The Constitution set forth a new national government that completely rejected the structure of the Articles of Confederation. The Articles had been founded upon the idea that the United States should be a federation of individual republics, tied by the confines of geography and the requirements of defense into a nation. Each state had been given independent authority over its functions and laws. The Constitution granted powers to the national government that the period under the Articles of Confederation had proven necessary. For instance, the Congress under the Articles had been unable to get total cooperation from the states, and thus had not been able to pass import duties or taxes necessary to the sustenance of the national budget. As a result, the Constitution granted Congress the right to levy and collect taxes. The case of interstate commerce and diplomacy were similar in that the national government had failed to act decisively in either arena due to restrictions on power, which were lifted by the Constitution.

The final form of government represented a compromise between those who advocated power for the states and those who advocated power for the national government. The Constitution set forth a government far more empowering to the states than either the Virginia Plan or the New Jersey Plan had suggested. Undoubtedly, the Constitution established a government system under which the national government was far superior to that of the state, but the final result was a republican balance, which acknowledged the need for some level of state autonomy.

The tripartite format of government laid out by the Constitution was the central feature of the new government. The three separate branches of the national government helped to clearly define the major functions of the central government and enabled the framers to design the system of checks and balances that would protect the people from the corruption of any one branch of government. The system of checks and balances has been hailed ever since the drafting of the Constitution as perhaps the most important contribution of the founders toward the goal of good government.

Slavery proved a divisive issue for the Constitutional Convention, with some radicals even calling for its abolition by the Constitution. For reasons of economics and political tradition, abolition was basically out of the question, but the framers were forced to deal with issues regarding slavery, such as representation and fugitive slave laws. However, the Constitution nowhere clearly states the opinion of the framers on the morality, legality, or future of slavery. This would prove to be an important admission, as the proponents and opponents of slavery squared off over the legality of slavery in an ever increasing zeal that spread through the decades before the civil war. The very mention of slavery in the Constitution convinced many that the framers had accepted the institution of slavery and intended it to be legal. Opponents of slavery claimed that the fact that the framers had given Congress the power to ban the importation of slaves after 1808 proved that abolition had been the framers' ultimate goal. The evidence suggests that the framers, much like their descendents, were split on the topic of slavery, but that most accepted the institution as a necessary evil.

Perhaps the most important effect of the drafting of the Constitution was its reaffirmation of the American people, in the broadest sense, as the ultimate source of political legitimacy in the nation, responsible for the selection of their leaders, and shapers of the future of the nation. Additionally, the framers recognized the need for the Constitution to be a living, evolving document, which the people would have access to and be able to change as the need arose.

RATIFICATION

Though accepted by the convention, the Constitution had to be ratified by the people of the United States before it could take effect as the law of the land. The framers devised a system by which special state conventions of popularly elected delegates would be created to ratify the Constitution. Only two-thirds (nine) of the states needed to ratify the Constitution to put the new government into operation. Since those states that did not ratify the constitution would remain under the authority of the Articles of Confederation this situation presented the possibility of the division of the United States into two separate nations.

As the process of ratification began, the majority of Americans were hesitant to support the Constitution, which represented a drastic shift away from the Articles of Confederation, whose weaknesses many common citizens had not been in a position to observe. The long process of ratification began with the entrenchment of opposing sides. The supporters of the Constitution called themselves the Federalists, and their opponents, who supported states rights over centralized power, were dubbed the Anti-federalists. The main contention of the Anti-federalists was that the Constitution failed to balance the power of state and national governments, erring in the direction of granting too much power to the national government. The Anti-federalists claimed that the Constitution doomed the states to be dominated by a potentially tyrannical and uncompassionate central government. Federalists, for their part, defended the necessity of a strong national government and pointed to the Constitution as the best possible framework for the United States' government.

With the aid of funding and experience, the Federalists pushed ratification through eight state conventions between December 1787 and May 1788. Only Rhode Island and North Carolina rejected the Constitution outright. However, by May 1788, along with New Hampshire, neither Virginia nor New York, both states crucial to the Union in terms of population and economics, had made a move toward rejecting or ratifying the Constitution. The Union, for all intents and purposes, could not function without the membership of both states. When, on June 21, 1788 New Hampshire ratified the Constitution, making it effective as the framework of national government, neither Virginia nor New York had reached a decision. Both states were torn by debate between solid constituencies of both Federalists and Anti-federalists. On June 25, 1788 Virginia finally ratified the Constitution by a narrow 53 percent margin. In New York, the debate raged on until Alexander Hamilton's Federalists finally emerged victorious by nearly as slight a margin on July 26, 1788.

The fierce debates over the issue of ratification, particularly in Virginia and New York, mobilized both Federalists and Anti-federalists in media campaigns to convince the population of the value of their causes. The writings of the political leaders of this period have become an important part of American history. The most notable works produced are collectively entitled The Federalist Papers. The Federalist Papers contain a series of newspaper articles written by John Jay, James Madison, and Alexander Hamilton. The articles most likely played little part in the ratification of the Constitution, but clearly lay out the arguments in favor of the Constitution and against the Anti-federalists.

The framers realized that if they sent the Constitution straight to the state legislatures, it would no doubt be defeated, as it took power from the states and gave it to the national government. Additionally, the framers intended the source of governmental legitimacy to be the population at large rather than the states. In keeping with this ideal and with concern for the state legislatures' bias toward rejection, the framers established the system of ratification which eventually took place. The people would elect representatives, not to govern, but to decide on the form of government. However, the framers knew that the process of ratification would not be easy. They anticipated the resistance that sprung up among the Anti-federalists.

The Anti-federalists' arguments against the Constitution represented deep-seated mistrust of centralized government, which found its source in Enlightenment thinking, and more concretely, in the colonial experience leading up to the revolution. The principle contention of the Anti-federalists was that the national government could never be as responsive and compassionate to the needs of the citizens as could state governments. The Anti-federalists claimed that the people would not submit to being governed by a geographically distant central government controlled by politicians who had little incentive to vote for the best interests of individual states. They saw the submission of state government to national government as representative of the submission of the interests of the individual to the dangerous interests of the nation. Indeed, one of the Anti-federalists' main points of contention with the Constitution was that it nowhere guaranteed the protection of individuals' civil rights, and nowhere explicitly guaranteed that the national government would not attempt to unjustly limit and usurp the power of the states. Indeed, the absence of a bill of rights was a common criticism of the Constitution, and turned many to the Anti-federalist side.

Conversely, the Federalists' political values were grounded more recently in the experience of government under the Articles of Confederation. They extolled the Constitution as the perfect balance between state and national power, and claimed that the system of checks and balances would keep the government honest and limited in its power. The Federalists had many advantages on their side. Most of the nation's wealthiest and best respected men, including George Washington and Benjamin Franklin, were Federalists. Most newspapers supported the Constitution, and Federalists dominated the national networks of experienced politicians. The results of the early conventions may well have been more a reflection on the aggressiveness and organization of the Federalists than the actual opinions of the people.

Though the Anti-federalists lost the battle to prevent the ratification of the Constitution, they did make significant progress in some areas. Virginia, Massachusetts, and New York all ratified the Constitution with the request that the government adopt a bill of rights. This became an immediate goal of the government. And, as the government began to take shape, Anti-federalist forces remained vigilant as a counter-balance to the Federalist tendency to accord great powers to the central government. The division of the nation into Federalists and Anti-federalists during the ratification of the Constitution set the stage for the continuing deepening of the rift between those in favor of a strong central government and those wary of the limitation of states' rights.

DEFINING THE NATIONAL GOVERNMENT

The first Congress under the Constitution convened in New York, the new capitol, on March 1, 1789. George Washington had been elected as the nation's first president, and took the oath of office on April 30. The founding members of the national government found there were many details that the constitution had left to them to work out. Issues requiring immediate attention included the setting of the legislative agenda, defining the role and details of operation of the cabinet, the establishment of the judicial branch, and meeting the popular call for a bill of rights.

By way of interaction with Congress, George Washington did very little. He suggested few laws, leaving the setting of legislative agenda to the Congress. He only rarely spoke publicly on the topic of public policy, leaving domestic policy in the hands of Congress alone. Instead, Washington focused primarily on matters of finance, diplomacy, and the military. Washington only vetoed two bills in all eight years of his presidency.

The form and function of the President's cabinet was left up to the first Congress to determine. The first cabinet consisted of four departments, headed by the secretaries of state, war, and treasury, as well as the attorney general.

Washington's initial cabinet consisted of Thomas Jefferson as Secretary of State, Henry Knox as Secretary of War, Alexander Hamilton as Secretary of Treasury, and Edmund Randolph as Attorney General.

Similarly, the federal-court system was left in the hands of Congress to shape. Congress passed the Judiciary Act of 1789 to create the federal-court system. The act established a federal district court in each state that ran according to local legal tradition. The Supreme Court exercised final jurisdiction in all legal matters. The federal-court system, and the Supreme Court specifically, had to wait until the mid 1790s to fully explore their powers. In Hylton v. US in 1796, the Supreme Court first established its power to determine the constitutionality of congressional statutes. This was only the first of many decisions important in the evolution of the Supreme Court as a government body.

Perhaps the most important item on the national agenda was the drafting of a bill of rights to guarantee the civil rights of US citizens. James Madison led the group that drafted the first ten amendments to the Constitution, collectively known as the Bill of Rights, which the state legislatures ratified in December 1791. The First Ameendment guaranteed freedom of expression. The Second gave each state the right to form a citizens' militia, and the third protected the citizens from the imposition of a standing army. The Fourth through Eighth Amendments dealt with fair treatment in judicial proceedings. The Ninth and Tenth Amendments restricted the powers of the national government by declaring that the enumeration of Constitutional rights could not be used to deny citizens of other rights, and that all power not explicitly delegated to the national government fell to the states.

More than anything else, the creation of the executive office worried those who feared despotic government. Many feared the president would amass too great an amount of power and turn into an unstoppable tyrant. Many aspects of the presidency were left vague by the Constitution, and the nation watched in great anticipation to see how Washington and Congress would interpret the role of the president. Washington's reluctance to interfere with Congress sprang largely from his knowledge of the fears of the people, and his desire to avoid setting any precedent that might lead future presidents to overstep their bounds. The creation of the cabinet was undertaken carefully for similar reasons, and the establishment of four distinct departments was part of the effort on the part of both Washington and Congress to clearly define the domain of the executive branch. The cabinet departments, especially those of treasury and state, would play heavily into the functioning of the Washington administration.

The solution to the problem of establishing a federal-court system was a compromise between the desire for broad access to federal justice and the desire on the part of citizens to maintain state traditions. Many citizens feared the extension of a federal-court system would do away with the unique procedures that had operated at the state level for decades. Many citizens therefore initially rallied against the development of the federal-court system within the states. Bearing in mind these fears and objections, Congress passed the Judiciary Act of 1789, which both increased access to federal justice and assuaged fears that state traditions would be lost.

The demand for the Bill of Rights sprang from the fear, stoked by the Anti-Federalists, that a strong central government would neglect the rights of citizens in the pursuit of what officials thought to be the greater good. While the Anti-federalists had not been able to stop the creation of a strong national government, they hoped the Bill of Rights would serve to limit the powers of the government and protect individuals from despotism and tyranny. The Federalists, on the other hand, insisted that the Bill of Rights, while guaranteeing personal liberties, would not deprive the national government of powers essential to the fulfillment of its duties.

The Ninth and Tenth Amendments seem to be the only major concessions made by the Federalists in the drafting of the Bill of Rights. However, their wording was vague enough that it left loopholes that would allow the national government to avoid the restriction of any significant power. The Tenth Amendment especially, leaving all power to the states not explicitly granted the national government, seemed a great success for the Anti-federalists. However, it would prove far less useful than its wording suggested. Time after time the national government avoided adherence to the Tenth Amendment by invoking what became known as the elastic clause of the Constitution, which granted Congress the authority to pass any measure which was "necessary and proper." A loose interpretation of this clause allowed the national government to effectively ignore the Tenth Amendment.

The interpretation of the elastic clause would prove to be a bone of much contention during the Washington administration and well beyond.

ALEXANDER HAMILTON AND FINANCE IN THE WASHINGTON ADMINISTRATION

Despite the growing concern throughout the nation over a string of acts asserting national over state power, the Washington administration remained dominated by Federalists, led by Secretary of Treasury Alexander Hamilton. Hamilton's initiatives aroused the ire of those who maintained the politics of the Anti-federalists. Hamilton's main goals were to achieve the financial stability necessary to fight another war should one arise with the foreign threats of Britain and Spain, and to dull assertions of state power that might diminish national power. In his Report on Public Credit, submitted to Congress in January 1790, Hamilton calculated the US debt at $54 million, with individual states owing an additional $25 million. American credit abroad was poor, and continued to fall with every day the debt was left unpaid. Hamilton suggested funding the debt by selling government bonds, and further proposed that state debts be assumed by the national government.

Hamilton advocated the selling of western land to pay off US debt to European nations in order to rebuild credit, but suggested that the debt to US creditors be maintained as a perpetual debt. He argued the US could continue paying interest on its domestic debt, thus maintaining good credit, if the US creditors would accept the debt as a secure investment which paid yearly interest. This plan generated opposition from many, objecting to the fact that under the plan, astute wealthy speculators who had bought the debt certificates of others, many at great discounts, would benefit, while the Americans who actually financed the war would lose out.

Heavy opposition arose to Hamilton's proposal that the national government assume the debts of the states as well. Opposition ran especially high in the South, which, excluding South Carolina, had paid off 83 percent of the region's debt. Southern states saw in Hamilton's proposal a plan to alleviate the tax burden on northern states lagging in their debt payments, while southern states had already reduced their debt at great internal cost. In the end, Hamilton pushed his proposals through Congress with the aid of much political wheeling and dealing. The nation reaped the economic rewards of Hamilton's efforts to improve credit, as Europeans increasingly purchased US government bonds and invested elsewhere in the US economy.

In December 1790, Hamilton began his second controversial policy campaign. Having increased the amount of capital available for investment, he planned to establish a national bank. One-fifth of the bank's stock would be owned by the US Treasury, which would have one fifth control of the board of directors. The remainder would fall into private hands. Hamilton claimed the Bank of the United States would, at negligible cost, provide a secure depository for federal revenue and a source of federal loans, as well as issue currency. The bank would regulate the activities of the nation's banks and extend credit to US citizens in order to expand the economy.

The proposal for the national bank brought Hamilton more opposition than had any previous initiative. Most notably, Thomas Jefferson, the Secretary of State, joined the ranks of Hamilton's opponents. Jefferson and other political leaders recalled how the Bank of Britain had undermined democracy, and feared that the creation of the bank would tie private individuals too closely to public institutions. They predicted that politicians would manipulate bank shareholders and that members of Congress who held bank shares would vote for the best interests of the bank over those of the nation. Hamilton's opponents further pointed out that the Constitution did not grant the federal government the power to grant charters. Despite this opposition, Congress approved the bank by a thin margin, and the Bank of the United States obtained a twenty-year charter in February 1791.

Alexander Hamilton, a veteran of the Revolutionary War, was an idealist who had become disillusioned by the faltering morals that many of his countrymen had exhibited during the revolution and following decade. He believed that Americans could not be motivated by self-sacrifice, but rather, had to be motivated by appeals to their own self-interest. Thus he advocated building ties between the government and wealthy and influential individuals, who he believed would support the nation were it in their own interest. Distrustful of the masses, he argued for the consolidation of power in the hands of the national government.

Hamilton's proposals as Secretary of Treasury reflected this ideological standpoint. The funding of the US debt through the sale of US government bonds would undoubtedly fill the nation's treasury. The assumption of state debt, he further claimed, would prevent states from failing to repay debts, thus injuring US credit abroad. However, the true motive of his Report on Public Credit was to win the loyalty of state creditors to the national government and take the matter of debt out of the hands of the states. Even knowing Hamilton's aims, legislatures in debt-wracked states could not resist the offer to alleviate their debt.

Hamilton's proposal to maintain a perpetual national debt meant that the US could act almost as a bank, securely keeping the savings of the wealthy and paying a competitive interest rate. Thus the fate of the wealthy and powerful owners of the US debt would be tied to the fate of the nation. Through this appeal to economic self-interest, Hamilton thought he could harness the wealth and power of these individuals for purposes of public good. Astutely, the opponents of Hamilton's plan to maintain a running debt claimed the plan was antagonistic to the concept of equality, since it rewarded public creditors over common Americans. Also, many feared that the plan would give the wealthy creditors undue influence in the national government, a seemingly valid fear considering Hamilton's true intentions.

Hamilton's most controversial proposal was the creation of the Bank of the United States. For Hamilton, the creation of the bank was yet another way in which the national government could take control of the nation's day-to-day operations and rely less on private institutions for services such as loans. To his opponents, Hamilton's proposal grossly overstepped the bounds of the executive branch and the national government. Any claim that Congress could create the Bank of the United States relied upon a loose reading of the Constitution, especially the elastic clause. Article I, Section VIII of the Constitution states that Congress shall have the power "to make all laws which shall be necessary and proper for carrying into execution...powers vested by this Constitution in the government of the United States." The opponents of the bank argued that a strict interpretation of the Constitution was necessary to protect against tyranny. These so-called strict constructionists, led by Thomas Jefferson, focused on the latter part of the clause, claiming that nowhere did the Constitution give Congress the power to grant the bank a charter, so that the passing of the bank charter could not be considered necessary and proper. Loose constructionists, on the other hand, focused on the beginning of the clause, claiming it gave Congress the power to do anything not expressly forbidden by the Constitution. Though Hamilton's proposals succeeded in becoming law, the debates his proposals instigated were by no means settled.

The debate over Hamilton's measures in regard to public credit and the bank exposed the differing ideologies developing in the United States, and set the stage for future conflicts between the strict and loose constructionists. Moreover, the debates over Hamilton's proposals demonstrated how more and more, the differing ideologies developing in the United States were merely a matter of the differing desires and needs of North and South. The industrial North had rallied to Hamilton's cause, supporting the measures to improve credit and increase investment. Meanwhile, the agricultural South saw no need for the national government's usurpation of power to these ends, and was content to govern itself by local rule. This rift would steadily widen well into the nineteenth century, dominating (and dividing) US politics.

INCREASING TENSIONS AND THE WHISKEY REBELLION

Alexander Hamilton did not stop with the creation of the Bank of the United States. His next initiative was to encourage industrialization and a higher degree of national self-sufficiency. In his December 1791 Report on Manufacturers, Hamilton proposed the passage of protective tariffs to spur domestic production. Further, he called for the reduction of duties on goods carried by American ships.

Thomas Jefferson, and his newest political ally, James Madison, opposed efforts to encourage protectionist economic policy. They feared the policies would weaken competition and create industries that were dependent on government aid. Tariffs would lead to higher prices and decrease innovation. Congress refused to approve high new tariffs. However, Hamilton did push legislature through Congress to set higher import duties on goods not imported on American ships. At Hamilton's behest, Congress also approved subsidies for a number of floundering New England fisheries.

Along with building political opposition to Federalist policy, there was some degree of public outcry. One element of Hamilton's policy had been the establishment of an excise tax on domestically produced whiskey. Americans, who consumed an average of six gallons of hard liquor per person each year, did not take kindly to this tax, which amounted to 25 percent of the retail value of Whiskey. Nowhere was the effect of this tax felt more than in western Pennsylvania, where whiskey was distilled and transported east. The excise tax was enforced most stringently and cruelly in western Pennsylvania, as opposed to most other areas of the country where it was more or less ignored. Additionally, anyone charged with tax evasion was sent to trial in federal court, which meant small family farmers had to travel hundreds of miles to Philadelphia, to be tried by men who knew little of their situation.

Popular opposition to the Whiskey tax mounted, and episodes of violence against tax collectors broke out in many areas of western Pennsylvania. Large-scale resistance began in late July 1794 in what became known as the Whiskey Rebellion. During a short period of time, over a hundred men attacked a US Marshall, the chief revenue officer for Allegheny County saw his house and stables burned to the ground, and organized, militant farmers threatened to form a separate country. President George Washington responded swiftly, calling 13,000 militiamen from Mid-Atlantic States to march with him to western Pennsylvania. Washington led the march into Pennsylvania himself, crushing the rebellion convincingly and returning order to the land. However, Washington was shaken by the experience of the rebellion. The whiskey tax was reduced and trials for tax evasion became the jurisdiction of federal courts as a result of the public outcry, even before full-fledged rebellion began.

Hamilton's efforts to pass protectionist policies magnified the already growing gap between his supporters and opponents. The proposal was yet another attempt to gain the loyalty of wealthy and powerful industrial merchants and traders, at the expense of the population at large. Hamilton proved widely successful in his effort to amass political support by appealing to economic self-interest, establishing strongholds of Federalists in New England, New Jersey, and South Carolina, all of which benefited from his economic policies. Manufacturers and merchants in these areas were able to raise prices and better compete with European goods in a protected market. However, not all Americans welcomed price increases.

However, significant opposition to the Federalism rose throughout most of the South and West. Most southern and western inhabitants benefited little from Hamilton's economic initiatives, and if anything, were hurt by the rise in prices that resulted from efforts at protectionism. They saw Hamilton's policies as catering to the wealthy businessmen of the northeast (which they did), and felt that they were neglected and abused by national financial policy. This coalition of southern and western opponents to the economic policy of the national government, which increasingly included citizens of Mid-Atlantic states, presented an increasing obstacle to Federalist control of the government.

The Whiskey Rebellion was the public embodiment of the political opposition to Federalism as exercised by Washington and Hamilton. Hamilton's political opponents claimed his policies singled out individual groups unfairly for reward. The rebellion arose partly because western Pennsylvania farmers saw themselves singled out and exploited for revenue. Political opponents to Federalism further claimed that the Federalists wished to concentrate power in the hands of the central government at the expense of the state governments, which they claimed would be less responsive to the needs of the citizenry. The Whiskey Rebellion arose partly because the farmers felt that the tax had been imposed, and was enforced, by men who knew nothing of their situation and needs. These elements of the Whiskey rebellion lent the weight of easy comparison to the American Revolution by the opponents of Hamilton's fiscal policies. The claims of arbitrary taxation and an uncompassionate central government, matched with the threat of secession, allowed Thomas Jefferson and his followers to recall the events of the past that had forced the British government out of the colonies' favor.

The one positive result of the Whiskey Rebellion for the Washington administration was the effectiveness of Washington's response. The Whiskey Rebellion was the first major test of the national government's ability to enforce its laws within the states. This it did, and in inspiring fashion. George Washington led the troops himself, symbolizing the broad reach of the national government, and its commitment to dealing with the states on a close, rather than remote, basis.

EXPANSION AND CONFLICT

On June 1, 1792, the State of Kentucky was admitted to the Union, and four years later, on the same day, Tennessee also joined. During the 1790s, the US attempted to expand its territory into the west (which constituted the land just west of the Appalachian Mountains), where opposition lay in the foreign powers of Spain and Britain, both of which desired control of parts of North America. Also, Native Americans populated most of this coveted land. Each of the three nations, as well as the Natives, struggled against the others for control of the western territory.

The US tried to strike a balance between trying to form an alliance with the Indians and attempting to forcibly remove them. The US tried to force peace through military action in 1790 and 1791. These military efforts yielded little success, and the campaign ended with the November 4, 1791 defeat of the US troops, when the Miami Indians killed 900 men out of a force of 1400. Having failed militarily, President Washington authorized Secretary of War Henry Knox to proclaim that the Indian title to land would be formally recognized by the US and would not be revoked without "free consent." Laws punishing trespassers on Indian land accompanied this policy, as did the beginning of an initiative to "civilize the natives. However, as in the past, Indians resisted this initiative and clung to their cultures. The attempt to alter relations with the Indians ended in continued stalemate.

Meanwhile, the French went to war with Britain and Spain in 1793. Northern merchants pressed for an anti-French foreign policy, and southern planters encouraged the government to ally itself with France. The nation was torn between two options. French diplomat Edmond Genet traveled to the United States to argue the French case to the US government, but he was unsuccessful in evoking government action. On April 22, 1793, Washington issued the Proclamation of American Neutrality, refusing to be drawn into the war. Despite this proclamation, Genet was able to persuade southwestern settlers to offer limited military support to the French against the Spanish in Florida and the Mississippi Valley. Additionally, Genet enlisted nearly 1,000 Americans to function as privateers at sea, terrorizing the British navy.

Washington exhorted his people to cease their attacks on British vessels, but it was too late. British ministers decided that only a massive show of force would rectify the situation. Accordingly, the British navy seized over 250 American vessels during the winter of 1794. At the same time, British naval officers began the practice of inspecting American vessels for British subjects, who, if they were found, were impressed into service in the royal navy. American sailors were often seized as well. Britain further challenged US neutrality in February 1794. Canada's royal governor denied US claims to the land north of the Ohio River and encouraged the Indians there to resist expansion. British troops built Fort Miami on US territory, and the Spanish, following suit, built Fort San Fernando on US lands in the southwest.

On the brink of war, Washington dispatched negotiators to attempt to win peace with the encroaching forces. The first to experience success was General Anthony Wayne, who led troops into the Northwest Territory and routed a large contingent of Indian warriors at the Battle of Fallen Timbers on August 20, 1794. The next August, twelve Indian tribes signed the Treaty of Greenville, which ended hostilities and opened the area now known as Ohio to settlement. Shortly after, Jay's Treaty was signed in Britain. John Jay negotiated a settlement which removed British troops from American land and reopened trade with the West Indies. Finally, Thomas Pinckney negotiated the Treaty of San Lorenzo with Spain, which granted the US unrestricted access to the Mississippi River and removed Spanish troops from American land.

US relations with the Native Americans had grown increasingly dire by the early 1790s. Washington's military efforts in the north proved to be a complete failure, the southern tribes had resumed hostilities with the inhabitants of the frontier, and the Indians were unresponsive to attempts at "civilization." Convinced that the only way to avoid the continued exile from their land at the hands of the US government, Indian tribes allied themselves with America's enemies. US citizens, especially those along the frontier, saw the coalitions being built between the natives and the foreign armies. Many believed that the only way to contest the forces of Britain and Spain, both supported by Natives, was through an alliance with France. Many southern and western inhabitants pressed for pro-French foreign policy, hoping that France, supported by the US, could achieve victory in Europe, distracting the British and Spanish governments from their preoccupation with the American West.

American feelings toward France were generally strong, in one direction or the other. The conservative North generally disapproved of the recent French Revolution, while more liberal southerners generally supported it. Northern merchants realized that trade with Britain was, more than anything else, the force sustaining their economy. The largest portion of US trade went through British ports. New England businessmen thought an alliance with France might force British retaliation in the form of constriction of trade and/or all out war, while a pro-British stance might invite an expansion of trade. Southerners, on the other hand, saw reliance on British trade as a weakness of the national economy, and favored the expansion of trade with France. Additionally, southern plantation owners feared the intentions of the British toward the institution of slavery. Many based their opinions on this subject on rumors that claimed the British had begun a bloody slave uprising on the French-controlled island of Saint Domingue. They feared the British would attempt to abolish slavery in the American South, and thus advocated a pro-French foreign policy. The conflict over foreign policy in the early to mid 1790s was yet another struggle emblematic of the division of the nation into quarreling factions, largely based on the division between North and South.

Jay's Treaty, perhaps the most important diplomatic achievement of the Washington administration, was received poorly in the US, where critics saw it as a weak attempt at negotiation, allowing the British to continue to impress sailors and to restrict US trade with French ports in the Caribbean. Jay himself was criticized heavily by the public and denounced as a diplomatic failure. However, in retrospect, the treaty accomplished quite a lot, considering the circumstances. Most importantly, it halted the advance toward war with Britain before the outbreak of serious violence. Second, it ended the occupation of American land by British forts, which had lasted for twelve years. Finally, the treaty made crucial headway in resolving squabbles between the two nations revolving around the collection of prewar debts, which had gone on for over a decade.

In retrospect, the Washington administration accomplished a great deal in the realm of diplomacy. It defended American territorial rights, avoided war, and opened the crucial port of New Orleans. Though the administration had made great strides in the establishment of the US as an international power, internal divisions over policy showed that foreign policy was simply yet another area that gave rise to political conflict between American citizens.

DIVISION INTO PARTIES AND GEORGE WASHINGTON'S FAREWELL ADDRESS

The framers considered political parties to be self-serving factions that cultivated dissent and were ultimately detrimental to good government. Though the framers had not written provisions into the Constitution dealing with political parties, by the end of George Washington's second term, the issues of national government had divided the nation into two distinct and hostile factions: the Federalists and the Republicans.

The Federalists, led by Alexander Hamilton, advocated strong central government. Concentrated in the northeast, they preferred a system under which the population would choose their government officials based on merit and reputation rather than politics, and in which elected officials would rule without the direct influence of the people. Thomas Jefferson, James Madison, and others who found Federalist thought offensive, developed a markedly different view of good government under the Washington administration. With their stronghold in the South, Republicans claimed that liberty could only be protected if political power were rested firmly in the hands of the people and those government officials closest and most responsive to the people

Republicans attempted to arouse the political awareness of the common people, who generally viewed national politics with an attitude of apathy, in order to present a challenge to the Federalists, who wielded the majority of power in the national government. They did so through a media campaign, centered on the publication of America's first opposition newspaper, The National Gazette. Additionally, Republicans organized a number of societies and clubs throughout the nation, which spread criticism of Washington's political decisions. The birth of the Republican Party may be traced to 1793, when Thomas Jefferson resigned from Washington's cabinet in opposition to Federalist policy decisions, especially those undertaken by Alexander Hamilton. As Republican influence in the government grew, Washington allied himself clearly with the Federalists in 1794, at which point the nation fully recognized the existence of two distinct parties. That same year the Republicans won a slight majority in the House of Representatives, signaling the arrival of the party as a legitimate political movement.

The parties grew increasingly hostile toward one another during the final years of Washington's presidency. A battle raged in the press, each side attacking the other's political values, and spreading rumors. The Federalists alleged that Republicans wanted to destroy the government and hand the nation over to France, and that the Republican clubs and societies were revolutionary organizations created to carry out this mission. Meanwhile, Republicans charged Federalists with attempting to create a government of aristocracy at the common taxpayer's expense, and even started rumors that the Federalists planned to establish an American dynasty by marrying John Adams' daughter to Britain's King George III.

In the midst of building hostilities, Washington decided to resign from office after his second term. On September 19, 1796, the American Daily Advertiser published Washington's Farewell Address to the nation. The basic premise of the address was a condemnation of political parties. Washington warned that the development of parties would destroy the government, and worried that special interest groups and foreign nations would easily dominate the factions. On this note, he implored future generations to avoid embroilment in the affairs of other nations, and concentrate on the development of "efficient government" at home, free from foreign influence. Washington left office in March 1797, leaving the nation still very much divided.

As of the early 1790s, most Americans remained convinced that political parties were a detriment to good government. The framers had neither desired nor planned for the rise of political divisions. In fact, in Federalist No. 10 of the Federalist Papers, James Madison, one of the leaders of the Republican party, had argued that one of the strong points of the Constitution was that it would prevent the formation of political factions. It was commonly assumed that should factions rise to a position of political power, they would act to achieve selfish goals at the expense of the public good. However, this concept of political parties began to crumble as opposition arose to Hamilton's initiatives as Secretary of Treasury. Many political leaders began to view an opposition party as necessary to check the power of the ideological majority in the national government, and as a means to provide a more fully encompassing examination of the issues presented to the national government. Thus, gradually, political parties took their place as an integral part of American government.

The political parties in the US developed due to differing responses to the events of the early 1790s. Federalists shuddered at the thought of disorder, and thought events such as the Whiskey Rebellion, or, in France, the French Revolution, proved that if left with too much power the people would foster disorder and rebellion against the government. Republicans, on the other hand, rejoiced in the Whiskey Rebellion and French Revolution as assertions that the true source of political power was the population at large. Observing the actions of the Washington administration, especially of Alexander Hamilton, republicans became convinced that the assumption of broad power by the central government would only foster inequality and misery among the people of the separate states.

More than anything else, the division of the nation into political parties exemplified the growing rift between North and South. The conservative, industrial North was decidedly Federalist, while the more liberal and agricultural South was overwhelmingly Republican. Historians most often attribute this split to the differing economic modalities of the regions. Clearly, the industrial North was far more supportive of Hamilton's financial policy, which benefited merchants and shippers more than others. However, perhaps more important in the division into parties were the differing social concerns that grew out of industrial and agricultural economies. In the North, as in every industrial economy, those with economic power sought to protect that power from those who did not have as much, namely the masses in the workforce. Thus, to the powerful businessmen of the North, an ideology that closely linked the wealthy to the government and put political power in the hands of elites who were free from the influence of the masses sounded very attractive. In contrast, the workforce in the South was made up primarily of slaves, with no chance to rise in the economic ranks and vie for the power of the plantation owners. Moreover, southern plantation owners did not have an antagonistic relationship with small farmers. To the contrary, they trusted their abilities to be elected by the small farmers and to lead them in peace, should they be given the chance. Thus, for southerners, an ideology that placed the power of the government in the hands of the people did not seem dangerous; it seemed logical.

Washington's Farewell Address was a direct response to the fractioning of the American people. From a clearly Federalist point of view he extolled the virtues of neutrality. He pleaded for American political neutrality, that citizens not be forced to choose between political alternatives, but rather choose their leaders on the basis of merit and reputation. He further pleaded for international neutrality, exhorting Americans to avoid "political connection" with Europe, hoping such avoidance would remove the divisiveness of foreign policy from the American political dialogue and allow US leaders to concentrate on domestic goals. While he could not stop the rise of political parties, which had already become a fact of American political life, his plea for neutrality and vision of an isolated America would inform American foreign relations into the twentieth century.

CHAPTER 5 - THE ARTICLES OF CONFEDERATION (1781-1789)

IMPORTANT TERMS, PEOPLE, AND EVENTS

Terms

- Confederacy - A confederacy is a form of government in which independent states are loosely joined, typically for common defense. Each independent state maintains power over the majority of its own affairs.

- Confederation Congress - The governing body that consisted of representatives from each of the 13 states. Congress governed the affairs of the United States between the ratification of the Articles of Confederation in 1781 and the ratification of the U.S. Constitution.

- Conservatives - Political leaders who favored the formation of a strong central government and who thought the Articles of Confederation should grant more powers to the national government than to the state governments. Conservatives tended to fear the power of the masses and to favor government by the elite.

- Impost - A form of tax applied to goods that are imported into a state or country. Imposts are typically used to make money, protect a home industry, or retaliate against another state or country.

- Radicals - Political leaders who favored strong state governments and thought the Articles of Confederation should remove most power from the national government, placing more power in the hands of the people. Radicals feared the formation of another strong central government, similar to the British government, which would favor the elite, strip people of their right to equal representation, and violate their freedom.

- Ratify - To formally approve and accept a legal document, such as a constitution.

- Sovereignty - Sovereignty means that an independent state has the power to govern its own affairs. A sovereign state maintains the power to govern its own affairs without interference from other states or other bodies of power.

- Second Continental Congress - The Second Continental Congress met for the first time in Philadelphia in May of 1775, and continued to meet until the full ratification of the Articles of Confederation on March 1, 1781. This congress produced the Declaration of Independence, drafted the Articles of Confederation, and served as an unofficial national government, managing the war effort, finances and foreign affairs, while the Articles were debated by the states. It was succeeded by the Congress of the Confederation.

People

- Benjamin Franklin - A printer by vocation, inventor, philosopher and author by hobby, Benjamin Franklin played many vital roles in establishing both the independence of the United States and in ensuring the success of the young nation. Elected as a delegate to the Albany Congress of 1754, his Albany Plan outlined the balance of power between local independence and colonial union, and has been said to be prophetic of the U.S. Constitution. He served as a delegate to the Second Continental Congress, was chosen for the committee to draft the Declaration of Independence, was sent as a diplomat to France to procure military assistance during the Revolution, and was appointed as one of three to negotiate the Treaty of Paris. Franklin also served as a delegate to the convention that produced the U.S. Constitution.

- Thomas Jefferson - Known mostly as the author of the Declaration of Independence, Thomas Jefferson also served as an influential statesman of Virginia and as a diplomat to France. He contributed important legislation and ideology during the early years of the new nation. He strongly believed in the importance of legislation that limited the power of government and strengthened the rights of the people. Jefferson proposed and passed important legislation dictating the separation of church and state and was integral in both Virginia's decision to cede its northwestern territory to Congress and in drafting the land ordinances that would serve to manage the land equitably.

- John Dickinson - Serving as a delegate from Pennsylvania to the Second Continental Congress, John Dickinson became part of the committee assigned to author the first draft of the Articles of Confederation. Dickinson, who had extensive writing experience, was chosen as the chairman and the primary author of this document, although he had been one of the delegates who did not sign the Declaration of Independence. Favoring a strong central government similar to that of Great Britain, much of Dickinson's draft was changed before ratification, although his insistence on a strong central government resurfaced later in his support of the U.S. Constitution.

- Richard Henry Lee - An influential planter and statesman from Virginia, Richard Henry Lee proposed the resolution that led both to the formulation of the Declaration of Independence and the Articles of Confederation. He served as a delegate to the Second Continental Congress, once serving as its president, and was one of a committee of three to review the Articles of Confederation for completeness before it was sent to the states for ratification. He later served as a delegate to the Constitutional Convention and received credit for drafting the 10th Amendment, which guaranteed states' rights.

- Daniel Shays - A farmer from western Massachusetts and a former captain in the Continental Army, Daniel Shays staged a protest and led a rebellion against what he perceived to be unfair taxation and debt repayment legislation.

- George Washington - The Commander-in-Chief of the Continental Army, this Virginia-born planter served a great symbolic role in early American history. He was keenly in favor of a strong national government, and exerted his influence toward that end when possible. He hosted the first successful interstate commerce meeting at his plantation home, Mount Vernon, and contributed tremendous prestige to the Constitutional Convention by agreeing to serve as one of the delegates from Virginia.

Events

- Annapolis Convention - Held in September 1786 at the request of Virginia, this meeting of the states aimed to improve the uniformity of commerce. Only twelve delegates came, and they proceeded to call a second meeting, to be held in May of 1787, for the purpose of revising the Articles.

- Jay-Gardoqui talks - John Jay, as diplomat to Spain, attempted to negotiate for American access to trade along the Mississippi River. Threatened by Americans moving westward, the Spanish diplomat Diego de Gardoqui recommended instead that Spain would establish trade with eastern U.S. ports, assist in removing Great Britain from the Great Lakes and assist in combating the Barbary Pirates. Southern and Western delegates in Congress viewed with contempt this plan that seemed to sacrifice their interests to the commercial interests of the Northeast.

- Maryland ratifies the Articles - Although the Articles of Confederation had been approved by 12 states by 1779, they could not go into effect until Maryland's ratification on March 1, 1781.

- Mount Vernon Conference - This name was applied to a meeting between Maryland and Virginia statesmen at George Washington's Mount Vernon Plantation. Originally scheduled to meet at Alexandria to discuss free navigation of the Potomac and Pocomoke Rivers, the delegates ended up resolving far broader issues of trade and mutual policy between the two states.

- Land Ordinance of 1784 - Proposed by Thomas Jefferson just a month after Virginia officially handed over western lands to congress, this ordinance established the process by which new lands would be divided into states, the process for surveying and sale, and the qualifications of new states to enter into Congress. This ordinance set the precedent to prohibit any attempts to colonize newly ceded lands.

- Northwest Ordinance - A revision of the earlier Land Ordinance of 1784, the Northwest Ordinance of 1787 refined some of the earlier qualifications for statehood. It further provided that a certain amount of land had to be reserved for public education, and that slavery was to be prohibited in this territory north of the Ohio River.

- Shays' Rebellion - Daniel Shays organized farmers throughout New England to protest legislation that increased taxes and demanded immediate debt-repayment. When the state legislature refused to respond, Shays and his armed followers closed the courts in western Massachusetts in protest of foreclosed properties. The rebellion came to a head when Shays was defeated while trying to seize a federal arsenal of weapons in Springfield, Massachusetts, on January 25, 1787. This rebellion demonstrated the weaknesses of the Articles of Confederation, and convinced many states of the need for a stronger central government.

- Treaty of Paris - This treaty, negotiated by Benjamin Franklin, John Jay and Samuel Adams, formally acknowledged the independence of the thirteen American colonies, and set the boundaries of the new nation at the Atlantic Ocean in the east, the Mississippi River in the west, Florida in the south, and Canada in the north.

As the first official document that defined the United States government, the Articles of Confederation both reflected the ideals and philosophies of the American Revolution and highlighted the practical difficulties of democratic government.

The idea of a union formed for mutual defense began in 1643 with the founding of the first colonial union, called the New England Confederation. Recognizing that a union would help the colonists to defend themselves against the threat of Indian attacks and French invasion, this confederation established the idea that unified strength was an effective power on the North American continent.

As the governments of the colonies evolved and established more power, they continued to rely on unions for mutual defense. At the beginning of the French and Indian War in 1754, additional colonies attended the Albany Congress for the purpose of forming a unified defense strategy against the French and Indians. The colonists learned an important lesson from this experience, and began to instinctively rely on the power of unions any time their rights were abused during the pre-Revolutionary era.

The governing body that eventually created the Articles of Confederation was based on this tradition of defensive unions, but was formed in a time of peace--not actually preparing for war. However, the Second Continental Congress, originally formed for the purpose of mutual defense of the thirteen colonies, suddenly found itself in 1776 waging a full-scale war and governing a nation.

Congress managed to successfully direct the Revolution effort and to prevent domestic anarchy by relying more on improvisation than on any codified system of laws. Consensus worked for the thirteen states when faced with the imposing task of defeating the British; however, when Congress approached the topic of drafting a constitution that would serve to direct the affairs of the nation, numerous controversies erupted over how to establish a balance of power between individual states and a national governing body. Despite all their experience in organizing unions for mutual defense, the representatives had no reliable source from which they could draft the plans for a new and democratic form of government.

The source of most of the controversies lay in that Americans held sharply contrasting interpretations of the implications of the American Revolution. Radicals believed that the purpose of the Revolution was to establish a government, unlike any other at the time, that placed power solidly in the hands of the people. Therefore, they interpreted the confederation to be like past unions, given power solely to provide for mutual defense. Sovereignty, they claimed, belonged close to the people in the hands of state governments, not in a strong central government. Conservatives, on the other hand, viewed the Revolution as an opportunity to remove control from a foreign elite and place it solidly in the hands of a centralized government in America. Like radicals, they believed in the importance of mutual defense, but wanted to extend the union's power to be able to manage all affairs of the new nation.

The shape of the new government, as established by the Articles of Confederation was largely influenced by the radicals' point of view. The Articles were submitted to the states for ratification in the midst of war with Great Britain. Most Americans greatly feared the possibility that their new American government would be as strong and as destructive to individual rights as the British one, and that the war would thus have been fought in vain. The government established and approved by the people in 1781, therefore, consisted of a national congress with extremely limited powers and thirteen independent state governments that held the balance of power.

The significance of the Articles of Confederation is that it provided enough of a structure for the nation to survive during those eight years, while the American people learned about the requirements to run an effective national government. The weaknesses inherent in the Articles of Confederation eventually provided the means for change.

In the midst of frustrating economic chaos and political confusion, individuals began to assert their own power against ineffective and unfair government created by the Articles. In Shays' Rebellion, Massachusetts farmers rebelled against a state legislature that seemed no different than Parliament in its unwillingness to change tax regulations and debt- repayment laws. Respected leaders from many states met at the Annapolis Convention in 1786 to try to determine a uniform system of commerce amongst themselves in the absence of a national policy. In both cases, Americans had realized that their liberties were threatened when not protected by a strong enough central government.

When delegates of the states met to revise the Articles of Confederation at the Constitutional Convention in May of 1787, they had gathered enough experience about the intricacies of government to more clearly define what the next government of the nation should and would do. It would not abandon the ideas of the American Revolution by placing too much power in the hands of the central government, but it also would not allow numerous competing government systems to tear the union apart.

Once again, the concept of union had evolved. Having learned from the failures of the government created by the Articles of Confederation, the delegates at the Constitutional Convention created a government that not only provided mutual defense against outside threats, it also created a central government strong enough to reign in and withstand internal threats and represent unified national interests to the world.

The representatives of the thirteen states agree to create a confederacy called the United States of America, in which each state maintains its own sovereignty and all rights to govern, except those rights specifically granted to Congress.

As these thirteen states enter into a firm "league of friendship" for the purpose of defending each other, there are standards that the states should follow to help maintain good relationships. Each state must recognize the legal proceedings and official records of every other state, and that the citizens of one state have the rights of citizenship in any state. Additionally, a state must help return runaway criminals to the state in which the crime was committed.

States have the right to select and send two to seven delegates to Congress each year. Each state has one vote in congress, and delegates can only serve for a period of three years in any interval of six years. Delegates have certain privileges while serving in Congress. They are guaranteed the right to freedom of speech and are immune from arrest for most petty crimes.

States are not allowed to conduct relationships with foreign nations without the permission of congress. They cannot wage war, negotiate peace, raise an army or navy, conduct diplomacy, or make an alliance with another state. However, they can make imposts on goods, as long as they do not interfere with foreign treaties. States must keep a local militia, and they may wage war if they need to quickly defend themselves.

During war, states have the right to appoint officers of colonel rank and below. Congress pays for war from a treasury that states contribute to relative to the value of land in their state.

Congress has the sole power to deal with foreign nations, including making war and peace, and to deal with Indian (Native American) affairs. Congress must maintain uniform standards of coins and measures, make the rules for the army and navy, and run the post office. Congress will help resolve interstate disputes only as a last resort, and has the sole right to hold trials for crimes committed at sea.

Congress can appoint a provisional Committee of the States to serve when Congress is not in session. Congress can appoint other committees made up of civilians to help run the nation, and a president who can serve for one year every interval of three years.

Congress determines the budget and will publish it regularly, along with the proceedings of its meetings. When Congress must request troops, it will do so relative to the number of white inhabitants in each state, and the states must provide those troops on the date indicated.

On the most important issues of foreign affairs, nine of thirteen delegates must agree.

If Canada chooses to join the United States, it will be admitted as an equal state.

Congress takes full responsibility for all debts from the American Revolution.

All states agree to follow the rules of the Articles and the decisions of Congress and to never violate the union.

Any changes to the Articles of Confederation must be agreed to in congress and approved by every state.

TIMELINE

- 1643: Formation of the New England Confederation Consisting of the Massachusetts Bay, Plymouth, New Haven and Connecticut colonies, this was the first union formed for the purpose of mutual defense against the French and Indians and as a forum for inter-colonial disputes. See more...

- June, 1754: Formation of the Albany Congress With delegates representing Massachusetts, New Hampshire, New York, New Jersey, Pennsylvania (including Delaware), Maryland, Virginia, Rhode Island, and Connecticut, this congress provided for unified negotiations with the Six Nations of the Iroquois Confederation.

- July 10, 1754: Publication of the Albany Plan of Union Drafted by Benjamin Franklin, this was the first document to detail a proposal of inter- colonial unity and to aim for a permanent union of American colonies.

- 1765: The Stamp Act Congress meets in New York City This congress developed a unified colonial strategy to appeal and protest the unfair legislation of Parliament. See more...

- 1774: Meeting of the First Continental Congress Meeting in Philadelphia, the First Continental Congress organized a unified colonial boycott, and agreed to meet again if their terms were not met.

- 1774: Presentation of the Galloway Plan to Congress This proposal for union included a plan to establish an American Parliament that would provide legislative authority over the colonies and empowered with veto power over the British Parliament in regards to colonial matters.

- May, 1775: The Second Continental Congress meets in Philadelphia This congress met to discuss further unified colonial appeals, to plan protests and to manage the beginnings of military action against the British. See more...

- January,1776: Publication of Articles of Confederation and Perpetual Union Benjamin Franklin drafts a plan of union that based representation in congress and contributions to the common treasury on the number of males in each state between sixteen and sixty years of age.

- June 7, 1776: Richard Henry Lee proposes independence in Congress Lee proposes a resolution that calls for drafting a declaration of independence and a plan of government and confederation.

- June 12, 1776: Committee appointed to draft Articles of Confederation Congress appoints a committee chaired by John Dickinson to draft the plan of confederation.

- July 2, 1776: Draft of the Articles submitted to Congress John Dickinson's draft of the Articles of Confederation is submitted to Congress for debate and revision.

- July 4, 1776: U.S. declares independence Thomas Jefferson's Declaration of Independence is published to the world.

- November 15, 1777: Congress completes the Articles of Confederation The final version of the Articles of Confederation is adopted by Congress and submitted to the states for ratification.

- July 9, 1778: Eight of the thirteen states officially ratify the Articles The delegations from New Hampshire, Massachusetts Bay, Rhode Island, and Providence Plantations, Connecticut, New York, Pennsylvania, Virginia and South Carolina sign and ratify the Articles of Confederation.

- February 22, 1779: Delaware ratifies the Articles Delaware ratifies the Articles of Confederation, and Maryland is the only state yet to ratify. The confederation does not take effect until all states have ratified.

- January 2, 1781: Virginia cession of land Virginia cedes a portion of its land west of the Appalachian Mountains to Congress.

- March 1, 1781: Establishment of the U.S. Government Maryland ratifies the Articles of Confederation, formally establishing the first government of the United States.

- October 17, 1781: Surrender at Yorktown British General Charles Cornwallis surrenders to the Continental Army at Yorktown, Virginia, ending the war between the United States and Great Britain.

- 1782: Establishment of the Bank of North America Founded by the Secretary of Finance, Robert Morris, this bank helped to stabilize the commerce of the United States.

- March, 1783: Newburgh Mutiny The army stationed at Newburgh threatened mutiny because they had not received their pay and were only stopped by George Washington's effective persuasion to remain loyal to the patriotic cause.

- June, 1783: Congress forced from Philadelphia A mutinous group of Pennsylvania troops, demanding pay, forced Congress to leave Philadelphia. President John Dickinson refused the assistance of all on the state militia, as he feared they were not reliable. Congress retreated to Princeton.

- September 3, 1783: Signing of Treaty of Paris The Treaty of Paris establishes the terms of peace between the United States and Great Britain.

- March 1784: Acquisition of the Northwest Territory Congress officially acquires the land ceded by Virginia north and west of the Ohio River.

- April 23,1784: Passage of the Land Ordinance Drafted by Thomas Jefferson and accepted by Congress, this ordinance is the first to establish the process to administer newly acquired lands.

- March 25, 1785: Meeting of Mount Vernon Conference Representatives of Maryland and Virginia met at George Washington's plantation to resolve conflicts over the navigation of the Potomac and Pocomoke Rivers.

- September 11, 1786: Meeting of the Annapolis Convention New York, New Jersey, Pennsylvania, Delaware and Virginia, meet to discuss uniform trade regulations, but agree to appeal to all states to meet again to discuss broader reforms.

- January 25, 1787: Shays' Rebellion Daniel Shays and other armed farmers from western Massachusetts are defeated in their attempt to conquer an arsenal of weapons in Springfield, Massachusetts.

- May 25, 1787: First meeting of the Constitutional Convention Delegates from all states except Rhode Island meet in Philadelphia for the purpose of revising the Articles of Confederation.

- July 13, 1787: Passage of the Northwest Ordinance This serves as a revision of the earlier ordinance and establishes, amongst other things, that slavery is prohibited from the new region.

- September 17, 1787: Draft of constitution submitted to the states The Constitutional Convention sends its draft of the U.S. Constitution to the states for ratification.

ARTICLES 1-2 (STATE SOVEREIGNTY)

By signing the document, the delegates of each state agree to the form of government described in the Articles of Confederation and therefore commit their state to the permanent union of states that will be called the United States.

The form of government created by this document is called a confederacy, or a loose organization of independent states. Each state will maintain sovereignty, which means that the state maintains the power to run its own affairs. Any rights, privileges and powers that are not specifically given to the Congress by the Articles of Confederation are maintained by the state.

Where the balance of power would rest in the newly formed union--whether it would rest in the state governments or in a centralized national government--proved to be one of the most challenging and divisive issues that the Second Continental Congress faced. The debate between state power and central or national power continued to occupy politicians throughout the nation's early history, and vestiges of it are found in today's big government versus small government debate.

When Richard Henry Lee proposed independence and the establishment of a new government to replace the King and Parliament, the debate was largely theoretical. Did the central authority that previously rested in the hands of the King and Parliament get passed down directly to the Second Continental Congress? Or did the power to govern rest directly with the people protected by the authority in each independent state? Those who favored the argument for a strong central government were called conservatives, and feared that the absence of a strong central government would lead to anarchy in the states. Those who favored states' rights were called radicals, and felt that simply replacing one strong central government with another defeated the purposes of the American Revolution.

The original draft of the Articles of Confederation was written by the conservative John Dickinson and described a confederation that placed a significant amount of power in the hands of the central government, or Congress. In this first draft, states were allowed to keep as many of their laws, rights and customs as they choose, and to have the sole authority to regulate their internal police, as long as this power did not interfere with the Articles. Congress would represent the supreme authority on any issue. This was quickly criticized by radicals in Congress for providing no distinct authority to the states separate from that of Congress and for giving states no protection against an all-powerful central government. By the time the articles were distributed for review by state legislatures, the radicals had insisted that the balance of power be shifted to favor the states over the central government. This shift was reflected in the wording of Article II.

The Second Continental Congress operated mostly as a strong central government without any legal authority before the Articles of Confederation, but radicals were unwilling to put that strength into written law. Not only had the Congress raised a military, appointed military leaders, requisitioned supplies and administered all war efforts, it had also tended to foreign diplomacy, establishing currency and a post office, and had even begun to establish administrative departments to manage certain areas of national government. The power of Congress to do these things during wartime was never questioned. But when it came time to write a constitution that would govern during times of peace, radicals could not see the necessity of having so much power concentrated in the hands of the central government.

This dislike of a centralized government was rooted in the radicals' belief that the union of states was formed solely for the purpose of common defense against Great Britain. Radicals argued that the purpose of the Revolution was to form more democratic governments, by definition requiring a close relationship between the people and their government. They argued that a strong centralized government exerting its power over many thousands of people would simple cease to be democratic, because the authority would lie too far from the people. Let the states govern their own affairs, they said, and the liberties of the people are most likely to be protected. To radicals, the only purpose of the confederation was to provide a foundation for mutual defense and foreign policy should they be threatened by an outside power again. They interpreted the Articles of Confederation as a pact between thirteen separate states that agreed to delegate certain powers for specific purposes, not one that granted general powers to a central government.

After the American Revolution, many people feared the prospect of another strong central government that would simply replace the British government. This fear was reflected in the final draft of the articles, which not only strongly claimed that sovereignty rested with the state (in Article II), but also effectively stripped the congress of any effective powers whatsoever in the remaining articles of the document.

The ineffective and disunited governance that resulted between 1781 and 1789 proved to the people that they could effectively disempower the national government by placing many checks and controls on its power. However, it also demonstrated to most people that their rights and liberties would be threatened in the absence of a national government that could serve as a supreme authority over all of the states.

By successfully removing all significant powers from congress, the radicals won the first round of the nation versus state debate. However, a few years of experience in self-government convinced many that, in practice, the theory of basing power in the hands of the people did not work. By 1786, many who had been radicals would clamor for giving more effective power to the central government and to place sovereignty with the nation. As such, the spirit expressed by Dickinson's original draft of the Articles of Confederation, which he could not persuade others to accept on purely theoretical terms, was later expressed in the U.S. Constitution.

ARTICLES 3-4 (INTERSTATE RELATIONS)

Each of the thirteen states that make up the United States commit to a firm "friendship" with each of the other states. They are united for the purposes of defending themselves against military threats, protecting their independence, and ensuring the general well being of all of the states and good relationships between them. Each state commits to help any other state to defend itself against any attack on the basis of their religion, their right to self-government, their freedom to trade, or for any other reason.

To ensure friendly relationships and good business between people living in different states, any free person living in one state, not counting slaves, has the same rights as a free person living in any other state.

If a person charged as a criminal or traitor in one state runs away to another state, the government of the first state has the authority to bring the criminal back to the state in which the crime was committed.

Any official records, documents, trials and decisions made by the court system in one state will be recognized by each of the other states.

Delegates to congress expressed a lofty idealism when they talked about the "friendship" of the thirteen states and of the states' willingness to work together for their mutual benefit and towards the common good. The reality of the situation was that each state jealously guarded its own power, had no qualms about usurping power from or abusing the power of less powerful states, and ruthlessly supported its own cause at the expense of the common good. The bonds of friendship, rather than being enforced by a structured and centralized government, faltered because of the unwillingness of states to focus on their role as part of a bigger nation.

The Articles of Confederation were worthless in enforcing good interstate relations because they did not endow Congress with the authority to regulate interstate trade or to intervene in questions of interstate disputes, except as a last resort. The Articles also made it too difficult for Congress to easily pass legislation beneficial to the common good. Furthermore, Congress itself was so plagued by poor interstate relations and low morale that it was often unable to address areas that did fall under its direct control.

The failure of a supreme authority to regulate interstate commerce became a problem because, although Congress was endowed with the sole authority to negotiate foreign treaties, it did not have the power to control trade between individual states and foreign countries. States were solely granted the right to levy imposts on foreign goods, and they freely interpreted this to mean goods from other countries as well as other states in the United States. States insisted on printing their own paper money and requiring it in kind for payment of tariffs of purchase of goods. Bordering states that shared the same rivers struggled to exert control by imposing competing tolls. In addition to a variety of different customs regulations and currencies, state governments sought commercial advantage over other states, and based their policies on what would bring their state the biggest rewards, not what was best for the common economic good.

These interstate trade wars developed because states with clear commercial advantages abused their power. The disadvantaged states without ports could not import goods directly into their state and had to rely on neighboring states with ports. These neighboring states often charged to transport goods either into or out of the state. The only recourse for the states without ports was to retaliate by enacting their own tariffs on imported goods. Therefore, the consumer was caught up in a confusing and costly interstate battle resulting from interstate jealousies and a system of commerce that lacked uniformity. Consumers, farmers, and merchants bore the brunt of these policies, but appeals for change accomplished nothing.

Committees of merchants organized to appeal for a more regulated system of commerce. Nationalist politicians did what they could to make improvements to the system. Alexander Hamilton tried in 1781, and again in 1783, to draft an amendment that granted Congress the right to levy and collect an impost. This would not only provide some regulation to the world of trade, but would also provide Congress with a much-needed source of revenue. Many states were surprisingly eager to relinquish their control of commerce in order to relieve some of the confusion, but it required unanimous approval before it could become law. Unfortunately, Rhode Island opposed both measures, insisting that this infringed upon the sovereignty of the states. The inability of Congress to make much needed change without a unanimous decision, not to mention their inability to regulate commerce, fueled interstate tension further. Rhode Island especially irked the majority of states for not graciously succumbing to the desires of the other twelve states.

Rhode Island again became the source of interstate frustration when it passed debt-repayment laws that required all creditors to accept the highly inflated and worthless Rhode Island currency. This attempt to quickly pay of its debt demonstrated a naivete about the fine points of finance, and appalled commercial men in other states. It would have been better for Rhode Island's line of credit had the state tried to pay off the actual value it owed over a longer period of time. Instead, creditors from other nations and other states were forced either to take full payment in paper currency, of a greatly diminished value, or give up their repayment altogether. Rhode Island established criminal penalties for refusing to accept its currency and removed the right to trial-by-jury in cases related to debt-collection. Acting solely in its own interest, Rhode Island jeopardized not only the United States' line of credit with foreign creditors but also threatened to remove civil liberties. Without a strong central government to control the behavior of individual states, there was no recourse when an individual state acted against the general welfare of the United States.

The same lack of "friendship" between states existed between delegates to Congress as well. Sometimes openly hostile to delegates from other states, openly criticizing others in letters and other public forums, the delegates did not behave like friends, or even like polite acquaintances. A general lack of camaraderie plagued Congress in the form of low attendance and states refusing to compromise their own best interest. Congress was often unable to exert the few powers it did have to sooth interstate rivalries simply because of lack of a quorum. In other cases, Congress was unable to act objectively because it was so easily manipulated by powerful states. When appealed to by one state, Congress had to carefully weigh that state's influence (especially financial) when deciding whether to intervene. For example, when Vermont, which had been formed by land taken from New York, appealed to Congress to be accepted as a new state, New York withheld its requisitioned funds to pressure Congress into deciding on its behalf. The "perpetual union of firm friendship" lacked both the friendship and the coercive power necessary to regulate interstate relations. Relying on the pure motives of states, motives that were in fact driven by self-interest and jealousy, destroyed the possibility of a firm league of friendship.

Ironically, one of the only attempts of self-regulation between two states actually succeeded in becoming a uniform policy and became the first step towards a revision of the Articles of Confederation. This self-regulation was also deemed technically illegal by the Articles, which did not allow states to contract treaties outside of the forum of Congress. Nevertheless, leaders from Maryland and Virginia agreed to meet in Alexandria to discuss a mutually agreed upon regulation of commerce on the Potomac and Pocomoke Rivers. As was typical of the time, the Virginia delegation did not get the message and failed to attend. When the Maryland delegates arrived with no reception, they contacted two of the Virginia delegates and persuaded them to go ahead with the meeting anyway, which they did at Mount Vernon. The results of the meeting went far beyond the original goals; not only did the delegates resolve the dispute relating to the two rivers, they also established a uniform policy of commerce and trade regulations in all areas of exchange between the two states. Additionally, their success inspired them to call a convention of all states interested in discussing issues of common commerce in Annapolis. This Annapolis Convention is what eventually led to the call for a Constitutional Convention in May 1787. Ironically, it seems that the states were eager to befriend each other in order to work towards their mutual interests, but somehow the Articles reinforced jealousies rather than effectively encouraging the friendship necessary to enact uniform policies towards the common good.

ARTICLE 5 (REPRESENTATION IN CONGRESS)

Each state can decide how it wants to select its delegates, but it must do so once a year, prior to the annual meeting of Congress on the first Monday of November.

States can send between two and seven delegates to Congress. A delegate cannot serve for more than three years in every six-year period. A delegate cannot hold another position in the United States government for which he receives any kind of payment or benefit, either directly or indirectly.

Each state has one vote in Congress, irrespective of how many delegates are sent.

Delegates' freedom of speech is protected while they are serving in Congress. Delegates may not be arrested or put in prison while they are in Congress, or traveling to and from, unless they have committed treason, a felony, or have been guilty of breach of the peace.

Article 5 strongly supports the sovereignty of states clause of Article 2. Instead of outlining a national system of elections to Congress, which would be more reflective of the overall population of the United States, the Articles of Confederation require that each state provide at least two delegates, regardless of the amount of land, population size, or wealth of that state.

Although John Dickinson's original draft of the Articles of Confederation included equal representation in Congress regardless of state size, other conservatives were deeply troubled by the implications of this form of representation. This issue became another debate between the radicals on one side and the conservatives on the other. The radicals argued that since the government of the United States was a loose confederation of equal and sovereign states, they must be equally represented in that confederation. Furthermore, radicals insisted that Congress did not have the authority to determine how elections were to be carried out in the individual states, each of which had its own constitution and means for holding elections.

Conservatives, on the other hand, hoped for a strong centralized government and felt that only a system of "national" representation would effectively represent the people. In this form of representation, elections would be administered by Congress and would be the same in each state: the people would be represented by a number of delegates proportionate to the population in their state. This method of representation places sovereignty more firmly in the nation than the state, and was deeply opposed by radicals.

The evolution of Benjamin Franklin's thinking on the topic of representation is interesting because it reflects the transition between a colonial mindset and a young national mindset. When Franklin drafted the Albany Plan of Union in 1754, he called for equal representation from each colony to that congress (two per colony). However, when he drafted the Articles of Confederation and Perpetual Union in early 1776, he called for a system of representation in which delegates were chosen annually in proportion to their population of males between the age of sixteen and sixty (one delegate to every five thousand). Franklin clearly distinguished between the union created during the colonial period, which didn't have much overall authority to begin with and could be a loose confederation, and the necessity for the young nation to place more authority in the hands of a central government.

Article 5 also established some precedents for our current national government. The years a delegate could serve were restricted (term limits), they had limited immunity from legal proceedings while Congress was in session, and their freedom of speech was guaranteed while in Congress.

ARTICLE 6 (POWERS DENIED TO STATES)

States are denied certain powers under the Articles of Confederation. States may not send ambassadors to foreign countries, receive foreign ambassadors, or make any kind of arrangement, meeting or treaty with any king, prince or state. No person or state may accept any gift, including titles of nobility, from a foreign state. Neither Congress nor any state can give people noble titles.

A state may not enter into any treaties or alliances with another state without the approval of Congress.

A state may not make imposts on trade that will interfere with the terms of foreign treaties made by Congress.

A state cannot maintain any warships, or other military forces (troops) during peacetime unless Congress has determined it necessary to defend that state, its trade or forts in that state. Each state must maintain a "well-regulated and disciplined" militia, and a sufficient amount of supplies for that militia.

A state does not have the power to make war without the permission of Congress, unless it is forced to defend itself against a surprise attack and cannot wait for the permission of Congress.

While the focus of Article 6 is on the limitations of state power, it also reflects certain historical realities that faced the young nation, and addresses the threats, both internal and external, that the nation was vulnerable to in its early years.

One of the most important and agreed upon ideas in the Articles of Confederation was its anti- nobility sentiment. Colonists, even the most conservative, understood how a system of hereditary nobility would serve to sharpen class distinctions, limit economic and political freedom, and corrupt a democratic government. They wanted to break from the tradition of the British parliament, where the House of Lords, made up only of nobles, had clear advantages over the House of Commons, comprised of people elected from each region. Although many colonists still favored an "elite" group holding greater power than the masses, they preferred that the elite group be defined by actual property holdings and wealth, rather than by a title of nobility.

Another strongly held belief by most colonists was the importance of protecting the state, and therefore the people, through the establishment of a well-regulated militia. Based on the tradition of the minutemen, the militia clause recognizes the constant need of a state to be on guard against military threats and invasion. Although states could not raise armies and navies, they were required to have a group of soldiers prepared in case of threats from within or without. This would also protect the state governments against a strong national military.

During the time of the Articles of Confederation, the states faced many sources of potential invasion. The nations that had fought in the American Revolution and still occupied parts of North America were the most threatening. Great Britain, although agreeing to abandon the forts in the Great Lakes region, refused to leave. They therefore posed a military threat from the north (Canada) and the west. Not only were they able to amass troops on the northern and western borders of the United States if they chose, but they also maintained their trade posts in the Great Lakes Region and could provide Native American tribes with weapons to be used against the states.

Great Britain could also serve as an outside alliance for disgruntled states. When Ethan Allen formally declared Vermont independent from New York, Great Britain promised to recognize its independence if it would become an ally. Vermont tried to use this proposed alliance to force Congress to accept its independence at this time, but Great Britain lost interest in Vermont once the war ended. However, the potential for powerful outside alliances was there, and threatened the internal stability of the United States.

Spain, holding territory to the south and west of the United States also posed a threat. Although Spain had been an ally of the United States during the American Revolution, it feared the expansion of the United States west beyond the Mississippi. Spain tried to woo those westerners into Spanish citizenship in order to strengthen its hold on the Mississippi River region. In the Jay-Gardoqui talks, Spain attempted to block all American trade from the Mississippi River, in hopes of coercing American farmers living in the western regions of the United States to become Spanish citizens in order to sustain their livelihood.

Furthermore, most Native American tribes were allies of the British, and felt threatened by the American tendency to grab great amounts of western land for their ever-increasing population. Border states, especially to the South (Georgia, North Carolina), constantly feared the threat of a Native American attack or invasion. The qualification that states are not empowered to wage war, unless under imminent attack, refers to the very distinct possibility that a state would find itself under attack without a formal declaration of war, or enough time to ask for permission of Congress to defend itself.

A more remote fear of internal division is alluded to in the clause about states entering into alliances with each other. Those who drafted the Articles were well aware of the power of unity in opposing a governing force. They anticipated that states might become unhappy with the central government. In this light, the writers of the Articles attempted to eliminate the possibility that states could join in unity against the government. However, the wording is weak and emphasizes the inability of Congress to enforce its rulings. This clause implies that as long as states inform congress of their alliance, the alliance is okay. Even if Congress prohibited the alliance, how could it force the alliance to end?

The trade meeting between Maryland and Virginia that took place at Mount Vernon in 1786 is a perfect example of what was disallowed by the Articles of Confederation. Congress did nothing at all to stop this meeting or alliance, and when an additional meeting was scheduled at Annapolis, inviting all of the states into a commercial alliance, Congress still did nothing. Congress had good reason to perceive this alliance as a threat, since it served to undermine its authority by re-making the Articles of Confederation. However, in its powerless position, Congress did nothing.

Article 6 is also significant in the way in which it expresses the relationship between Congress and the states with regard to commerce. States are not allowed to partake in any sort of foreign diplomacy or treaty making--that power is reserved for Congress. However, Congress is not granted the power to make imposts on foreign trade. Therefore, each state is allowed to determine its own imposts, as long as it doesn't interfere with the terms of foreign treaties made by Congress.

The phrasing of the clause on imposts leaves a huge flexibility of interpretation, allowing states to determine their imposts. The allowance of such flexibility demonstrates the powerlessness of Congress when it came to taxes of any kind. All of the other clauses in this Article assert that a state may not do something (such as make war), without the approval of Congress. In the impost clause the necessary approval of Congress is noticeably missing because Congress does not possess any authority over imposts. Therefore, the judgment is left to the states, not to Congress, about the permissibility of each impost.

Article 6, in attempting to define the limitations of state powers, actually does more to indicate the threats facing the young nation and the powerless nature of Congress. Even the powers given exclusively to Congress, such as making war and peace, are transferable to a state when Congress approves. A weak Congress lacking the power of enforcement could have been powerless to stop a state that usurped the congressional power of making war. Fortunately, the only usurpation of power that it was unable to stop, the Mount Vernon Conference, ultimately resulted in a strengthening of national power.

ARTICLES 7-8 (WAR PREPARATION)

When raising an army to defend the United States, each state legislature has the authority to name all colonels and lesser officers in any way they choose to lead the troops recruited from that state.

The common treasury will supply any money needed to pay for war or to defend the country, when allowed by Congress. Each state has the responsibility of contributing to the common treasury based on the relative value of all the land within that state. Congress will determine the method of surveying land and estimating the total value per state. The taxes to support the common treasury will be made and collected by each state legislature by a date decided by Congress.

Probably the most taboo topic throughout the duration of the American Revolution was taxation. Because it served as the impetus that brought the colonists to declare their independence from Great Britain, "taxation without representation" was a rallying cry that few forgot when visualizing their ideal government.

Most agreed that taxation was necessary to support a stable government. However, they also believed that the power to tax should be in the hands of the government that represents the people. Since the radicals had successfully placed sovereignty solidly in the state governments, people accepted, in theory, the right of the state legislature to levy taxes. However, they outright rejected the possibility of a central government levying any sort of taxes whatsoever.

Since one of the primary purposes of the Confederation Congress was to provide for mutual defense, it also had to establish a financial means to support its purpose. Hamstrung without the power to tax, Congress relied on requisitions of money from each state. Powerless to enforce its requisitions, Congress and the administrators of finance often resorted to begging states to pay. While this served to substantially weaken the ability of Congress to carry out its few responsibilities, it also reflected the unresolved debate of how states should be taxed.

One of the most divisive debates that occurred in the ratification process of the Articles of Confederation was the means by which the amount of a state's tax contribution would be determined. This issue was also closely linked to representation in congress and the requisitioning of troops. At issue was the means by which political and economic power would be measured. For the purposes of taxation, Congress had to decide whether labor or land was the best indicator of economic strength. This debate between land and labor faced head-on the issue of sectionalism and slavery.

Northern states had well-cultivated and productive land, but southern states had tremendous labor resources in the form of slavery. Southern states also held immense tracts of land, but they did not have the same productivity value of northern states because they were not as densely populated or cultivated. In order to protect its own best interests, states supported the means of taxation that required them to pay the least taxes.

Northern states argued that taxation should be based on the number of laborers in each state, including slaves, because only through labor is land turned into economic value. Southern states countered this argument by stating slaves were property, and unless Northern states agreed to count their horses and cows for the taxation purposes, slaves could not be fairly counted. Aside from this obviously derogatory statement about the nature of slavery, the southern point of view clearly demonstrates that they would count slaves if it was to their advantage for representation purposes, but not when it would take a large chunk out of their profit from slavery.

Southern states strongly argued that it was the value of property that determined the potential wealth of a state, because property was more permanent than laborers. The land argument put the burden of taxation on the Northerners, who obviously resented that they would have to shoulder the burden of debt while the lucrative southern industry of cash crops would continuously prosper. Congress retained the power to determine the value of land, and therefore determine the relative contribution of taxes from each state. However, without the power to enforce the collection of taxes, which was a sole power of the state, Congressional finances became a large and problematic issue under the Articles of Confederation.

ARTICLE 9 (POWERS OF CONGRESS)

Only Congress has the right to make peace and make war (except in those cases described in Article 6), to send and receive ambassadors, and to make treaties and alliances with foreign nations. Congress also has the exclusive right to give permission to private ships to attack enemy ships, and to oversee trials related to crimes on the sea.

Congress will help resolve conflicts between states relating to boundaries, jurisdiction and other issues, but only as a last resort.

Other powers of Congress include the right to determine how much precious metal is in each coin, and the value of coins made by them or any state. Congress determines the standard of weights and measures. Congress has authority over trade and other affairs involving Indians, as long as the Indians are not residents of any of the states and that Congress does not infringe on the states' rights by getting involved. Congress establishes the post offices in each state, and can charge postage on items handled by the post office to help pay expenses. Congress appoints all officers of the army except regimental officers appointed by states, commissions all officers that serve in the army or navy, makes the rules to regulate the army and navy, and has the sole power to direct the army and navy.

The Congress has the authority to create a committee called the Committee of the States that serves in place of Congress when Congress is not in session. The Committee is made up of one delegate from each state. The Congress can also appoint other committees and civil officers as needed to manage the affairs of the United States. Congress can appoint a president, but he may only serve for one year every interval of three years. Congress has the authority to determine how much money is needed to run the United States, to spend the necessary amounts, and to borrow money on the credit of the United States. Every six months, a finance report will be published for all the states. The Congress has the right to build the army and navy, deciding how many forces are needed and requesting the amount from each state, proportional to the number of white inhabitants in that state. Once the request for troops is made, the state has the responsibility to appoint the regimental officers, organize and equip the soldiers, and march to the designated place at the time requested by Congress.

In order for Congress to act on the specifically listed powers above, nine of the thirteen states must agree. Issues of any other type, except for the request to adjourn from day to day, must be decided by the majority of states.

Congress has the power to stop a session of Congress or move it to any other place in the United States, but Congress cannot be out of session for more than six months at a time. Each month, Congress will publish their proceedings, unless a matter of security requires secrecy. These proceedings will include the voting patterns of each delegate if it is recorded by request of a delegate, and each delegate may get a copy of the proceedings to present to the state legislature.

What seems at first glance to be a lengthy list of powers granted to Congress under the Articles of Confederation was in actuality little more than a grant of limited powers necessary for the mutual defense of the United States. The Articles did not grant Congress the powers necessary for the effective governance of the United States.

In Article 9, the debate over the strength of the state versus the nation is articulated in a detailed list of precisely which powers Congress does and does not have. Although granted with the sole power to act in affairs of an international nature, Congress holds little authority over the day-to-day management of a nation. The radicals wanted it that way, inserting as many checks against strong governmental power as they could.

The most glaring deficiency of power is that the Congress served only a legislative role, and only in a narrowly defined area. Evolving out of a congress that united solely for the purpose of winning a war, the final draft of the Articles of Confederation did not recognize the need for a more expansive central government.

The only power of taxation belonging to Congress came in the form of postage, the revenue of which could solely be used to support the post office. Congress only possessed judicial power in cases involving felonies and piracy on the high seas and in cases related to the regulations it established for the army and the navy. The Articles imply that Congress had the authority to judge matters related to the boundaries of states or their jurisdiction, but only as a last resort. And, Congress lacked the executive power to enforce such decisions. Even if Congress were to rule in matters of interstate conflict, it would be up to the states to abide by that ruling.

Closely related to boundary disputes, but conspicuously absent from the Articles of Confederation, is whether Congress had the authority to acquire and administer land claimed by multiple parties. As the single most divisive issue facing the Congress when they drafted the Articles, it also served to delay Maryland's ratification, thereby delaying the Articles being put into effect, by four years.

At issue was a conflict between "landed" states, whose original charters granted them land west of the Appalachian Mountains (and in some cases to the Pacific Ocean), and the "landless" states, whose boundaries were clearly defined and finite. The situation was made even more complicated by the Proclamation of 1763, in which King George III dictated that land west of the Appalachian Mountains was off-limits to American settlers even if it was included in their colonial charters. Private speculators and corporations took advantage of this no-man's land to purchase property directly from Native Americans, banking on the fact that when the area was opened up, they would already own huge stakes of it.

The declaration of war complicated things further. Did the declaration of war return land to each state as originally chartered? Did the declaration of war automatically endow Congress, as the successor to the British king, with authority over the land referred to in the Proclamation of 1763? The "landless" states believed that the land belonged to Congress, and further bolstered their argument by claiming that disputed land should be shared by all the states. The "landed" states, which also happened to favor state sovereignty, argued that the declaration of war meant that each state returned to the sovereignty, rights, and privileges as granted in its original colonial charter. In other words, the "landed" states claimed the land as legally theirs.

The "landless" states had a variety of concerns regarding this situation. Primarily, they were concerned that influential speculators living within their states would lose the land they had purchased from Native Americans before the war. Additionally, Congress decided to allow soldiers to be compensated with land instead of cash, and "landless" states did not have the excessive land to give that states like Virginia and North Carolina did. This unfair economic advantage threatened the economic future of the "landless" states as well.

Fiercely jealous of the income potential of the "landed" states, "landless" states frequently argued that they would be swallowed up by their more powerful neighbors. "Landed" states could not only gain an economic advantage from the land, but with a broader base of income to draw revenue from, they could also use lower taxes to entice residents away from the "landless" states. The "landless" states would be left in an unfair position of being economically disadvantaged, and would be forced into a perpetual cycle of levying higher taxes on a increasingly smaller population until they went broke.

States like Maryland, Delaware and New Jersey claimed that Congress had to resolve the competing claims over western lands as part of the Articles of Confederation. Congress strongly resisted doing so, and individual "landed" states proceeded to deal with the land as though it belonged to them. Virginia even went so far as to hold trials to determine if the claims of speculation companies were legal. In all cases, Virginia determined that the land was unlawfully sold and purchased, and that any claims but those authorized by Virginia were worthless.

Finding no remedy in the Articles, Maryland withheld its signature in protest. Although this concerned the other states, the "landed states" still refused to give up their land to Congress. Instead, the solution was born out of military necessity. When the southern states began to feel the power of the British invasion late in the war, a French diplomat threatened to remove the protection of the French navy from Maryland's seas if Maryland did not sign the Articles. Meanwhile, some Virginians began to see that it would be more of a burden, and potentially bad for democracy, to have to govern over too much land. Around the same time as Maryland signed the Articles, Virginia ceded its land north of the Ohio River to Congress.

The Virginia cession of land is significant in that it allowed Congress to pass the Land Ordinance of 1784 and the Northwest Ordinance of 1787, both providing a process for the fair and equal entry of new states to the union. The cession also partially increased congressional authority in the acquisition of new lands. In conjunction with the clause relating to congressional jurisdiction over Native American tribes (who did not live in one of the states), Congress gained almost sole authority over land and issues west of the Appalachian Mountains.

However advantageous this authority was to new American settlers on this western land, it severely limited the rights of Native Americans. Native American tribes, although many lived within the boundaries of the United States, were defined and classified as "foreign nations." This precedent continued throughout U.S. history, as Native Americans were continually denied citizenship and inclusion in the U.S. Government. Having the authority to deal with "Indian Affairs," it is a shame that Congress did not make better use of it.

Other precedents were established in Article 9 as well. The Articles provide for a president to be elected from amongst the delegates in Congress. Although this president is not endowed with any executive authority, he is limited in the number of terms he may serve. Furthermore, the practice of publicly communicating both the proceedings of Congress (including voting records), and the financial state of the union were good democratic policies and precedents because they made Congress accountable to the people who elected them.

Although the western land issue was one of the most controversial issues relating to the Articles of Confederation, Article 9 also included the outcome of the controversy relating to the requisitioning of troops. The Articles dictate that troops will be requisitioned in proportion to the total number of white inhabitants of each state. Non-slave states opposed this as unfair because while white males in slave states went off to war, their slaves could continue to work on the plantations. In contrast, when white males in non- slave states went off to war, the productivity of their farms would suffer due to the loss of the chief laborer. This issue was related to issues of representation in Congress and the requisition of funds as discussed in other articles.

Within Article 9 is perhaps one of the biggest stumbling blocks that Congress experienced in trying to run the daily affairs of the government. The Articles dictate that in most matters over which Congress has authority, nine of the thirteen states must agree to any particular action. This extremely high percentage made it difficult for Congress to act or pass legislation; the problem was further complicated by the Congress' frequent inability to reach a quorum (mandatory minimum attendance) because of low attendance.

Despite the lengthy description of powers in Article 9, Congress was actually quite weak. It was a political body crippled by an inability to execute its laws, hemmed in by a limited range of authority, impeded by the absence of delegates, and trapped without the necessary unanimity to extend its legislative reach to matters beyond providing for the mutual defense.

ARTICLE 10 (THE COMMITTEE OF THE STATES)

When Congress is not in session, a committee called the Committee of the States has the full authority to act in its place, and take on additional powers as necessary if nine of the states agree. However, the Committee of the States can never adopt any powers that specifically require the consent of nine states while Congress is in session.

Under John Dickinson's draft of the Articles of Confederation, this body was called the Council of State, and was endowed with permanent bureaucratic and executive control over a variety of matters. It was changed to the Committee of the States and vested with minimal powers to sufficient only to simply manage the affairs under the authority of Congress when Congress was not in session.

Dickinson's Council would have been in charge of any matter agreed upon by nine of thirteen states, and was probably inspired by the bureaucratic committees that had existed during the war to help with administrative duties. Dickinson's Council could have been empowered to administer matters of commerce, trade, education, or any other area that Congress deemed appropriate. However, radicals viewed this vague extension of congressional authority as threatening to the state's sovereignty.

Therefore, the Committee of the States, as described in the final draft of the Articles, had even stricter restrictions placed on it than Congress. The Committee could never make war or peace, could never coin or regulate money, and could never appoint the military commanders. In their zeal to protect themselves from centralized power falling into the hands of a body not directly controlled by the states, the radicals also stripped the national government of the only semblance of executive authority it had.

Under the guise of managing matters that fell under the authority of Congress, bureaucratic committees operated both during and after the war. Originally, delegates to Congress were required to sit on committees. Over time, this policy evolved toward bureaucracy, first to the establishment of committees or boards that included appointed outsiders, and then to the appointment of a non-delegate as single head of each department. This secretary system outlasted the Continental Congress, and the Confederation Congress appointed a Secretary of War and Foreign Affairs, a Secretary of the Post Office, and a Secretary of Finance.

The Committee of the States met only once during the summer of 1784 and suffered the same low attendance as Congress. It never reached its required quorum to accomplish any of the administrative tasks assigned to it.

ARTICLE 11 (CANADA)

If Canada chooses to declare its independence and agrees to the terms of the Articles of Confederation, it can join the union and become a fully sovereign state like the other thirteen states. This offer does not include any other colony but Canada, unless nine states agree to extend this offer to another colony.

Establishing both the means by which a new state could enter the "union" on equal footing, and an attempt for military security, Article 11 specifically targets one issue in a way that no other article does.

Annexing Canada and formally absorbing it into the folds of the United States would have increased the power of the U.S. tremendously. The inclusion of Canada in the union would significantly increase the U.S. resources of land, people, types of industry, and available ports. It would increase the tax base of Congress as well as contribute its valuable resources to the overall economic good of the U.S. Furthermore, the annexation of Canada would help to significantly eliminate the biggest threat to American Independence: the presence of Great Britain on the North American continent.

If Canada had overthrown British rule in the 1780s and joined the United States as a sovereign state, the British would have had no further holdings of land in North America. However, after the war, the British continued to violate the Treaty of Paris by maintaining forts in the western territory of the United States. The British controlled the Great Lakes, which bordered the U.S. and Canada and the St. Lawrence River, thereby giving them powerful control over trade in the interior of North America. The United States aimed to eliminate the presence of as many of its competitors as possible. Unfortunately, Canada had no interest in joining the United States and remained a British colony. The British presence north and west of the United States continued to be a problem, and eventually led to the War of 1812.

What this Article did accomplish, however, was to establish the precedent by which new states would be absorbed into the union. With this precedent, rather than representing a governing body with fixed limits, the United States would be able to expand and absorb sovereign states on an equal basis, instead of as colonies. This idea was later put into practice in Thomas Jefferson's Land Ordinance of 1784, which provided new states with the same right to self-governance and representation in congress as those enjoyed by older states.

ARTICLE 12 (DEBTS OF CONGRESS)

The United States takes full financial responsibility for all the debts accrued and money borrowed under the authority of the Second Continental Congress during the American Revolution. The United States solemnly pledges to repay all these debts.

In an attempt to maintain the good credit of the United States in the eyes of foreign nations and creditors, the Confederation Congress guaranteed that all debts contracted by the Continental Congress would be repaid. However, this commitment to repay debts is not matched in the Articles by any articulated means of repayment.

Other than the taxes that the states were supposed to supply, Congress had no independent source of revenue with which to repay its creditors. Because many individual states had their own debts from the war, they were typically more inclined to pay those first before contributing to repayment of the national debt. These issues were compounded by the fact that each state printed its own paper money and established its own set of commerce regulations. Furthermore, inflation raged out of control in both the national and state currencies.

Given the limited range of authority in matters of finance, it is amazing that the U.S. Congress managed to stay financially afloat at all. Much of this could be contributed to the abilities of the first Secretary of Finance, Robert Morris, who tried to work within the confines of the system as much as possible. In 1782, he established the Bank of North America. Although this was suspected by some to be an illegal extension of the authority of Congress, it passed Congress and greatly assisted in financial stability. However, his attempts, along with Alexander Hamilton, to pass an amendment empowering Congress to collect a 5% impost failed in both 1781 and 1783.

Without an established source of revenue, Congress also could not pay the soldiers in the Continental Army. This moved troops close to mutiny on two separate occasions. At Newburgh in March of 1783, troops protesting their lack of pay came close to mutiny until George Washington intervened. In Philadelphia in June 1783, another group of mutinous troops demanding pay forced Congress to retreat to Princeton. During this year, Robert Morris resigned from the position, haunted by accusations of corrupt politics and inability to perform his job due to the limitations of Congress.

The issue of debt repayment deeply worried individual states as well. Massachusetts levied high taxes and imposed strict regulations about debt repayment after the war. In 1787, these taxation methods resulted in an armed protest of Massachusetts farmers, led by Daniel Shays, a former captain in the Continental Army. The Massachusetts legislature's unyielding attempts to immediately repay its debts abused the rights of citizens in much the same way as the British Parliament had a decade earlier: the Massachusetts farmers rallied under the same cry as the American Revolutionaries, "no taxation without representation," and relied on similar military tactics.

When the legislature failed to respond to their petitions for change, Shays and his followers closed the courts and attempted to capture a federal arsenal of weapons in Springfield, MA. Referred to as Shays' Rebellion, this group of farmers, although defeated by the local militia, proved to many that issues of taxation would continue to stir up internal conflict unless managed by a strong national government. Reactions to Shays' Rebellion largely propelled politicians to favor a strengthening of the national government and encouraged their participation in the Constitutional Convention of 1787.

ARTICLE 13 AND CONCLUSION (PLEDGE OF PERPETUAL UNION)

Each state must accept and agree to follow the decisions of the United States in Congress assembled. The states must follow all of the rules as stated in the Articles of Confederation. The union of states is meant to last forever. No alterations can be made to the Articles without the agreement of Congress and the confirmation by each of the state legislatures.

Each of the delegates that sign this document has the power to commit the state that they represent to all of the Articles and their specific contents. The people of each state will agree to follow the rulings of Congress on all matters they discuss, and each of the states agrees to never violate the union. We have signed this as members of Congress, meeting in Philadelphia, Pennsylvania on July 9, 1778, the third year of American Independence.

Article 13 and the conclusion provide the means by which the Articles will be enforced and establishes the process for amendment to the Articles of Confederation.

The authority of the government established by the Articles rests in the pledge of all of the delegates to respect the union of thirteen states forever. This forces each individual state to rely on the honor of each of the other states to fulfill their mutual commitments. This reflects a notion similar to the "friendship" promise of Article 2, which had already been demonstrated to be ineffective.

The farther removed the states felt from the threat of war, the less they cared about honoring their pledge to abide by the Articles. In the absence of a strong and coercive power to force states into compliance, states failed to send delegates to Congress, were delinquent on contributions to the general treasury, negligent regarding the matters of foreign commerce, and eager to take power into their own hands. When the need for mutual defense was removed, there seemed to be little need for a central government whose authorization solely covered things related to the common defense.

The significance of this portion of the Articles of Confederation lies not only in demonstrating the weakness of the government from 1781-1789, but also because it provided the means through which the Articles could be revised and the U.S. Constitution could be formed.

Although this Article states that the union cannot be violated by any state, it does allow for amendment to the Articles through agreement in Congress and approval by each of the state legislatures. The convention of all states, except for Rhode Island, in Philadelphia in May 1787, met under this guise to "amend" the Articles, not replace them. When the new and radically different document was adopted by this convention, it had to be ratified by all of the states before it took effect.

It is questionable whether this transition between the Articles of Confederation and the Constitution was legal at all. The Articles stated that Congress had to agree to amendments, and the convention was not Congress. However, given the weakness of the Congress and the strength of the states, it would have been futile to try to stop it. Plus, Congress, more than any other group, probably understood the difficulties inherent in a powerless central government, and therefore welcomed the chance for increased powers after being so long held captive by the supreme sovereignty of the states.

The transition from Articles to constitution was somewhat in the spirit of Thomas Jefferson's Declaration of Independence, which stated that a people have a right to overthrow a government that does not protect its fundamental rights. This time, however, the people did not demand a more democratic government that put sovereignty solely in the state, but clamored for a stronger central government that had a better chance of protecting their property from the chaos of too many competing state governments.

CHAPTER 6 - THE CONSTITUTION (1781–1815)

After their victory in the American Revolution, America's leaders were leery about establishing a powerful centralized government, fearful that such a government would only replace the tyranny of King George III with a new form of tyranny. As a result, the first U.S. constitution, the Articles of Confederation, created a decentralized new government. The Articles established the United States as a confederation of states—a system in which the states were largely independent but were bound together by a weak national congress.

Ultimately, the Articles of Confederation proved ineffective, giving Congress little real power over the states, no means to enforce its decisions, and, most critically, no power to levy taxes. As a result, the federal government was left at the mercy of the states, which often chose not to pay their taxes.

Sensing the need for change, delegates from nearly all the states met in 1787 to revise the Articles of Confederation but ended up drafting an entirely new document: the Constitution. The Constitution created a new government divided into three branches: legislative (Congress), executive (the president), and judicial (headed by the Supreme Court). After much debate, the delegates compromised on a two-house Congress, consisting of an upper house (Senate) with equal representation for each state, and a lower house (House of Representatives) with proportional representation based on population. Congress also was given new abilities to levy national taxes and control interstate commerce.

Although most states ratified the Constitution outright, some, especially New York, had reservations. In response, Alexander Hamilton, John Jay, and James Madison argued the case for the Constitution in a series of essays called the Federalist Papers. These eighty-five essays are now regarded as some of the most important writings in American political thought.

However, many skeptics, or Anti-Federalists, remained unconvinced, believing that a stronger government would endanger the freedoms they had just won during the Revolution. As a compromise, the framers of the Constitution promised to add a series of amendments to guarantee important liberties. Sponsored by James Madison, the first ten amendments became known as the Bill of Rights. Their liberties secured, Anti-Federalists in the last remaining states grudgingly voted for the Constitution.

The 1790s were rocky for the United States: the new government functioned well, but disputes arose about how the government should act in situations in which the Constitution was vague. The foremost of these disagreements involved the question of whether or not the federal government had the right to found a national bank. "Strict constructionists" such as Thomas Jefferson interpreted the Constitution literally, believing that the document forbade everything it did not expressly permit. "Loose constructionists" such as Alexander Hamilton believed that the Constitution's "elastic clause" permitted everything the document did not expressly forbid—such as the founding of a bank.

Hamilton and Jefferson disagreed often during George Washington's presidency, and eventually their ideas spread through the country and coalesced into the nation's first two political parties, the Hamiltonian Federalists and the Jeffersonian Democratic-Republicans. Although Washington begged Americans not to separate into dangerous political factions—for he believed that factions and political parties would destroy the republican spirit and tear the Union apart—the party system developed. Indeed, Washington's successor, the Federalist John Adams, tried to ruin the opposition party with his 1798 Sedition Act, which ultimately only made the Democratic-Republicans stronger.

When Adams's bitter rival Jefferson was elected president in 1800, many European observers thought the American "experiment" in republicanism would end. But when the transfer of power proved to be peaceful, many Europeans, seeing that republicanism could be viable and stable, began to believe the system might work for them too. The U.S. triumph over Britain and success in establishing a stable government had already encouraged the

French to overthrow their own monarch in the French Revolution of 1789. Later, republicanism and democracy would spread beyond France to Britain and the rest of Europe. Thus, the drafting of the Constitution and the years that followed were enormously important in world history as well as American history.

THE ARTICLES OF CONFEDERATION

After declaring independence from Britain in 1776, the delegates at the Second Continental Congress immediately set to the task of creating a government. In 1777, Congress submitted the nation's first constitution, the Articles of Confederation, to the states, who finally ratified it a few years later.

PROBLEMS UNDER THE ARTICLES

Congress proved unable to manage the country's economic affairs under the Articles. Because most state currencies had become useless due to wartime inflation, Congress printed its own continental dollars to keep the economy alive, but these faltered as well. Congress also proved unable to raise enough money from the states, because the federal government had no way of forcing the states to pay taxes. Most states also ignored Congress's attempts to resolve numerous interstate disputes that arose.

In addition, many Americans became fed up with their incompetent state legislatures and demanded debt relief and cheaper money. A few even revolted, as in Shays's Rebellion in 1786–1787, which culminated in Daniel Shays leading 1,200 western Massachusetts farmers in an attack on the federal arsenal at Springfield. Although the rebellion was quickly dismissed, it convinced many American leaders that change was needed if the U.S. were to survive.

DRAFTING THE CONSTITUTION

To resolve these problems, delegates from most of the states met at the Annapolis Convention in 1786. When nothing was resolved, they agreed to reconvene in 1787 at a Constitutional Convention in Philadelphia. At this second convention, it was quickly decided that an entirely new constitution was needed rather than just a revision to the Articles.

A major point of contention was the structure of the new legislative branch. Small states supported the New Jersey Plan, under which all states would have equal representation in the legislature. Large states advocated the Virginia Plan to create a bicameral (two-house) legislature in which representatives would be appointed according to population. The Great Compromise among the states created a bicameral Congress in which states would be equally represented in the Senate and proportionally represented in the House of Representatives.

The framers of the Constitution believed strongly in checks and balances and separation of powers to prevent any one branch of government from ever becoming too powerful. As a result, the new government would also have a strong executive branch and an independent judiciary branch.

THE FEDERALIST PAPERS AND THE BILL OF RIGHTS

When the delegates submitted the Constitution to the states for ratification, heated debates erupted between the Federalists, who supported the Constitution, and the Anti-Federalists, who thought it gave the federal government too much power. Federalists Alexander Hamilton, John Jay, and James Madison coauthored the Federalist Papers in 1787–1788 to convince Anti-Federalist Americans, especially in New York, that the Constitution was necessary. Eventually, the Anti-Federalists conceded on the condition that a Bill of Rights be written to preserve liberties, such as freedoms of speech and religion and the right to trial by jury.

STRICT VS. LOOSE CONSTRUCTIONISM

The Electoral College unanimously chose George Washington to be the first president, with John Adams as vice president. Soon after, the new secretary of the treasury, Alexander Hamilton, wanted to repair the national credit and revive the economy by having the federal government assume all the debts of the individual states. He also wanted to establish a national Bank of the United States. The Constitution said nothing about a national bank, but Hamilton believed that the Constitution allowed many unwritten actions that it did not expressly forbid. Thomas Jefferson, the secretary of state and a strict constructionist, believed that the Constitution forbade everything it did not allow. These ideological differences within Washington's cabinet formed the basis of what later became full-fledged political parties—the Hamiltonian Federalists and the Jeffersonian Democratic-Republicans.

DOMESTIC UNREST IN THE 1790S

Despite the passage of the Indian Intercourse Acts, beginning in 1790, Native Americans frequently raided American settlements west of the Appalachians until federal troops crushed several tribes in the Battle of Fallen Timbers in 1794.

Later, when farmers in western Pennsylvania threatened to march on Philadelphia to protest the excise tax on liquor in 1794, Washington dispatched 13,000 federal troops to crush the insurgents. The Whiskey Rebellion, however, ended without bloodshed.

WASHINGTON AND NEUTRALITY

Events in Europe also affected the United States. The French Revolution of 1789 and France's subsequent war with Britain split American public opinion: some wanted to support republican France, while others wanted to help England. However, under the Franco-American alliance of 1778, the United States was obligated to assist France.

Unprepared for another war, Washington issued the Neutrality Proclamation of 1793. Citizen Genêt, the French ambassador to the United States, ignored the proclamation and, immediately upon his arrival in the United States, began commissioning privateers and planning to use U.S. ports in the French campaign against Britain. Outraged over the Citizen Genêt affair, Washington requested Genet's recall.

Meanwhile, Spain threatened to block Americans' access to the vital Mississippi River, while Britain still refused to withdraw from American territory in the Ohio Valley. These issues were not resolved until Jay's Treaty with Britain in 1794 and Pinckney's Treaty in 1795.

Finally, in his famous Farewell Address in 1796, Washington warned against entangling alliances with European powers and potential political factions in the United States.

ADAMS'S TERM

In 1797, Washington was succeeded by his Federalist vice president, John Adams, who faced continued challenges from Europe. When Adams sent an ambassador to Paris to restore Franco-American relations, three French officials demanded a bribe before they would speak with him. This incident, the XYZ Affair, shocked Americans and initiated two years of undeclared naval warfare.

To prevent unwanted French immigrants from entering the country, Adams and a sympathetic Congress passed the Alien Acts in 1798. They also passed the Sedition Act, which banned public criticism of the government in an attempt to stifle political opposition and wipe out the Democratic-Republicans. Thomas Jefferson and James Madison responded with the Virginia and Kentucky Resolutions, which nullified the Sedition Act in those states. They argued that because the states had created the Union, they also had the right to nullify any unconstitutional legislation.

THE ELECTION OF 1800

The Democratic-Republicans defeated the Federalists in the election of 1800. Despite years of mutual hatred, the Federalists relinquished the government to their political enemies in a peaceful transfer of power. Thomas Jefferson, champion of western and southern farmers, became president and immediately advocated a reduction in the size and power of the federal government.

INCREASES IN FEDERAL POWER

In reality, federal power increased in many ways during Jefferson's eight years in office. The Supreme Court reasserted its power of judicial review in the 1803 Marbury v. Madison decision. Jefferson's Louisiana Purchase more than doubled the size of the country despite the fact that the Constitution said nothing about new land purchases.

THE EMBARGO ACT

Jefferson continued to face challenges from Europe, as neither Britain nor France respected American shipping rights as a neutral country. Both countries seized hundreds of American merchant ships bound for Europe, and British warships impressed (captured for forced labor) thousands of American sailors. To end these practices, Jefferson and Congress passed the Embargo Act in 1807, closing all U.S. ports to export shipping and placing restrictions on imports from Britain. Unfortunately, the boycott backfired, and the U.S. economy slumped as Britain and France found other sources of natural resources.

THE NON-INTERCOURSE ACT AND MACON'S BILL NO. 2

Congress repealed the Embargo Act in 1809 but replaced it with the Non-Intercourse Act, which banned trade only with Britain and France. A year later, with James Madison in office as president, the American economy still had not improved, so Congress passed Macon's Bill No. 2, which restored trade relations with all nations but promised to revive the Non-Intercourse Act if either Britain or France violated U.S. shipping rights.

THE WAR OF 1812

Meanwhile, War Hawks in Congress from the West and South pressed Madison for war against the British and Tecumseh's Native American Northwest Confederacy. Tecumseh's forces were defeated at the Battle of Tippecanoe in 1811. Since the British were still seizing American ships and impressing American sailors, Congress declared war on Britain in 1812.

The War of 1812 was primarily a sectional conflict supported by Americans in the West and South and condemned by those in the Northeast. In 1814, delegates from the New England states met at the Hartford Convention to petition Congress and redress grievances. By the time Congress received their complaint, however, the war had ended and the Treaty of Ghent had been signed.

KEY PEOPLE & TERMS

People

John Adams

A prominent Boston lawyer who first became famous for defending the British soldiers accused of murdering five civilians in the Boston Massacre. At the Continental Congresses, Adams acted as a delegate from Massachusetts and rejected proposals for self-governance within the British Empire. He served as vice president to George Washington and then as president from 1797–1801.

Samuel Adams

A second cousin of John Adams and a failed Bostonian businessman who became an ardent political activist in the years leading up to the Revolutionary War. Samuel Adams organized the first Committee of Correspondence and was a delegate to both Continental Congresses in 1774 and 1775.

Alexander Hamilton

A brilliant New York lawyer and statesman who, in his early thirties, was one of the youngest delegates at the Constitutional Convention in 1787. An ardent Federalist, Hamilton supported the Constitution during the ratification debates even though he actually believed that the new document was still too weak. He helped write the Federalist Papers, which are now regarded as some of the finest essays on American government and republicanism. He served as the first secretary of the treasury under George Washington and established the first Bank of the United States.

William Henry Harrison

A former governor of Indiana Territory and brigadier general in the U.S. Army who rose to national stardom when he defeated the Northwest Confederacy at the Battle of Tippecanoe in 1811. Harrison went on to be elected president in 1840.

Patrick Henry

A fiery radical who advocated rebellion against the Crown in the years prior to the American Revolution, as in his famous "Give me liberty or give me death" speech. Later, Henry was a die-hard Anti-Federalist who initially opposed ratification of the Constitution.

Andrew Jackson

A hero of the War of 1812 and the Creek War who later entered the national political arena and became president in 1829. Jackson, nicknamed "Old Hickory," was the first U.S. president to come from a region west of the Appalachians.

John Jay

A coauthor of the Federalist Papers, which attempted to convince Anti-Federalist New Yorkers to ratify the Constitution. Jay served as the first Chief Justice of the Supreme Court and became one of the most hated men in America after he negotiated Jay's Treaty with Britain in 1794.

Thomas Jefferson

A Virginia planter and lawyer who in 1776 drafted the Declaration of Independence, which justified American independence from Britain. Jefferson went on to serve as the first secretary of state under George Washington and as vice president under John Adams. He then was elected president himself in 1800 and 1804.

James Madison - A Virginia Federalist who advocated for the ratification of the Constitution, coauthored the Federalist Papers, and sponsored the Bill of Rights in Congress. After ratification, he supported southern and western agrarian interests as a Democratic-Republican. After a brief retirement, he reentered politics and was elected president in 1808 and 1812. As president, Madison fought for U.S. shipping rights against British and French aggression and led the country during the War of 1812.

James Monroe - A Virginia officer, lawyer, and Democratic-Republican who was elected president in 1816 and inaugurated the Era of Good Feelings. An excellent administrator, Monroe bolstered the federal government and supported internal improvements, and was so popular in his first term that he ran uncontested in 1820. The "good feelings" ended, however, during the Missouri Crisis that split the United States along north-south lines. Monroe is most famous for his 1823 Monroe Doctrine, which warned European powers against interfering in the Western Hemisphere.

Tecumseh - A member of the Shawnee tribe who, along with his brother Tenskwatawa (often called the Prophet), organized many of the tribes in the Mississippi Valley into the Northwest Confederacy to defend Native American ancestral lands from white American settlers. Even though the tribes had legal rights to their lands under the Indian Intercourse Acts of the 1790s, expansionist War Hawks in Congress argued the need for action against Tecumseh, and eventually William Henry Harrison was sent to wipe out the Confederacy. Tecumseh's forces were defeated at the Battle of Tippecanoe in 1811.

George Washington - A Virginia planter and militia officer who led the attack that initiated the French and Indian War in 1754. Washington later became commander in chief of the American forces during the American Revolution and first president of the United States in 1789. Although he lost many of the military battles he fought, his leadership skills were unparalleled and were integral to the creation of the United States. In his noteworthy Farewell Address, Washington warned against factionalism and the formation of political parties, believing they would split the nation irreparably.

Terms

Alien Acts

A group of acts passed in 1798, designed to restrict the freedom of foreigners in the United States and curtail the free press in anticipation of a war with France. The Alien Acts lengthened the residency time required for foreigners to become American citizens from five years to fourteen years and gave the president the power to expel aliens considered dangerous to the nation. It was passed simultaneously with the Sedition Act, and together they provoked the Virginia and Kentucky Resolutions, written the same year in protest. These resolutions stated that individual states had the right to nullify unconstitutional laws passed by Congress.

Annapolis Convention

A meeting of delegates from five states in Annapolis, Maryland, in 1786 to discuss the bleak commercial situation in the United States, growing social unrest, and Congress's inability to resolve disputes among the states. The conference dissolved when Alexander Hamilton proposed holding the Constitutional Convention in Philadelphia the next year to revise the Articles of Confederation.

Anti-Federalists

Primarily farmers and poorer Americans in the West, a group that strongly opposed ratification of the Constitution. The Anti-Federalists were suspicious of governments in general and a strong central government in particular. Rather, they believed that state legislatures should maintain sovereignty. Although they eventually lost the ratification battle, their protests did encourage the first Congress to attach the Bill of Rights to the Constitution.

Articles of Confederation

The first U.S. constitution, adopted in 1777 and ratified in 1781. The Articles established a national Congress in which each state in the Union was granted one vote. Congress had the right to conduct foreign affairs, maintain a military, govern western territories, and regulate trade between states, but it could not levy taxes. Because most states refused to finance the Congress adequately, the government under the Articles was doomed to fail. After Shays's Rebellion in 1786–1787, delegates met to discuss revising the Articles of Confederation, which ultimately led to the drafting of the Constitution.

Bank of the United States

A plan proposed by Alexander Hamilton for a treasury for federal money funded by private investors. The Bank sparked a debate between "strict constructionists" and "loose constructionists" regarding interpretation of the Constitution.

Bill of Rights

The first ten amendments to the Constitution, sponsored in Congress by James Madison, to guarantee basic freedoms and liberties. The Bill of Rights protects freedoms of speech, press, religion, assembly, and petition, and the rights to have trial by jury, bear arms, and own property, among others. Moreover, the Ninth Amendment states that the people have additional rights beyond those written explicitly in the Constitution; the Tenth Amendment awards state governments all the powers not granted to the federal government. The promise of a Bill of Rights helped convince many Anti-Federalists to ratify the new Constitution. Today, these rights are considered fundamental American liberties.

Checks and Balances

A term referring to the overlapping of powers granted to the three branches of government under the Constitution. For example, Congress has the power to pass laws and regulate taxes, but the president has the ability to veto, or nullify, those acts. On the other hand, Congress may override a president's veto if two-thirds of its members support the bill in question. The Supreme Court, meanwhile, has the power to review all laws but must rely on the president to enforce its decisions. The framers of the Constitution included this system of checks and balances to prevent any one branch of government from having too much power over the others.

Constitution

A 1787 document that established the structure of the U.S. government, drafted at the Constitutional Convention in Philadelphia by prominent statesmen from twelve states (minus Rhode Island). Unlike its predecessor, the Articles of Confederation, the Constitution established a strong central government divided into three separate but equal branches (legislative, executive, and judiciary). This separation of powers, combined with a system of checks and balances, was designed to prevent the new government from becoming too strong and tyrannical.

Constitutional Convention

A 1787 meeting in Philadelphia in which delegates from twelve states convened to revise the Articles of Confederation. The Convention quickly decided that the Articles should be scrapped and replaced with an entirely new document to create a stronger central government binding the states. The result was the Constitution.

Declaration of Independence

A document written by Thomas Jefferson in 1776 that proclaimed the creation of the United States. The Declaration sets forth a persuasive argument against King George III, claiming that the king ruled the colonies poorly and unjustly. The document thus served not merely as a declaration but also as a rational justification for breaking away from Britain.

Democratic-Republicans

Successors of the Anti-Federalists who formed a party under Thomas Jefferson's leadership during Washington's and Adams's presidencies. The Democratic-Republicans generally favored westward expansion, the formation of an agrarian republic, and an alliance with France, and were strict constructionists and advocates of states' rights. Political battles between the Democratic-Republicans and the Federalists were frequent during the first years of the nineteenth century. Though the Federalist Party died out during the War of 1812, the Democratic-Republicans lived on during the Era of Good Feelilngs and eventually became the Democratic party.

Elastic Clause

A nickname for Article I, Section VIII, Paragraph 18 of the Constitution, which states that Congress has the power "to make all laws which shall be necessary and proper" to carry out its proscribed duties. Alexander Hamilton and the Federalists interpreted this clause to mean that the Constitution allows everything it does not expressly forbid, and used it to justify the creation of the Bank of the United States. George Washington agreed, and the clause has since given presidents and Congress ample justification for expanding federal power. The clause has been dubbed "elastic" because it gives federal policymakers great flexibility when drafting laws.

Electoral College

A body of representatives appointed by states to cast their votes for president. The presidential candidate who receives the most Electoral College votes, regardless of how many popular votes he or she receives, becomes president. The framers of the Constitution created the Electoral College out of fear that the whimsical American masses might one day popularly elect someone "unfit" for the presidency.

Excise Tax of 1791

A liquor tax proposed by Alexander Hamilton in 1790 to raise revenue so that Congress could pay off all national and state debts. The excise tax was immensely unpopular with western farmers, whose protests eventually culminated in the Whiskey Rebellion of 1794.

The Federalist Papers

A series of eighty-five articles written by James Madison, Alexander Hamilton, and John Jay in 1787–1788 to convince New Yorkers to ratify the Constitution. The Federalist Papers are now regarded as some of the finest essays on the Constitution, American government, and republicanism.

Federalists

Primarily from the wealthier and propertied classes of Americans along the eastern seaboard, a group that supported ratification of the Constitution and creation of a strong central government. The Federalists eventually became a full-fledged political party under the leadership of John Adams and Alexander Hamilton. Adams was the first and only Federalist president, as the party died after Federalist delegates from the Hartford Convention protested the War of 1812 and were labeled traitors.

Great Compromise

An agreement between the large and small states at the Constitutional Convention of 1787 to create a bicameral (two-house) Congress with one chamber of delegates assigned based on population (the House of Representatives) and another chamber in which all states had two representatives regardless of population (the Senate). The agreement ended the deadlock among the states and set a precedent for compromise in American politics.

Hartford Convention

An 1814–1815 meeting of delegates from five New England states in Hartford, Connecticut, to discuss possible secession from the Union due to discontent with the War of 1812. The delegates ultimately decided to remain in the Union but sent a petition to Congress, requesting amendments to the Constitution in order to alter the office of the presidency and to change the distribution and powers of Congress. None of their demands were met, however, because the petition arrived at Congress during celebrations over Andrew Jackson's victory at the Battle of New Orleans and the signing of the Treaty of Ghent. Nonetheless, the convention demonstrated the sectional nature of the war and the growing differences between the North and the South.

Indian Intercourse Acts

A series of acts passed in the 1790s that attempted to smooth relations between the United States and Native American tribes along the western frontier. The act attempted to regulate trade between these groups and promised that the United States would acquire western lands only via treaties. Most American settlers ignored this bill, which produced bloody clashes between tribes and settlers.

Judiciary Act of 1789

The first act that Congress passed, which created the tiered U.S. federal court system. The Supreme Court, under Chief Justice John Jay, was at the head of the court system, supported by three circuit courts and thirteen district courts. Even though the Judiciary Act strengthened federal judicial power, it also upheld local and state courts by stipulating that most cases heard in federal courts would be appeals cases.

Land Ordinance of 1785

An ordinance passed by the national Congress under the Articles of Confederation that established an efficient system to survey and auction lands west of the Appalachian Mountains.

Loose Constructionists

People such as Alexander Hamilton, who believed that the Constitution allowed the government to take any actions that were not expressly forbidden in the document. The loose constructionists' interpretation was challenged by Thomas Jefferson and other strict constructionists, who believed that the Constitution must be read literally.

Macon's Bill No. 2

An 1810 bill that restored U.S. commerce with Britain and France (after their interruption under the Embargo Act and Non-Intercourse Act) but threatened to revive the terms of the Non-Intercourse Act if either country failed to respect U.S. neutrality and shipping rights.

New Jersey Plan

Also known as the small state plan, a proposal at the 1787 Constitutional Convention to create a unicameral (single-house) legislature in which all states would be equally represented. The New Jersey plan appealed to smaller states but not to more populous states, which backed the Virginia Plan to create a bicameral legislature in which representatives were apportioned by population. The Great Compromise solved the dilemma by creating a bicameral Congress featuring one house with proportional representation and another with equal representation.

Non-Intercourse Act

An 1809 act that replaced the ineffective Embargo Act in an attempt to revive the faltering American economy by boosting U.S. exports. The Non-Intercourse Act banned trade only with France and Britain (unlike the Embargo Act, which banned exports completely) until both nations agreed to respect American sovereignty. When this bill also failed, Congress passed Macon's Bill No. 2.

Northwest Confederacy

A confederation of Native American tribes in the Mississippi Valley, led by Tecumseh and his brother, for mutual defense against white settlers. Although the tribes of the Northwest Confederacy had legal rights to their lands under the Indian Intercourse Acts of the 1790s, expansionist War Hawks in Congress nonetheless prevailed, and William Henry Harrison was sent to wipe out the Confederacy. Tecumseh's forces were defeated at the Battle of Tippecanoe in 1811.

Northwest Ordinance of 1787

A framework passed by the national Congress under the Articles of Confederation to decide which western U.S. territories (Ohio, Michigan, Wisconsin, Illinois, and Indiana) could become states. Because the ordinance also abolished slavery and established basic civil liberties (trial by jury, freedom of religion) in the Northwest Territory, it is often seen as an important first step toward the creation of the Bill of Rights.

Second Continental Congress

A meeting of colonial delegates that convened in different places from 1775 to 1789 to establish a new U.S. government after declaring independence from Britain. In 1777, the Congress drafted the Articles of Confederation as the first U.S. constitution.

Sedition Act

A 1798 act (passed simultaneously with the Alien Acts) that banned all forms of public expression critical of the president or Congress. President John Adams approved the act, fearing the influence of French immigrants in the United States and also hoping the free speech ban would harm his political opponents, the Democratic-Republicans. Ironically, the act only made the opposition party stronger. Thomas Jefferson and James Madison wrote the Virginia and Kentucky Resolutions the same year in protest, arguing that individual states had the right to nullify unconstitutional laws passed by Congress.

Separation of Powers

A term referring to the fact that each of the three branches in the American federal government has separate and distinct powers. The legislative branch, for example, has the sole ability to propose and pass laws, while the executive branch has the power to enforce those laws, and the judiciary the power to review them. The writers of the Constitution separated these powers to prevent any one part of the new government from becoming too powerful.

Shays's Rebellion

A 1786–1787 revolt by western Massachusetts farmer Daniel Shays, who led 1,200 other men in an attack on the federal arsenal at Springfield, Massachusetts. Shays and others like him throughout the United States were dissatisfied with the ineptitude of state legislatures during the economic depression after the American Revolution. Shays's Rebellion and other revolts spurred leading Americans to meet and discuss revising the Articles of Confederation.

Strict Constructionists

People such as Thomas Jefferson who believed that the Constitution forbade the government to take any actions that it did not expressly permit. The strict constructionists' interpretation was challenged by Alexander Hamilton and other loose constructionists, who believed that the Constitution allowed the government many implied powers.

Three-Fifths Clause

A nickname for Article I, Section II, Paragraph 3 of the Constitution, which states that representation in the House of Representatives is determined by counting all free persons and "three-fifths of all other persons," or slaves. The three-fifths clause was created as part of the Great Compromise between states with few slaves and those with many slaves.

Treaty of Ghent

The December 1814 treaty that ended the War of 1812 between Britain and the United States. The treaty stated that the war had ended in a stalemate and that neither side had gained or lost any territory. Ironically, the Battle of New Orleans—the greatest American victory in the war—was fought about two weeks after the treaty had been signed, as General Andrew Jackson had not gotten word of the war's end.

Virginia and Kentucky Resolutions

Two resolutions, passed in 1798–1799 and written by Thomas Jefferson and James Madison, that declared that the individual states had the right to nullify unconstitutional acts of Congress. The resolutions stated that because the individual states had created the Union, they also reserved the right to nullify any legislation that ran counter to their interests.

Virginia Dynasty

A nickname that arose because four of the first five presidents (Washington, Jefferson, Madison, and Monroe) all hailed from Virginia. Many northern states resented this fact, as demonstrated by the Hartford Convention's 1814 request that presidents should not come from the same state as their predecessor.

Virginia Plan

Also known as the large state plan, a proposal at the 1787 Constitutional Convention to create a bicameral (two-house) legislature in which delegates would be appointed according to the population of the state they represented. Large states with greater populations supported this plan, unlike small states, which backed the New Jersey Plan to create a unicameral legislature in which all states were equally represented. The Great Compromise solved the dilemma by creating a bicameral Congress featuring one house with proportional representation and another with equal representation.

War Hawks

A younger generation of statesmen, primarily from the West and South, who replaced the Founding Fathers in the first decade of the 1800s. The War Hawks favored westward expansion and a nationalist agenda and thus encouraged war against both the Northwest Confederacy and against Britain (in the War of 1812). Despite their early zeal, many War Hawks, such as Henry Clay, eventually settled down to become some of the most revered statesmen in American history.

XYZ Affair

A bribery scandal that caused public uproar during the Adams administration in 1798. After several naval skirmishes and French seizures of American merchant ships, Adams sent ambassadors to Paris to try to normalize relations. When the emissaries arrived, however, French officials demanded $250,000 before they would even speak with the Americans, let alone guarantee a truce. These officials, whom Adams dubbed X, Y, and Z, outraged Congress and the American public. Adams's popularity skyrocketed, and Congress braced for war. Although no war declaration was ever made, the United States and France waged undeclared naval warfare in the Atlantic for several years.

SAMPLE REVIEW QUESTIONS

1. In general, Native American groups prior to contact with Europeans
   a. had developed dry farming techniques.
   b. had adapted to a variety of geographic and climate conditions.
   c. had developed large-scale cities with hierarchical governments.
   d. lived in scattered groups.
   e. had extensive trade networks that linked North and South America.

2. Which of the following was NOT a factor in the success of the Spanish in conquering Native American peoples?
   a. Spanish exploitation of rivalries among native peoples
   b. Spanish use of firearms and horses
   c. focus of other European nations on their own internal political and religious issues
   d. Native Americans' lack of immunity to European diseases
   e. the importation of Africans

3. All of the following were reasons the English were interested in colonization EXCEPT
   a. English merchants were looking for new markets
   b. English landlords wanted to import their enclosure movement to the Americas to make money
   c. the English, convinced there was a Northwest Passage to Asia, wanted to establish posts to supply ships going and back through the Northwest Passage
   d. the English needed a base from which to attack Spanish treasure ships sailing back to Spain
   e. religious rivalry between Protestant England and Catholic Spain motivated England to establish a Protestant empire in the Americas

4. Which of the following was NOT a direct result of the dumping of precious metals from the Americas into European markets?
   a. introduction of joint-stock companies
   b. the commercial revolution
   c. widespread inflation
   d. lower standard of living for most Europeans
   e. increased profits for merchants

5. Which of the following is a true statement about Puritanism?
   a. Puritanism attracted few followers among the growing English middle class of merchants and commercial farmers.
   b. Puritanism was based on a set of religious, political, and social values.
   c. Puritans renounced the Calvinist concept of the work ethic.
   d. Rigorous adherence to social mores for their own sake was a cornerstone of Puritanism.
   e. In leaving England, the Puritans renounced any political ambitions.

6. The first published poet in the North American colonies was
   a. Phillis Wheatley
   b. Emily Dickinson
   c. William Bradford
   d. Jonathan Edwards
   e. Anne Bradstreet

7. William Penn called his colony a "Holy Experiment" because he
   a. intended to buy land from Native Americans rather than seize it
   b. wanted to establish a self-governing colony with political and religious freedom
   c. intended to keep a journal history of the development of the colony
   d. welcomed people of various faiths
   e. banned indentured servants

8. The Bodies of Liberty, the first set of laws in the English colonies, was passed by the
   a. Virginia House of Burgesses
   b. Massachusetts General Court
   c. First Continental Congress
   d. Proprietors of Georgia
   e. Maryland General Assembly

9. Tobacco was the most important export commodity in the late seventeenth century for which of the following?
   a. Massachusetts
   b. New York and New Jersey
   c. Georgia
   d. Virginia and Maryland
   e. North and South Carolina

10. Which of the following is NOT a true statement about life in the English colonies?
    a. Families tended to be large, because many children meant many workers.
    b. Women had little opportunity outside the home but played a central role within the family.
    c. The English had fairly open immigration policies.
    d. Colonial culture tended to be similar to that of England.
    e. The colonies had no colleges, so young men had to go to England for higher education.

11. Which of the following was fought between colonists and Native Americans?
    a. King Philip's War
    b. Bacon's Rebellion
    c. Shays's Rebellion
    d. Stono Uprising
    e. First Seminole War

12. A major difference in government structure between royal colonies and charter colonies was
    a. the monarch paid the governor's salary in a royal colony, whereas in a charter colony the legislature paid his salary
    b. royal colonies had no local legislative representation, whereas charter colonies elected a colonial legislature
    c. the colonists elected their own governor in charter colonies, whereas the monarch appointed the governor in a royal colony
    d. town meetings made decisions for towns in charter colonies, but in royal colonies all government decisions were made by the royal governor and council
    e. royal colonies limited the right to vote and participate in government to white, male property owners.

13. The development of enslaved Africans as the chief labor supply after Bacon's Rebellion occurred because of
    a. greater availability of slaves
    b. the inability to find Europeans willing to be indentured servants
    c. Indian resistance to working as laborers
    d. the labor-intense nature of tobacco agriculture
    e. the growing number of white landless and discontented former servants

14. The first colony in the 1600s to require that each town establish a public primary school was
    a. Pennsylvania
    b. Massachusetts
    c. New York
    d. Virginia
    e. Georgia

15. While the English were the largest group of people to immigrate to the colonies, the second largest group were
    a. Irish
    b. Scots Irish
    c. French Huguenots
    d. Germans
    e. Welsh

16. A significant characteristic of the social class structure in the English colonies was
    a. its lack of social mobility
    b. the size and wealth of the middle class
    c. the lack of importance given to wealth
    d. an upper class of wealthy merchants and professionals only
    e. the lack of a lower class of poor

17. The child depicted in this painting reflects what idea of Puritans?

   a. Children were gifts from God and should be well cared for and well dressed.
   b. Children were considered small adults.
   c. Children wore many layers of clothing for modesty's sake.
   d. Dressing children like their parents were God-like.
   e. No expense should be spared in clothing children, because their outfits were another indication that the parents were saved.

18. "The stench of the hold while we were on the coast was so intolerably loathsome, that it was dangerous to remain there for any time, and some of us had been permitted to stay on deck for the fresh air . . . "This quotation probably describes
   a. an American warship during the American Revolution
   b. the Mayflower
   c. an Irish immigrant ship in the early 1700s
   d. a slave ship bound for the Americas
   e. a German immigrant ship in the early 1700s

19. The religious group that had the greatest influence in New England after the initial phase of settlement was
   a. Roman Catholicism
   b. the Anglican Church
   c. Presbyterianism
   d. Congregational Church
   e. Methodism

20. Over time, which of the following rights were married women in the colonies able to exercise?
   a. vote
   b. conduct business
   c. attend college
   d. hold public office
   e. act as ministers

21. The Great Awakening spurred all of the following EXCEPT
    a. the development of religious pluralism
    b. establishment of nonsectarian colleges
    c. separation of church and state
    d. active participation in church affairs by ordinary people
    e. the banning of Anglicanism

22. A major difference between slavery in Virginia and in the Carolinas and Georgia was that
    a. landowners were less tolerant of slaves creating families
    b. there was more cultural diversity in the Carolinas and Georgia as a result of the blending of European and African cultures
    c. the major crop that slaves in Virginia cultivated was cotton, whereas in the Carolinas and Georgia, it was rice
    d. most slaves in Virginia had been born in the colony rather than imported
    e. there was a greater degree of diversity in the kinds of work that slaves did in the Carolinas and Georgia

23. Which of the following was a major advantage for the British in North America during the French and Indian War?
    a. The British colonies joined together through the Albany Plan of Union to wage war as a single unit.
    b. A number of Native American groups allied with the British.
    c. The British colonies had a homogeneous population loyal to Great Britain.
    d. The British had thirteen separate governments directing the war along with the government in London.
    e. The British colonies were populated with families willing to fight for their homes.

24. The British government did not enforce the Proclamation of 1763 because
    a. the French removal from Canada made the proclamation unnecessary
    b. it was to the benefit of the British empire to have the colonists move West
    c. the government did not want to enrich land speculators
    d. the colonists refused to obey the law
    e. the Native Americans turned on the British and the government wanted revenge

25. British policy toward its colonies in the 1600s and 1700s was based on the principle of
    a. popular sovereignty
    b. salutary neglect
    c. direct representation
    d. the price revolution
    e. mercantilism

26. The "power of the purse," colonial legislatures' ability to influence the actions of royal officials in the colonies, was eliminated by the
    a. Stamp Act
    b. Quartering Act
    c. Intolerable Acts
    d. Townshend Acts
    e. Declaratory Act

27. All of the following are examples of the influence of Enlightenment thinking EXCEPT
    a. Benjamin Franklin's scientific experiments
    b. John Locke's social contract theory
    c. the Declaration of Independence
    d. predestination
    e. the use of inoculations against smallpox

28. This quotation was most probably written by
    a. Marquis de Lafayette
    b. William Pitt
    c. George Washington
    d. Thomas Paine
    e. Edmund Burke

29. The battle of Saratoga in 1777 was important because it
    a. gave the British a much needed victory
    b. brought France into a formal alliance with the United States
    c. convinced the Iroquois Confederacy to side with the Patriots
    d. ended the war in New England
    e. ended any interest by Spain and the Netherlands in aiding England

30. The Peace of Paris called for all of the following EXCEPT
    a. Loyalists were to be paid for their confiscated property
    b. the British were to withdraw from all U.S. territory
    c. the Mississippi would serve as the western boundary of the United States
    d. Florida was given to the United States
    e. the United States was given fishing rights in the northern waters off Canada

31. The major difficulty of government under the Articles of Confederation was
    a. lack of a judiciary
    b. lack of a chief executive
    c. the inability to collect taxes
    d. the lack of a method for admitting additional states
    e. irregularly scheduled meetings of Congress

32. Which of the following provided the plan for all subsequent admission of territories to statehood in the United States?
    a. Bill of Rights
    b. Homestead Act
    c. Kansas-Nebraska Act
    d. Gadsden Purchase
    e. Northwest Ordinance

33. The Great Compromise reached at the Constitutional Convention resulted in
    a. the establishment of the office of president
    b. the counting of slaves as three-fifths of a person
    c. the establishment of the new nation's capital in an area between Virginia and Maryland
    d. the establishment of a legislature of two houses, a House of Representatives based on population and a Senate with equal representation among the states
    e. setting the date for the end of slavery as 1808

34. The major shortcoming of the new Constitution according to Anti-Federalists was
    a. lack of protection for individuals
    b. the method of ratification
    c. the use of the three-fifths compromise
    d. the small states would be overpowered by the large states in Congress
    e. that it gave the states too much power

35. Which of the following is the correct listing of the freedoms included in the First Amendment to the U.S. Constitution?
    a. freedom of religion, freedom of speech, right to due process, right to have an attorney
    b. freedom of the press, right to assemble, freedom of speech, right to bear arms
    c. right to vote; one man, one vote; right to assemble
    d. freedom of religion, freedom of speech, freedom of the press, right to assemble
    e. freedom of speech, freedom of the press

36. The authority of Congress to approve presidential nominees to the federal judiciary is an example of
    a. judicial review
    b. checks and balances
    c. the amendment process
    d. implied powers
    e. enumerated powers

37. The reason underlying Alexander Hamilton's proposal that the United States government redeem all bonds at face value and pay all state debts was
    a. to force the northern states to help southern states that had not paid their debts
    b. to enrich himself because he had bought bonds at a discount
    c. to enrich bond speculators who were his political supporters
    d. to convince wealthy Americans that the United States was a safe investment
    e. to convince other nations that the United States did not need foreign investment

38. Which of the following was the first test of the unity of the United States under its new Constitution?
    a. Whiskey Rebellion
    b. Shays's Rebellion
    c. Denmark Vesey's Conspiracy
    d. XYZ Affair
    e. War Hawks

39. Which of the following helped to lay out Washington, DC, and was a mathematician and astronomer?
    a. Benjamin Franklin
    b. Benjamin Banneker
    c. Joseph Henry
    d. Charles Wilson Peale
    e. Benjamin Rush

40. The Federalists party of the 1790s found its support among
    a. Northern merchants, New England farmers, and skilled workers
    b. Southern planters and frontier settlers
    c. poorer farmers in the North
    d. Southern planters and Northern merchants
    e. Northern merchants, farmers in North and South, and semiskilled workers

41. "'Tis our true policy to steer clear of permanent alliances, with any portion of the foreign world." This quotation is most likely from a speech by
    a. Benjamin Franklin
    b. Thomas Paine
    c. George Washington
    d. John Adams
    e. Abraham Lincoln

42. The Treaty of Greenville is significant because
    a. it ended the continuing British presence in the Ohio Valley
    b. the United States agreed to buy Florida from Spain
    c. Native Americans in the Old Southeast agreed to live within a certain area
    d. Native Americans in the Old Northwest ceded most of their lands to the United States
    e. it removed the Spanish from the Ohio Valley

43. The Sedition Act was used primarily against
    a. traders who supplied Native Americans with guns
    b. Republican printers and editors
    c. Federalist judges
    d. French immigrants
    e. British sailors

44. The Kentucky and Virginia Resolutions are significant because
    a. they institutionalized slavery in their respective states
    b. they were the first articulation of the doctrine of nullification
    c. they were written in support of the Constitution during the ratification process
    d. they were written in support of the passage of the Twelfth Amendment after the election of 1800
    e. they were written in support of war with France in 1798

45. The Supreme Court decision that established the principle of judicial review of acts of Congress was
    a. Brown v. Board of Education
    b. Plessy v. Ferguson
    c. Dred Scott decision
    d. Marbury v. Madison
    e. McCulloch v. Maryland

46. All of the following were results of the Louisiana Purchase EXCEPT
    a. it doubled the size of the United States
    b. it removed the French threat from the center of the continent
    c. it permanently opened New Orleans for trade with Americans in the interior
    d. it increased tensions over slavery
    e. it provided a Northwest Passage to the Pacific Ocean

47. The purpose of the Embargo Act of 1807 was to
    a. force France and Great Britain to end their boycott of American goods
    b. preserve the neutrality of the United States
    c. end impressment of British sailors by Americans
    d. punish Americans trading illegally with the British and French
    e. end smuggling from Canada

48. Which of the following groups lost significant influence as a result of the War of 1812?
    a. War Hawks
    b. Federalists
    c. Whigs
    d. Westerners
    e. Democrats

49. The War of 1812 was significant because
    a. it showed the superior firepower of the American forces
    b. it damaged the British economy, but did not harm the United States economy
    c. it ended Native American efforts to block the expansion of white settlement
    d. it made Andrew Jackson a national hero
    e. the new United States fought Great Britain to a standoff

50. Between 1780 and 1830, the population of the United States grew from 2.7 million to 12 million chiefly as a result of
    a. immigration
    b. the importation of Africans
    c. natural increase
    d. the inclusion of Native Americans in population figures
    e. acquisition of the Louisiana Territory

51. The Monroe Doctrine was a bold statement by the United States because
    a. it came so shortly after the end of the War of 1812
    b. the nation did not have the power to back it up
    c. it gave notice to all European nations to stay out of the affairs of the Americas
    d. it offered help to the newly independent nations of South America
    e. no one had asked the United States to intervene in the affairs of any other nation

52. Henry Clay's plan to finance a national bank, levy a protective tariff, and use federal funds to finance internal improvements is known as
    a. Era of Good Feelings
    b. Monroe Doctrine
    c. Compromise of 1820
    d. Hartford Convention
    e. American System

53. The Missouri Compromise was important because
    a. it established the principle of popular sovereignty as law
    b. it established a boundary line for the expansion of slavery
    c. it showed the extent of party rivalries
    d. it earned Henry Clay his nickname "the Great Compromiser"
    e. it ended the coalition between frontier and Northeastern politicians

54. The Democratic Party of Andrew Jackson attracted
    a. a coalition of wealthy merchants and landed gentry in all regions.
    b. former Federalists
    c. Free-Soilers
    d. those who favored a national government
    e. Southerners, Westerners, and Northern urban workers

55. The election of 1824 resulted
    a. in a president from one party and a vice president from another
    b. in passage of the Twelfth Amendment
    c. in "the corrupt bargain" between Henry Clay and Andrew Jackson
    d. in the House of Representatives' deciding the election
    e. in the beginning of the dominance of the presidency by New Englanders

56. The subject of the following cartoon is
    a. Jackson's lavish entertaining in the White House
    b. Jackson's appeal to the "common man"
    c. the damage Jackson was doing to the nation by his policies
    d. Jackson's misleading of the American people into thinking he was doing good when he was doing evil
    e. Jackson's use of the spoils system to reward supporters

THE POLITICAL BARBECUE

57. Which of the following transformed the economy of the Southern states?
    a. the transportation revolution
    b. the mechanization of textile production
    c. the introduction of tobacco agriculture
    d. the invention of the cotton gin
    e. the passage of protective tariffs

58. Jackson's Specie Circular resulted in
    a. a land boom
    b. the federal government's paying off its debt
    c. an economic depression
    d. state banks issuing more and more banknotes not backed by gold or silver
    e. the issuing of charters to banks by the states

59. "John Marshall has made his decision. Now let him enforce it." This quotation was most likely spoken by which of the following Presidents?
    a. George Washington
    b. Thomas Jefferson
    c. James Monroe
    d. Andrew Jackson
    e. Abraham Lincoln

60. The transportation revolution had all of the following effects EXCEPT
     a.   the South was more closely tied to the Midwest
     b.   the price of food fell in the Northeast
     c.   nationwide mail delivery was possible
     d.   manufactured goods took the place of homemade goods
     e.   less value was placed on women's work that did not generate income

61. All of the following resulted from the Second Great Awakening EXCEPT
     a.   the development of a sense of community and social belonging among followers
     b.   the rapid decline in the Methodist and Baptist churches
     c.   a desire among followers to reform society
     d.   the prominence of itinerant preachers
     e.   a newfound importance for women as moral pillars of their communities

62. The putting-out system was made possible only because of the adoption of
     a.   interchangeable parts
     b.   division of labor
     c.   master and apprentice model of medieval guilds
     d.   assembly line
     e.   water power

63. One of the biggest societal changes of the early 1800s was
     a.   the general acceptance of the value of public education
     b.   the increasing volume of print materials
     c.   the new concept of domesticity governing women's roles as wife and mother
     d.   the acceptance of unmarried women as teachers
     e.   the use of servants in middle-class households

64. Early union efforts were aimed at organizing
     a.   skilled and unskilled white male workers
     b.   skilled male workers—white and free African Americans
     c.   skilled and unskilled workers—men and women, white and free African American
     d.   skilled, white male workers
     e.   skilled white male and female workers

65. An author whose works helped to establish a national identity for American literature was
     a.   James Fenimore Cooper
     b.   Edgar Allen Poe
     c.   Horace Greeley
     d.   Walt Whitman
     e.   Emily Dickinson

66. Transcendentalists were interested in using their literary output
    a.   to create a romanticized view of American life
    b.   to foster the development of a national identity
    c.   to question natural law
    d.   to reform American life
    e.   to develop a rational explanation for life

67. By the 1830s, the greatest growth in printed material occurred in
    a.   Newspapers
    b.   religious literature
    c.   literary magazines
    d.   almanacs
    e.   sentimental novels

68. Which of the following artists painted romanticized versions of life on the western frontier?
    a.   John James Audobon
    b.   George Caleb Bingham
    c.   George Catlin
    d.   Thomas Cole
    e.   Asher B Durand

69. The campaign for local option laws was one aspect of which of the following movements?
    a.   prison reform
    b.   abolition
    c.   care of the mentally ill
    d.   schools for the blind and hearing impaired
    e.   temperance

70. Which of the following characteristics of European American society was not adopted by the Cherokee nation?
    a.   written language
    b.   enslavement of African Americans
    c.   individual's right to sell land to European Americans
    d.   Christianity
    e.   written constitution

71. All of the following are associated with the abolition movement EXCEPT
    a.   Frederick Douglass
    b.   William Lloyd Garrison
    c.   Elizabeth Cady Stanton
    d.   Sojourner Truth
    e.   George Washington Carver

72. All of the following were associated with the Underground Railroad EXCEPT
    a. Quakers
    b. Sojourner Truth
    c. the spiritual "Follow the Drinking Gourd"
    d. Canada
    e. the Deep South

73. All of the following split the abolitionist movement EXCEPT
    a. the exportation of slaves to and colonization in Africa
    b. Southern abolitionists versus Northern abolitionists
    c. the role of women in the abolitionist movement
    d. gradual versus immediate emancipation
    e. participation in the political process to change slave laws

74. Texas gained its independence as a result of
    a. the Mexican War
    b. the battle of San Jacinto
    c. the fight at the Alamo
    d. annexation by the United States
    e. a vote of all male Americanos and Tejanos property owners

75. Members of the Whig Party were most likely to disagree among themselves over the issue of
    a. protective tariffs
    b. social reforms
    c. continuation of the central bank
    d. extension of slavery into the territories
    e. immigration policies

76. The first example of the factory system in the United States was the work of
    a. Samuel F.B Morse
    b. Eli Whitney
    c. Francis Cabot Lowell
    d. Samuel Colt
    e. Robert Fulton

77. The first well-known woman scientist in the United States was
    a. Margaret Sanger
    b. Jane Addams
    c. Elizabeth Cady Stanton
    d. Maria Mitchell
    e. Alice Paul

78. Middle-class Americans at mid-century viewed public education
    a. as a civilizing influence on immigrants
    b. as a stabilizing force in a world of rapid change
    c. as a way to mold a subservient working class
    d. as a way to increase productivity while wiping out innovative thinking
    e. as still unnecessary for girls

79. Most fiction and nonfiction writers in the first part of the mid-nineteenth century
    a. wrote for the new magazines
    b. used themes from the nation's past
    c. supported abolition
    d. were social critics
    e. were "yellow journalists"

80. Which of the following is an allegory of good and evil?
    a. Leaves of Grass
    b. Moby Dick
    c. The Legend of Sleepy Hollow
    d. The Autobiography of Frederick Douglass
    e. Godey's Lady Book

81. This political cartoon
    a. is in support of the temperance movement
    b. plays off Andrew Jackson's humble beginnings
    c. plays off the Democrats' depiction of Harrison as living in a log cabin and drinking hard cider
    d. is in support of Harrison and Tyler
    e. is an example of the mudslinging that went on in the election of 1840

"WE STOOP TO CONQUER."

82. Labor had limited success in organizing in the 1840s and 1850s primarily because of
    a. lack of workers willing to lead organizing efforts
    b. periodic economic depressions that made workers afraid to organize
    c. the displacement of human labor by machines
    d. the lack of a history of successful labor organization in the United States
    e. the increasing ethnic diversity of the workforce as immigration increased

83. Americans who settled in Texas under Mexican rule plotted rebellion when Mexico tried
    a. to enforce its ban on slavery
    b. to collect the excise tax on goods exported from Texas
    c. to conscript Americanos into the Mexican army
    d. to encourage Native American attacks on Americanos settlements
    e. to end American immigration into Texas

84. The Seneca Falls Convention in 1848 took up the issue of
    a. temperance
    b. women's rights
    c. abolition of slavery
    d. prison reform
    e. universal education

85. Folk artists tended to use which of the following as themes for their works?
    a. portraits and scenes of family life
    b. ideas from the nation's past
    c. scenes from nature
    d. factory scenes
    e. scenes from Greek and Roman myths

86. "East by sunrise, West by sunset, North by the Arctic Expedition, and South as far as we darn well please." This quotation was another way of describing which of the following ideas?
    a. nativism
    b. manifest destiny
    c. manumission
    d. internationalism
    e. globalization

87. Those most likely to move into the class of Southern elite were
    a. middle-class professionals
    b. frontier farmers
    c. smaller farmers with a few slaves
    d. carpetbaggers
    e. politicians

88. Which of the following was NOT a utopian community?
    a. Deseret
    b. New Harmony
    c. Amana
    d. Brook Farm
    e. Oneida

89. Oberlin College is credited with being
    a. the first women's college
    b. the first coeducational college
    c. the first historically all-black college
    d. the first land-grant college
    e. the oldest college in the United States

90. All of the following underlay anti-immigrant feelings in the 1800s EXCEPT
    a. immigrants would hold back progress
    b. immigrants would take jobs away from the native-born
    c. immigrants would weaken the nation because they tended to live in their own communities
    d. many immigrants were Roman Catholic rather than Protestant
    e. immigrants might be revolutionaries fleeing the Europe after the unsuccessful revolutions of 1830 and 1848

91. Which of the following is an accurate description of the growth of cities by the mid-1800s?
    a. The largest centers of population had shifted to the Midwest.
    b. Cities were ringed by factories.
    c. Cities were becoming separated into neighborhoods based on socioeconomic levels.
    d. Sewer systems, regular garbage collection, and public water systems had come into wide use.
    e. Cities were safer because of street lights at night and traffic lights at intersections.

92. The Whig Party was replaced as a major party in the two-party system by the
    a. Democratic Party
    b. Democratic-Republican Party
    c. Loyalists
    d. Republican Party
    e. Bull Moose Party

93. The majority of pioneers in Oregon and the Puritans in Massachusetts had which of the following motivations in common?
    a. look for gold
    b. establish a theocracy
    c. escape repressive government policies
    d. better themselves financially
    e. convert the Native Americans to Christianity

94. Which of the following was meant to stop Congress from considering anti-slavery petitions?
    a. committee system
    b. censure
    c. filibuster
    d. cloture
    e. gag rule

95. Most white Southern families
    a. were plantation owners
    b. were tenant farmers
    c. lived on the frontier
    d. lived at subsistence level
    e. owned fewer than 20 slaves

96. All of the following were reasons that Southerners gave to justify slavery EXCEPT
    a. slavery helped slaves by guaranteeing them life-long employment and care
    b. the demand for cotton was on the increase
    c. raising cotton was very labor-intensive, so a cheap source of labor was needed
    d. the lack of a transportation network in the South meant there was no motivation to become industrialized
    e. slavery was cost-effective because the warm climate of the South allowed year-round cultivation of cotton

97. Which of the following was NOT true about life in the North for free African Americans?
    a. The basis of African American community life was the black church.
    b. Although African Americans lived in segregated areas, their children did not attend segregated schools.
    c. Free African Americans had few civil rights.
    d. Free African Americans faced discrimination in public facilities such as streetcars and theaters.
    e. Free African Americans had limited job opportunities.

98. "Can people of a Territory in any lawful way, against the wishes of any citizen of the United States, exclude slavery from their limits prior to the formation of a State constitution? I answer emphatically, . . . that in my opinion the people of a Territory can by lawful means, exclude slavery from their limits prior to the formation of a State constitution." The principle referred to in this quotation is
    a. nullification
    b. slave codes
    c. direct representation
    d. popular sovereignty
    e. virtual representation

99. All of the following increased tensions between North and South over slavery EXCEPT
    a. the Fugitive Slave Act
    b. Uncle Tom's Cabin
    c. "Bleeding Kansas"
    d. the rise of the Know-Nothing Party
    e. John Brown's raid

100. The Ostend Manifesto
    a. demanded that Spain sell Florida to the United States
    b. was the formal agreement handing over the Louisiana Territory to the United States
    c. set the boundary between Canada and the United States
    d. denounced the annexation of Texas
    e. threatened a U.S.-supported revolution in Cuba if Spain would not sell the island to the United States

101. The Wilmot Proviso was controversial because it proposed
    a. a ban on adding new states until a solution could be worked out about slavery
    b. a constitutional amendment giving Congress the power to ban slavery
    c. a ban on slavery in any state created out of land bought from Mexico
    d. federal funding for colonization efforts in Africa
    e. abolishing slavery and compensating slaveowners

102. Most goldhunters in the California gold rush of 1849
    a. came in family groups
    b. planned on finding gold and using it to buy land and settle down
    c. were immigrants
    d. expected to find gold and return home
    e. were from the Northeast

103. Of the various provisions of the Compromise of 1850, which one helped to turn many Northerners into abolitionists?
    a. admission of California as a slave state
    b. banning of the slave trade, but not slavery in the District of Columbia
    c. allowing people in Utah and New Mexico to decide whether they wanted to be admitted as free or slave states
    d. payment of $10 million to Texas in exchange for an end to its claim on parts of New Mexico
    e. the Fugitive Slave Law

104. The Republican platform of 1860
    a. supported John Brown's raid
    b. promised to stop the spread of slavery into new territories
    c. promised to provide access to public land for homesteaders
    d. promised to fund a transcontinental railroad
    e. promised to raise the tariff

105. The Civil War was most likely a result of
    a. racism on the part of Southerners
    b. political rather than economic differences
    c. incompetent political leadership on the national level
    d. opposing and intractable differences between North and South
    e. moral rather than political differences

106. Which of the following explains why Lincoln did not initially make emancipation a goal of the Civil War?
    a. He did not want to incite a general uprising of slaves.
    b. He did not believe that the Constitution gave the President the authority to end slavery.
    c. He was concerned that the British would support the Confederacy against the Union.
    d. He was concerned that the border states would join the Confederacy.
    e. He believed that slaveowners should be compensated for their lost property and the government didn't have enough money to pay them.

107. All of the following were disadvantages of the Confederacy EXCEPT
    a. high inflation
    b. lack of rail lines for transporting goods and supplies and moving soldiers
    c. little industrial production
    d. northern blockade of ships that severely limited trade
    e. they had to fight a defensive war

108. The major goal of the Confederacy's foreign policy was to
    a. gain the help of Great Britain in blockading Northern ports
    b. sell government bonds to foreign governments to raise money
    c. keep Mexico from invading Texas
    d. buy supplies from France
    e. gain recognition as an independent nation from foreign governments

109. The main goal of Lincoln's plan for Reconstruction was to
    a. remake Southern society to guarantee African Americans their rights
    b. grant voting rights to former male slaves
    c. punish the South
    d. restore the Union as quickly as possible
    e. return the same politicians to office as before the war in order to maintain continuity

110. All of the following were part of Johnson's Reconstruction plan EXCEPT
    a. Confederate debts would be repaid
    b. states could hold constitutional conventions without requiring a set number of voters take an oath of allegiances to the United States
    c. pardons for all who took the oath of allegiance to the United States except for certain officials and wealthy Southerners
    d. ratification of the Thirteenth Amendment
    e. repeal secession

111. After the Civil War, women were told to put aside their demand for voting rights and to work instead for
    a. property rights
    b. voting rights for African American men
    c. an end to the poll tax
    d. equal educational opportunities for African Americans
    e. passage of the Thirteenth Amendment

112. Andrew Johnson based his veto of the Civil Rights Act of 1866 on which of the following?
    a. The act did not include provisions against the black codes.
    b. It was unconstitutional because it violated states' rights.
    c. It did not include women's voting rights.
    d. Its provisions were covered in the Fourteenth Amendment.
    e. It would antagonize Northern supporters.

113. The most important goal for freed slaves was
    a. to take surnames
    b. to marry legally
    c. to search for family members who had been sold away
    d. to leave their plantations to prove they were free to travel
    e. to acquire land, a house, and a means of making a living

114. Which of the following was part of the Radical Republicans' plan for Reconstruction?
    a. A state could be readmitted to the Union when 10 percent of its voters took the oath of allegiance to the United States.
    b. The military governor of each district would appoint delegates to state constitutional conventions.
    c. State legislatures had to ratify the Thirteenth Amendment.
    d. The new state constitutions were to guarantee voting rights for African American males.
    e. Pardons would not be granted to former high-ranking Confederate officials.

115. "Seward's Folly" refers to
    a. the purchase of Alaska from Russia
    b. the annexation of Hawaii
    c. the Gadsden Purchase from Mexico
    d. the annexation of Texas
    e. the acquisition of Oregon

116. Redeemers were so-called because they
    a. worked for the Freedmen's Bureau
    b. were white Southern politicians who restored white supremacy in the South
    c. were members of a white supremacist group similar to the Ku Klux Klan
    d. oversaw the sharecropping system for absentee landowners
    e. were the civilian administrators for the military districts in the South during Reconstruction

117. Reconstruction ended in 1877 because
    a. all the Southern states had satisfied the requirements of Radical Reconstruction
    b. a deal was reached to name Hayes the winner of the presidential election of 1876 in exchange for an end to Reconstruction
    c. Northerners had grown tired of paying for military occupation of the South
    d. the Amnesty Act had made military occupation unnecessary
    e. Hayes, the Republican presidential candidate, had campaigned on a promise to end Reconstruction

118. Which of the following replaced the plantation system of agriculture in the South?
    a. sharecropping
    b. large-scale commercial farming
    c. small independently owned farms
    d. day labor on former plantations
    e. farm mechanization

119. White Southerners benefited from all of the following after the Civil War EXCEPT
    a. greater spending on public education
    b. improved transportation network
    c. introduction of more industry into the South
    d. more democratic state constitutions
    e. lower taxes

120. What did Presidents George Washington, Andrew Jackson, William Henry Harrison, Zachary Taylor, and Ulysses S. Grant have in common?

    a. None fought on the frontier.
    b. All were Southerners.
    c. All were Democrats.
    d. All were war heroes.
    e. All were slaveowners.

ANSWER

1. The correct answer is B. This is the only answer that applies to Native American groups IN GENERAL. The other answers are culture traits of only certain groups. TIP: Be alert to qualifiers like "in general." They can change the meaning of a question.

2. The correct answer is E. Choice E occurred after the Spanish had firmly established their hold on Native American areas. The other factors all contributed to the ability of the Spanish to take over Indian lands.

3. The correct answer is B. The only effect of the enclosure movement on the Americas, answer B, was to provide landless farmworkers with a reason to emigrate. The other answers are all true and, therefore, not correct for this reverse answer question.

4. The correct answer is A. Answer choices B through E were direct results of the dumping of gold and silver, most notably silver from Mexican mines. People may have decided to create joint-stock companies to take advantage of commercial opportunities, but they were not a direct result. TIP: Be careful of NOT questions. You are looking for what is NOT true or does NOT fit.

5. The correct answer is B. Think about the Massachusetts Bay Colony that the Puritans founded. The Puritans kept tight control over not only religious, but also political and social aspects of the colony. Choices A, B, and E are the opposites of what occurred. Choice D doesn't make sense; behavior to Puritans was an indication of whether one was saved or not.

6. The correct answer is E. The wrong answers are good distracters in that they are all known for their writings. Answer A is the first published African poet in the colonies; among her poems is one she wrote to George Washington. Answer B is well known, but wrote in the late 1800s, long after there was American poetry. Answer C was a contemporary of Bradstreet's, but he wrote a History of Plymouth Plantation. Answer D was a famous Puritan preacher whose sermons were published.

7. The correct answer is B. While answer choices A and D have elements of truth in them, answer choice B states Penn's intention. Answers C and E are just wrong.

8. The correct answer is B. You should have been able immediately to cross off choices C and D. Common sense would tell you that the First Continental Congress was too late in the history of the colonies. Proprietors, choice D, didn't have to pass laws; they decreed what needed to be done. The thing to remember about answer A is that the House of Burgesses was the first lawmaking body in the English colonies. Answer E passed the Act of Toleration, granting religious freedom to most faiths.

9. The correct answer is D. Discard choice C immediately. Georgia wasn't founded until 1732 and the question asks about the late seventeenth century. Remember John Rolfe's introduction of tobacco into the Virginia Colony in 1613 and how it saved the fledgling colony from extinction? The climate in choices A and B is too cold. Rice and indigo were answer choice E's export products.

10. The correct answer is E. The first century of colonization saw the founding of Harvard, William and Mary, and Yale. Other colleges such as Princeton (College of New Jersey) followed in the 1700s. Answer A is true for all frontier communities in the settlement of the United States as is answer B. TIP: This is another NOT question. Remember to look for the statement that is not true.

11. The correct answer is A. King Philip is his English name, but to his Wampanoag nation he was known as Metacom. He led a war against the colonists in New England over land rights. Answer B was a rebellion of frontiersmen against the

governor and House of Burgesses in the Virginia colony. Answer C was a rebellion on the frontier in the early days of the new United States. Answer D was an uprising of slaves in South Carolina and Georgia in 1739. Answer E was fought in Florida between Seminole and the U.S. Army, not colonists.

12. The correct answer is C. Answer A is incorrect, because the colonial legislatures paid the salaries of all governors. Answer B is false because all colonies had legislatures. Remember the Patriot mantra of "no taxation without representation." The royal governor and council had little impact on local government, so answer D is incorrect. All colonies limited voting, so answer E is incorrect.

13. The correct answer is E. Bacon's Rebellion attracted former indentured servants who wanted land and did not quibble about killing Native Americans to get it. Large and small planters alike came to see these discontented former servants as potential rebels who might come after them next. As a result, the planters turned to slave labor rather than indentured servants. While the pool of indentured servants, choice B, grew smaller over the decades, that was not the reason for the shift in labor pool. Choices A and D may be true in general, but not in relation to Bacon's Rebellion.

14. The correct answer is B. Eliminate answer E, Georgia, right away, because Georgia wasn't a colony until 1732. Based on what you know about Southern colonies—the agricultural base of their economies and their widespread settlements— eliminate answer D. Why would they care about establishing schools in far-off towns? That leaves the New England and Middle colonies. While any one might be a good choice, think ahead to the reformers of the 1800s. Massachusetts' educational system was so far advanced by the 1830s that Horace Mann, the first Massachusetts' secretary of education, organized the existing school districts into a statewide system. Answer B would be an educated guess and the right answer. By the way, answers A and C, Pennsylvania and New York, got on the education bandwagon in the 1800s.

15. The correct answer is B. By 1700, some 150,000 English had immigrated to North America. Answer B, the Scots Irish, had originally immigrated to Ireland from Scotland, and the end of the cloth-making industry in Ireland in the 1700s forced many of their descendants to emigrate. Answer D, the Germans were the first group of non-English speakers to immigrate in large numbers. Most of the 100,000 or so that came went to Pennsylvania. Answer A, the Irish, is the wrong time period; the Irish came in large numbers in the 1840s as a result of the potato famine. However, their numbers were never as great as the Germans. The same is true for answer E, the Welsh. Answer C, French Huguenots, came in the 1680s to escape religious persecution and settled mainly in Carolina colony.

16. The correct answer is B. About 70 percent of all white colonists were considered middle class. They were the small farm owners, shopkeepers, and craftworkers. Answer A is incorrect, because the ability to move up the social ladder was a characteristic of colonial society. Answer C is incorrect, because wealth still determined a person's place in the social structure. Answer D is incorrect because it leaves out wealthy planters. Answer E is incorrect because there was a large lower class of poor farm families, slaves, and indentured servants.

17. The correct answer is B. Puritans saw children as adults in miniature and dressed and treated them as such. Their personalities and childishness were to be bent to the teachings of God and all evidence of sin eradicated, often by the rod. Don't be fooled by answer A. Clothes were not important to Puritans; they would have been more likely to dress their children sensibly than fashionably, what well dressed implies.

18. The correct answer is D. This is a common sense question. Why would anyone ask a question about conditions on a ship if it weren't a slave ship? Look for clues in the quotation itself to confirm your idea. The words coast and permitted to stay signal that this was indeed written by someone who was captive on a slave ship. Africans were routinely captured inland and marched to slave factories on the coast and from there onto ships. Permitted indicates the writer didn't have any choice.

19. The correct answer is D. The early rigidity of the Puritans and Pilgrims gave way to a less strict adherence to religious tenets. However, the churches of New England continued to avoid any kind of hierarchy. Local congregations, or churches, managed their own affairs, hence the name. Roman Catholicism, answer A, although the faith of the Calvert proprietors of Maryland, had little influence anywhere, even in that colony. Answer B had the most influence among the planters of the Southern colonies. Answer C was limited mostly to the Scots and Scots Irish who settled the inland areas of the Southern colonies. Answer E had its greatest influence in the 1700s as a result of the Great Awakening religious revival in the colonies.

20. The correct answer is B. Single women and widows initially had more rights in the colonies, including the right to conduct business. This was a holdover from English common law. Over time, colonial legislatures and courts included married women in the right to conduct business, provided it was in connection with or for their husbands.

21. The correct answer is E. Answer choice E is antithetical to choice A. They can't both be true. Common sense points to choice A as being true and, therefore, choice E must be the answer. TIP: Be careful of EXCEPT questions. With these questions, you are looking for what is not true.

22. The correct answer is D. Answer A is incorrect, because slaves were encouraged to have families so that natural increase rather than importation would provide new workers for slaveowners. Answer B is the opposite of what occurred. Answer C is incorrect because the major colonial crop in Virginia was tobacco. Answer E is the opposite of what occurred; there was more diversity in jobs in Virginia.

23. The correct answer is E. French North America had few colonists. Most of the French immigrants were men who made their living as fur trappers and traders. Answer choice A is incorrect, although Benjamin Franklin attempted to join the colonies into a union during the war. Choice B is wrong; the British have only one ally, the Iroquois. Choice C is also untrue; the British colonies had a variety of ethnic groups within their borders.

24. The correct answer is B. Answer B is correct because the land beyond the settled colonies had riches that would ultimately benefit the British government through increased trade. Answer A makes no sense because the proclamation was issued because the French had been defeated and the area now was under British control. Answer C is the opposite of what would have happened if the proclamation had been enforced. Answer D is true, but was not the reason behind the government's lack of action. Answer E is incorrect; most of the Native Americans were British allies in the French and Indian War.

25. The correct answer is E. According to mercantilism, colonies exist for the benefit of the home country. Answer A relates to the establishment of slavery in new states in the 1800s. Choice B was the British government's attitude toward enforcing economic laws related to the colonies prior to the 1760s. Choice C was the colonists' argument against Parliament's attempt to tax the colonies. Choice D is what occurred in Europe in the 1500s as money poured into circulation and goods became scarce in relation to available money.

26. The correct answer is D. The revenues raised by the customs duties imposed in the Townshend Act were to be used to pay royal officials in the colonies, thus eliminating the bargaining chip that colonial legislatures held. Answer A refers to the direct tax on documents. Answer B required colonists to provide housing for British troops. Choice C are the laws passed to punish Boston and Massachusetts for the Boston Tea Party. Answer E was passed by Parliament reasserting its authority to make laws for the colonies.

27. The correct answer is D. The basic premise of the Enlightenment was that the natural world was governed by certain rules that were knowable by humans through observation. These rules could be applied to further the good of humankind. The Enlightenment encouraged scientific experimentation. Answer D, predestination, refers to the religious belief that people were either saved or damned by God and that their own good works were of no value in determining their salvation.

28. The correct answer is D. This is very inflammatory language and would hardly have been spoken by a French nobleman, choice A, or by choice B, William Pitt, the British Prime Minister, even though he was a defender of the American colonists. It is out of character for George Washington, answer C. Choice E, Edmund Burke, the Irish member of Parliament, supported the Americans, but in more reasonable terms. The sentiments fit the nature of Thomas Paine, answer D, the author of the inflammatory pamphlet Common Sense.

29. The correct answer is B. The battle of Saratoga was a turning point in the American Revolution. Answer A is the opposite of what occurred; the battle was a much needed American victory. Answer C is incorrect because most of the Confederacy were on the British side. General William Howe's departure from Boston in 1776 ended any fighting in New England, so answer D is incorrect. Spain and the Netherlands, answer E, were enemies of England.

30. The correct answer is D. Florida was given to Spain by Great Britain and did not become part of the United States until 1819.

31. The correct answer is B. Answer choices A, B, and C are true, but the question asks for the major problem of the Confederation government. That's answer A Think of the Confederation government as a body without a head. TIP: Establishing a way to admit new states was the only major achievement of the Confederation government.

32. The correct answer is E. The Ordinance of 1785 and the Northwest Ordinance of 1787 are considered the achievement of the Confederation government. Answer A refers to the first ten amendments to the U.S. Constitution and guarantees certain rights of individuals. Answer B set up a system to give land to families in the West who were willing to work it; passed in 1862 this act is too late to fit the question. Answer C also is too late in chronology to be correct; it was passed in 1854 and set up a way for residents of Kansas and Nebraska to decide whether they wanted their state to be free or slave. Answer D is the acquisition of land from Mexico in 1853 that makes up the current border between Mexico and the United States in southern Arizona and New Mexico.

33. The correct answer is D. Answer A, the establishment of an executive branch, or office of the president, was the result of a compromise among delegates to the Constitutional Convention, but it was not the Great Compromise. Answer B is known as the "three-fifths compromise." Answer C was the result of a compromise engineered by Alexander Hamilton and James Madison to ensure that the new United States pay all federal and state debts resulting from the Revolutionary War, however, it was achieved after the U.S. Constitution went into effect. Answer E is a misreading of Article 1, Section 9, Clause 1 of the Constitution, which states that Congress may not prohibit the importation of slaves into any state before 1808. The section did not end slavery.

34. The correct answer is A. Answers B and C are just distracters. They have something to do with the Constitution, but nothing to do with the right answer. Answer D was eliminated as a concern by the Constitutional Convention through the Great Compromise, also known as the Connecticut Compromise. Answer E doesn't make sense, because the purpose of federalism was to balance power between the national government and the states.

35. The correct answer is D. The First Amendment also includes the right to petition the government. In answer A, the right to have an attorney is guaranteed by the Sixth Amendment and right to due process is guaranteed by the Fifth and Fourteenth Amendments. In answer B, the right to bear arms is guaranteed by the Second Amendment. The right to vote, answer C, was extended to African American men by the Fourteenth Amendment and to women by the Nineteenth. "One man, one vote" refers to redistricting issues.

36. The correct answer is B. Answer B is correct. The delegates to the Constitutional Convention set up a system to ensure that no one branch of government became too powerful; this system is called "checks and balances." Answer A refers to the right of the Supreme Court to judge the constitutionality of Congressional laws and executive acts; this right was established in Marbury vs. Madison. Answer C is the process by which the Constitution is changed. Answers D and E are

terms given to certain clauses within Article 1, Section 8 of the Constitution. Answer E refers to Clauses 1 through 17, which list specific powers granted to Congress. Answer D is a term used to describe Clause 18, which gives the Congress the power to make all laws "necessary and proper" to carry out the business of the government. This is also known as the "elastic clause."

37. The correct answer is D. As the new Constitution went into the effect, there was still some doubt as to whether wealthy men in some states would support the Union or attempt to take their states out of the Union. Hamilton's proposal was meant to reassure this segment, answer D. Answer A is incorrect because it was the southern states that had repaid their debts for the most part. Answers B and C are not true. Answer E doesn't make sense, since the new nation needed investment capital from anywhere.

38. The correct answer is A. As part of Hamilton's plan to put the new nation on sound footing, he proposed and Congress passed an excise tax on whiskey. Farmers in the Pennsylvania backcountry rebelled because they turned much of the corn they raised into whiskey, which was easier to transport and sell. President George Washington called out the state militia to put down the rebellion against the federal government. Answer B, Shays's Rebellion, refers to an uprising in Massachusetts under the Articles of Confederation government. Answer C, Denmark Vesey's Conspiracy, was a planned uprising of enslaved African Americans in South Carolina to take control of Charleston, which was stopped before it began. Answer D, XYZ Affair, refers to an episode that almost led to war between the United States and France in 1797. Answer E, War Hawks, were a party in Congress that wanted the United States to declare war on Great Britain in the early 1800s. They finally achieved their wish with the War of 1812.

39. The correct answer is B. Answer A, Benjamin Franklin, had died by the time Washington, DC, was being surveyed and designed. Answer C, Joseph Henry, was a physicist and the first secretary of the Smithsonian Institution in Washington, DC, in the mid 1800s. Answer D, Charles Wilson Peale, was a famous painter of the period. Answer E, Benjamin Rush, was a Philadelphia colleague of Franklin's and a doctor. He was the first to diagnose insanity as an illness.

40. The correct answer is A. The Federalists were the party of industry and growth; think Alexander Hamilton. Therefore, its members would be drawn from those who would benefit from trade and industrial growth, answer A. Their opponents, the Republicans who were led by Thomas Jefferson favored an agrarian nation of small farmers. Answer B and C together would describe Republicans. Answers D and E are there to distract you from the correct answer; they're both wrong.

41. The correct answer is C. This sentence is from Washington's "Farewell Address." His warning against foreign entanglements is one of the most often cited pieces of his advice for the new nation. If you didn't know this, common sense would help you eliminate some answers. Answer A isn't logical since Franklin worked to achieve an alliance with France during the war. You know Thomas Paine, answer B, as the writer of pamphlets to incite colonists to rebel, but you don't know him as a foreign policy expert—and he wasn't. Abraham Lincoln, answer E, is associated with preserving the Union, not on foreign policy, so this answer doesn't make much sense. Answer D, John Adams, is a distracter.

42. The correct answer is D. The Shawnee, Miami, Sauk, Fox, and other Native American nations in the Old Northwest agreed to the treaty after their defeat in the battle of Fallen Timbers. Answer A was solved by Jay's Treaty by which the British agreed to leave the western frontier by 1796. Answer B was achieved in 1819. Answers C and E are distracters.

43. The correct answer is B. The Sedition Act, passed on July 14, 1789 made the publishing of "false, scandalous, and malicious writing" against the government illegal. The act was passed under the guise of protecting the U.S. from "dangerous" aliens, but in reality, it was a tool the Federalists used to hinder the growth of the Democratic-Republican Party.

44. The correct answer is B. The theory of nullification, that states could declare null and void any law passed by Congress, was at the center of the states rights' issue in the nineteenth century prior to the Civil War. Answer A is incorrect because slavery had been institutionalized by a series laws going back to the 1660s in Virginia. Answers C, D, and E are incorrect.

45. The correct answer is D. Answer A, Brown v. Board of Education, was decided in 1954 and eliminated the argument of "separate but equal" facilities and ended school segregation. Decided in 1896, answer B, Plessy v. Ferguson, established the doctrine of "separate but equal." Answer C, the Dred Scott decision, declared slaves property and protected the property rights of slaveowners. Its effect was to declare null and void the Missouri Compromise, which had banned slavery north of the 36th parallel in lands acquired under the Louisiana Purchase, and the popular sovereignty provision of the Kansas-Nebraska Act. In McCulloch v. Maryland, answer E, the Supreme Court broadened the powers of Congress to include implied powers in addition to the enumerated powers listed in Article 1. TIP: It's important to read all the answers. A good distracter like answer A here sounds familiar and has something to do with the topic, but isn't the right answer.

46. The correct answer is E. Once and for all, the Lewis and Clark expedition commissioned by President Thomas Jefferson ended the hope of a Northwest Passage.

47. The correct answer is B. The United States had declared its neutrality in the fight between Great Britain and France, which should have allowed its ships to trade with both nations. However, neither Great Britain nor France respected this declaration of neutrality and seized ships and goods bound for the other nation. Answer A is the opposite of the truth. Both Great Britain and France were highly dependent on U.S.-made goods. Answer C is the opposite of what was occurring; the British were impressing American sailors. Answers D and E are distracters. Both had something to do with the embargo but not as stated.

48. The correct answer is B. Answer B, Federalists, lost influence because they had protested the war. Answer A, War Hawks, a group of congressmen from the frontier states, were vocal supporters of the war. Answer D, Westerners, is similar to answer A and incorrect for the same reason. Answer C, Whigs, were later than the War of 1812. Answer E, Democrats, supported the war.

49. The correct answer is E. Answer A is incorrect; the United States had a small and poorly trained army. Answer B is incorrect because the United States lost tax revenues because of the loss of foreign trade and suffered high unemployment. Answers C and D are true but less significant than the war's effect on the national consciousness and sense of national identity of Americans. The United States was not yet two decades old and had taken on the most powerful nation in the world and fought it to a standoff. Neither side won and neither side lost.

50. The correct answer is C. Answer A would be a good guess, but the real waves of immigration came after 1840. Answer B is a bad guess because the importation of Africans was banned after 1808 by the Constitution. Answer D is a bad guess, too, because Native Americans were considered foreign nations during that period of history. Answer E is illogical because the United States bought empty land except for Native Americans.

51. The correct answer is B. The operative word in the question prompt is bold. What would make a nation's foreign policy be considered bold? Answer A doesn't give an adequate reason why time would make a difference. Answer C is part of what the Monroe Doctrine states, but that's not what the question asks. Answer D is not true of the Doctrine. Answer E is not true, because Great Britain had asked the United States to join it in issuing a declaration similar to the Monroe Doctrine, but Monroe decided to issue it in the name of the United States alone.

52. The correct answer is E. Answer A, Era of Good Feelings, was the term given to the administrations of James Monroe. Answer B, Monroe Doctrine, is the name given to the Monroe's warning to European nations to stay out of the Americas. Answer C, Compromise of 1820, also known as the Missouri Compromise, banned slavery below the 36th parallel in

states made from territory acquired in the Louisiana Purchase. Answer D, Hartford Convention, was a meeting called in New England to denounce the War of 1812.

53. The correct answer is B. Answer A is incorrect; that was the Kansas-Nebraska Act. Answer C is incorrect because the issue of the expansion of slavery and its solution was a result of sectional, not party, rivalries. Answer D is too obvious. Answer E is incorrect; there was no coalition.

54. The correct answer is E. Read "Andrew Jackson" and think West and the "common man."

55. The correct answer is D. Answers A and B were results of the election of 1800. Answer C has a familiar ring to it, but Jackson claimed that John Quincy Adams and Henry Clay had struck "the corrupt bargain" when Clay gave his support to Adams and Adams then made Clay his secretary of state. Answer E is the opposite of what has occurred. Between 1824 and 1960 when John Kennedy was elected, presidents came from all sections of the country except New England.

56. The correct answer is E. The title of this cartoon is "Office Hunters of the Year 1834." Jackson's introduction of patronage on a grand scale was a favorite subject of his political opponents.

57. The correct answer is D. Answer A, the transportation revolution, did not greatly affect the South. By 1860, it still had fewer miles of railroad track than either the Northeast or the Midwest. Answer B, the mechanization of textile production, made use of the increased amount of raw cotton available, but did not increase cotton agriculture. Answer C, the introduction of tobacco, is the wrong century; that's Jamestown Colony in the early 1600s. Answer E, protective tariffs, actually hurt the economy of the South.

58. The correct answer is C. The Specie Circular was an order issued by President Andrew Jackson that required that all federal lands be paid for in gold or silver (specie). Answers A, B, and D were all causes of Jackson's order, not results. Answer E is a good distracter. It refers to Jackson's fight to end the Second Bank of the United States, but is not related to the Specie Circular.

59. The correct answer is D. Some knowledge of chronology would help you here. John Marshall was the first Supreme Court Chief Justice, so it would be doubtful that he would still be alive when Lincoln was President. Eliminate Lincoln. Then consider the character of the men who are left. A sentiment as combative as that expressed here fits only Andrew Jackson. He used these words in referring to the Supreme Court decision in Worcester v. State of Georgia, which held that Georgia could not take Cherokee lands.

60. The correct answer is A. The transportation revolution connected the Midwest and the Northeast more closely. Answer B provided a clue. The price of food fell because food was shipped from the Midwest to the Northeast through the canal system.

61. The correct answer is B. The Second Great Awakening led to a rapid increase in membership in the Methodist and Baptist churches. Perhaps the most significant fact in these right answers is answer C. The Second Great Awakening provide the impetus for much of the reform movements of the first half of the nineteenth century.

62. The correct answer is B. Prior to the development of the putting-out system, one worker would do all steps in a process to make something like a shoe. With the putting-out system, a worker would do only one step in the process, such as cutting out the leather for shoes. Answers A and D relate to industrialization, as does answer E, the first source of power to run machinery in factories.

63. The correct answer is C. It was not until the early 1800s that the so called "traditional" family roles were established. It was at this time that husbands and fathers became the "breadwinners" whilst the wives became defined as "homemakers."

64. The correct answer is D. It was not until late in the nineteenth century that unions were interested in organizing unskilled workers, women, and African Americans. The Knights of Labor accepted African American men. The American Federation of Labor began organizing skilled and unskilled male and female workers, African Americans, and immigrants in 1890.

65. The correct answer is A. Cooper used the experience of the frontier in New York State as the subject matter for his novels. Answer B, Edgar Allan Poe, was a later author as was answer C, Horace Greeley, a famous journalist of the latter half of the nineteenth century. Answer D, Walt Whitman, is a good distracter because the American consciousness was his subject matter, too, but he wrote in the mid 1800s. Answer E, Emily Dickinson, wrote very personal poetry that was not indicative of a larger national identity.

66. The correct answer is D. As Emerson wrote, "What is a man born for, but to be a Reformer?"

67. The correct answer is A. The huge increase in the number of newspapers paralleled the increasing interest in politics among ordinary people. Political parties published their own papers and gave a decidedly partisan view of events. In the 25 years between 1810 and 1835, the number of papers almost quadrupled, from 376 to 1,200. Answer D, almanacs, were highly popular in colonial times.

68. The correct answer is B. Answer A, John James Audobon, painted detailed and realistic pictures of birds in their natural habitat. Answer C, George Catlin, painted Native Americans and tried to interest other white Americans in rectifying the ill-treatment they were receiving at the hands of the federal government and settlers. Answer D, Thomas Cole, founded the Hudson River School of landscape painting. Answer E, Asher B Durand, an African American, was a member of the Hudson River School.

69. The correct answer is E. Local option laws were laws that gave municipalities, that is, local governments, the option to ban the sale of alcohol within their boundaries.

70. The correct answer is C. The Cherokee were one of what was termed the "Five Civilized Nations" because they adopted various culture traits of white residents of the United States, while remaining a separate nation.

71. The correct answer is E. Answer E was an African American scientist who worked after the Civil War in the South. Don't be fooled by answer C. Stanton was an abolitionist and a feminist. Her experience with the male-dominated abolition movement helped her become a feminist.

72. The correct answer is E. Answer E, the Deep South, doesn't fit because the Underground Railroad didn't reach that far. Freedom in the North or Canada was too far away. Answer A, Quakers, were among the first to help African Americans escape their owners in an informal network that over time became the Underground Railroad. Answer B, Sojourner Truth, was known as "Moses" for helping so many of her fellow African Americans escape. Spirituals like "Follow the Drinking Gourd," answer C, were codes for instructions for escaping North. Answer D, Canada, was the destination for many escaped slaves.

73. The correct answer is B. The conflicts within the abolitionists movement split along ideological lines, not sectional lines, so answer B is the correct choice because it's wrong. TIP: Remember to look for the answer that doesn't fit when you are answering an EXCEPT or a NOT question.

74. The correct answer is B. Answer A, the Mexican War, settled the disputed boundary between the United States and Mexico along the southern border of Texas, but Texas already had been annexed by the United States. Answer C is illogical, because the Texans lost the battle. Answer D is incorrect because independence and annexation are not the same. Texas gave up its independence when it was annexed. Answer E is a nice try, but wrong.

75. The correct answer is D. The Whig Party solidly supported a strong role for the federal government in the nation's economic affairs, so answers A and C can't be right. Whigs also believed in the perfectibility of people, so answer B can't be correct either. Answer E is a distracter, because immigration was becoming an issue in national politics by the mid-1800s; however, it isn't relevant for the Whigs. The major split in the Whig Party came about over national expansion and slavery.

76. The correct answer is C. Remember Lowell, Massachusetts, and the textile factories that employed native-born young women from farms and then replaced them with cheaper immigrant labor. That town was named after Francis Cabot Lowell. Answer A invented the telegraph; answer B, the cotton gin; answer D, the Colt revolver and the use of interchangeable parts for manufacturing; answer E, established the first successful commercial steamboat service in the United States.

77. The correct answer is D. Maria Mitchell, answer D, was an astronomer who discovered a comet and several distant star groups. Answer A, Margaret Sanger, worked for women's access to birth control in the twentieth century. Answer B, Jane Addams, was a social reformer who began the settlement house movement to aid immigrants. Answer C, Elizabeth Cady Stanton, was an abolitionist and founder of the feminist movement; she was one of the co-organizers of the first women's rights conference held at Seneca Falls in 1848. Answer E, Alice Paul, led the fight for voting rights for women in the early 1900s.

78. The correct answer is B. Education was meant to turn out educated workers who could use the new machinery in factories while instilling good habits of character such as obedience and hard work. This was the stabilizing effect that middle-class Americans were looking for. However, education was not meant to stamp out innovative thinking, which led to greater productivity, so answer D is incorrect. That also means that answer C is incorrect. Answer A is not true, although at a later period education was seen as the way to turn immigrants into citizens. Answer E is not true.

79. The correct answer is D. While writers such as Nathaniel Hawthorne and Washington Irving did use themes from the past, this was not true of many writers, so answer B is untrue. While answer C may be true, answer D is a better answer because it includes answer C. Answer E is a term that belongs to the end of the nineteenth century.

80. The correct answer is B. Herman Melville's story of Captain Ahab's search for the white whale is social critique of American society. Answer A is a volume of poetry by Walt Whitman. Answer C is a short story by Washington Irving that draws on the rich history of the Dutch in New York. Answer D is an autobiography and, therefore, nonfiction, although certainly a story of good and evil. Answer E is the title of a women's magazine popular in the nineteenth century.

81. The correct answer is E. The election of 1840 ushered in a new form of political campaign complete with slogans, barbecues, negative campaigning, and political songs. If you chose answer A, it's a good guess, but you didn't read the text. Answer B is incorrect; Jackson wasn't an abolitionist or a Whig. Answer C is a misstatement of the truth; it was the Whigs, not their opponents who depicted their candidate Harrison as living in a log cabin. Answer D is illogical. TIP: Always remember to read all the answer choices. You might have read answer A, jumped to the wrong conclusion, and chosen it for your answer.

82. The correct answer is E. The ethnic and cultural diversity of the workforce worked against the development of a sense of unity among workers. Answer B hindered unionizing because workers were afraid to lose their jobs, but it wasn't the main reason. Answer C doesn't make sense. Answer D would be true for any country since there had been no industrialization before the nineteenth century.

83. The correct answer is A. Mexico had always banned slavery, but had not enforced the law and Americanos had ignored it. Answer B was enforced and while answer E did occur the reason for rebellion was answer A. Answers C and D are untrue.

84. The correct answer is B. The full name was the National Women's Rights Convention and passed a Declaration of Sentiments modeled after the Declaration of Independence. It proposed twelve rights for women including free speech, property rights, and the right to vote. This is one you need to know because any of the other answers fit the time frame.

85. The correct answer is A. Answer C better fits the works of artists painting in the Romantic style. Answer D would be true of realist painters, but they don't appear until later in the century.

86. The correct answer is B. The quotation is from a Philadelphia newspaper published in 1853 and is similar to the views expressed by an editor of a New York paper in 1845, which coined the term manifest destiny. Answer A, nativism, is a policy of favoring native-born over immigrants. Answer C, manumission, is the freeing of slaves. Answers D and E are anachronisms, that is, they are not terms that would have been used by mid-nineteenth century Americans; they belong to the rhetoric of a later century.

87. The correct answer is A. Middle-class professionals were doctors, lawyers, and merchants who had the money to invest in land and slaves and were sometimes paid in land and slaves. Answer D, carpetbaggers, is a negative term used to describe Northerners who moved South after the Civil War to make their fortunes at the expense of Southerners. Answer E is illogical since Southern politicians were usually from the upper class.

88. The correct answer is A. Answer A, Deseret, was the name given to the first Mormon state in what would become Utah Territory. Answer B, New Harmony, Indiana, was founded by Robert Owen. Answer C, Amana, was in Iowa. Answer D, Brook Farm, was in Massachusetts. Answer E, Oneida, was founded in New York State. TIP: Don't be confused by NOT questions. Remember to look for the answer that doesn't fit. It's wrong but right for a reverse question.

89. The correct answer is B. Answer A is Mount Holyoke founded by Mary Lyons in 1837. Answer C is Lincoln University in Pennsylvania. Both of these colleges still exist. The honor of answer E belongs to Harvard, founded in 1836.

90. The correct answer is A. Except for immigrants being Roman Catholic, the same arguments were used against all immigrants in the 1800s, whether Italian or Chinese.

91. The correct answer is C. In colonial times, socioeconomic classes lived in close proximity to one another. Shopkeepers and artisans usually lived where or close to where they worked. Answer A is incorrect; the major population centers were still in New England and the Mid-Atlantic states along the coast. Answer B is incorrect, because factories were not established in large numbers until later in the century. Answer D is incorrect; the lack of sewers, the prevalence of garbage thrown into the street, and the lack of safe water still plagued cities. Answer E requires electrical power and that wasn't invented until later in the century either.

92. The correct answer is D. Answer A is the party of Andrew Jackson, which is descended from answer B, the party of Jefferson. Answer C is incorrect, but might trip you up because it sounds familiar. It's the name given to supporters of Great Britain during the American Revolution. Answer E is the splinter party that Theodore Roosevelt founded when he bolted the Republican Party to run for President in 1912.

93. The correct answer is D. One of the basic motivations for emigration and immigration alike was to better one's self financially. Neither group was interested in answer A. Answer B was a motive only for the Puritans; a theocracy is a government system on the rule of God. Answer C is illogical since the pioneers in Oregon were going to an area claimed by the United States. Don't be confused because every history textbook seems to mention the Whitmans and their efforts to Christianize the Native Americans. That wasn't the motive of most emigrants to Oregon.

94. The correct answer is E. Answer A doesn't make sense because that's how Congress conducts business, by the committee system. Answer B, censure, is what Southern members of Congress tried to do to Senator John Quincy Adams who fought

an eight-year battle to repeal the gag rule. Answer C, filibuster, is a tactic used in the Senate to forestall a vote on a bill. Answer D, cloture, is a parliamentary procedure by which debate is ended and a vote taken on a bill.

95. The correct answer is D. Most white Southern families lived on farms and raised crops for their own use. Answer A is incorrect, because there were only about 50,000 plantations with from 20 to 200 slaves, whereas there were hundreds of thousands of small farmers. Answers B, C, and E are incorrect.

96. The correct answer is D. Believe it or not, answer A was actually used to justify slavery. Southern plantation owners pointed to the conditions in Northern textile factories and claimed slavery was more beneficent. Answers B, C, and E provided reasons for continuing slavery. With an increasing demand for cotton, there was no end in sight to the profitability of slavery, and, therefore, no reason to abolish it.

97. The correct answer is B. This wrong answer should have been easy to spot, because if African Americans lived in segregated housing, their children would have gone to segregated schools. TIP: For NOT questions, remember to look for what isn't correct or true.

98. The correct answer is D. Stephen Douglas spoke these words in a debate with Abraham Lincoln during the Senatorial election campaign in Illinois in 1858. Douglas's answer to a question from Lincoln has become known as the Freeport Doctrine. Answers C and E are two principles that were involved in the American Revolution. Parliament claimed answer E and the colonists demanded answer C. Answers A and B are distracters that are real terms but have nothing to do with the question.

99. The correct answer is D. The Know-Nothing Party was founded to restrict immigrants and keep Roman Catholics from holding public office. Don't confuse it with the Free-Soil Party that was founded to stop the expansion of slavery into the territories. Answer A was one of the five laws that comprised the Compromise of 1850. Answer B was written by Harriet Beecher Stowe and gave a face to slavery in the person of Uncle Tom. Answer C was the term given to the violence that erupted when it came time for Kansans to vote for or against slavery in their territory. John Brown, answer E, was an abolitionist who seized the federal arsenal at Harpers Ferry, Virginia, in an effort to start a slave insurrection.

100. The correct answer is E. The Ostend Manifesto was drawn up by three proslavery members of the Pierce administration to be submitted to Spain. The administration rejected the proposal as too inflammatory. The underlying purpose of the proposal was to gain additional slave states to support the South. Answers A, B, and D are distracters. The Adams-Onis Treaty in the correct match for answer C.

101. The correct answer is C. The Wilmot Proviso was never passed by both houses of Congress. Answer B is based on the decision in the Dred Scott case that Congress had no power to ban slavery without due process. Only states could decide whether they should ban slavery. However, this answer has nothing to do with the Wilmot Proviso. Answer E is similar to Lincoln's view that if slavery were abolished, slaveowners should be compensated. The other answers are just wrong.

102. The correct answer is D. Answer A is incorrect; most 49ers were white, single men, and native-born. Answer B is incorrect, although men attracted by the mild, sunny climate and rich farmland stayed to farm and ranch. Answer C is incorrect and illogical; this trip would cost money and most immigrants used whatever they had saved just to get to the United States. Answer E is incorrect; most of the goldhunters were from the Upper South and the Midwest.

103. The correct answer is E. Answer A is a misstatement; California was to be admitted as a free state. The other answers are stated correctly, and the one that turned Northerners into abolitionists was the Fugitive Slave Law. It seemed very unfair to turn over to slavecatchers men, women, and children who had risked death to escape slavery.

104. The correct answer is A. The 1860 platform promised something for everyone—or at least for a number of people with different interests. Answer C along with a severe denunciation of the Know-Nothings proposal to make naturalization

more difficult appealed to immigrants. It also appealed to easterners who wanted to make a new start. Answer D was meant to appeal to the same people and to existing Californians. Answer E attracted New England manufacturers.

105. The correct answer is D. Neither the North nor the South was willing to give in on the subject of slavery. Answer A enabled Southerners to enslave people, but it did not in itself lead to the Civil War. Answers B and E are incorrect because the Civil War encompassed moral, political, and economic differences. Answer C is illogical in context.

106. The correct answer is D. The border states—Delaware, Maryland, Kentucky, and Missouri—were slave-owning states and Lincoln was concerned that a bill freeing their slaves would drive them out of the Union and into the Confederacy. Answer A is the opposite of what the Radical Republicans hoped and not Lincoln's reason. Answer B is a distracter. Answer C is incorrect because Great Britain had outlawed slavery in its possessions almost 20 years before this, and the Radical Republicans hoped that freeing the slaves would keep Britain from trading with the Confederacy. Only half of answer E is correct. Lincoln did believe that slaveowners should be compensated, but the rest of the answer is incorrect.

107. The correct answer is E. Answer E is actually an advantage. The Confederacy had only to defend their land, not invade the enemy's territory as the Union had to. Both sides suffered from high inflation, answer A, but it was more severe in the South where by the end of the war a Confederate dollar was worth about one cent in gold.

108. The correct answer is E. If the Confederacy could achieve answer E, then it would have been able to accomplish answers B and D. Answer A is the reverse of the situation. The Union was successfully blockading Southern ports and cutting off the flow of cotton to British manufacturers, thus drastically damaging the South's economy. Answer C is a distracter.

109. The correct answer is D. Answer A was the goal of the Radical Republicans. Answer B is incorrect, because Lincoln did not propose granting voting rights to former slaves. Answer C is incorrect and out of character for Lincoln. Answer E is illogical.

110. The correct answer is A. Johnson's plan specifically calls for the cancellation of all Confederate debts, so that no one would receive back the investment in Confederate bonds or be paid for any goods supplied to the Confederacy.

111. The correct answer is B. Answer A, property rights, were a matter of states' granting certain rights to women rather than the federal government. If answer E had been the Fifteenth Amendment, which granted voting rights to African American men, it would have been correct. The Thirteenth Amendment ended slavery.

112. The correct answer is B. You can eliminate answer D because the Fourteenth Amendment was written and passed after the Civil Rights Act. Others besides Johnson thought that the 1866 act might be unconstitutional so they set about changing the Constitution. Answer A is incorrect, because the act's provisions were meant to address the violations of African Americans rights under the black codes. Answer E is illogical.

113. The correct answer is E. Being able to provide for themselves and their families would prove to former slaves that they were finally free. Answers A, B, C, and D were all important and activities that freed slaves engaged in, but economic independence was the long-term goal.

114. The correct answer is D. Answer A states the Ten Percent Plan, which was part of Lincoln's Reconstruction plan, not the Radical Republicans', who at one point called for 50 percent of voters to swear allegiance (Wade-Davis Act). Answer B is incorrect, because the voters elected delegates. Answer C is tricky; the state legislatures had to ratify the Fourteenth Amendment in the Radical Republicans' plan. It was the Thirteenth Amendment in Johnson's plan. Answer E is incorrect; they had to ask Congress for a pardon.

115. The correct answer is A. William Seward was secretary of state when Russia offered to sell Alaska to the United States for $7.2 million. When gold was found in the new territory in 1896, Seward didn't seem so foolish. How the United States

acquired answers B, C, and D is correctly stated. Answer E, Oregon, was part of a settlement over a disputed boundary with Great Britain.

116. The correct answer is B. By the end of Reconstruction, Redeemers had gained control of state government in all the former Confederate states. The Redeemers were not the old-line Southern politicians from before the Civil War, but businessmen interested in making money in the "New South."

117. The correct answer is B. Answer A is incorrect because Louisiana, Florida, and South Carolina were still under military control. Answer C is partially true; Northerners had grown tired of the corruption that was reported about Reconstruction governments. Answer D is illogical; the act pardoned most ex-Confederates so that they could vote and hold public office. Answer E is incorrect.

118. The correct answer is A. Because the slaves had been freed, landowners had no workers and no money to pay them, so a system of sharecropping was worked out. In exchange for land, tools, a mule, seed, and shack, a sharecropper and his family would give a third or a half of the harvest to the landowner. The system was set up so that the sharecropper was left little money at the end of the harvest and would have to borrow again for the next year. Answer A dominated the Midwest. Answers C, D, and E are distracters; they sound familiar but don't relate to the question.

119. The correct answer is E. In order to subsidize the rebuilding of the infrastructure of the South and to improve such aspects of it as transportation, Southern governments levied high taxes. Answer A was a great improvement. Prior to the Civil War, only one out of every eight white children went to school. Answer D is true—if you were white as the question prompt states.

120. The correct answer is D. Nominating and electing a war hero is a time-honored American political behavior. Answer A is incorrect because all fought on whatever was considered the frontier when they were in the army. Answers B and E are incorrect because Grant was originally from Ohio. All the other men were at least born in the South to slave owning families or in the case of Jackson acquired slaves on his own. Answer C is incorrect because Washington held Federalist opinions although he claimed no party; Harrison and Taylor ran as Whigs and Grant as a Republican.

Printed in the USA
CPSIA information can be obtained
at www.ICGtesting.com
LVHW081816210524
780976LV00013B/808